Steppin' Out

Contributions in American Studies
Series Editor: Robert H. Walker

The Supreme Court: Myth and Reality
Arthur Selwyn Miller

Television Fraud: The History and Implications of the Quiz Show Scandals
Kent Anderson

Menace in the West: The Rise of French Anti-Americanism
in Modern Times
David Strauss

Social Change and Fundamental Law: America's Evolving
Constitution
Arthur Selwyn Miller

American Character and Culture in a Changing World: Some
Twentieth-Century Perspectives
John A. Hague, editor

Olmsted South: Old South Critic/New South Planner
Dana F. White and Victor A. Kramer, editors

In the Trough of the Sea: Selected American Sea-Deliverance
Narratives, 1610–1766
Donald P. Wharton, editor

Aaron Burr and the American Literary Imagination
Charles J. Nolan, Jr.

The Popular Mood of Pre-Civil War America
Lewis O. Saum

The Essays of Mark Van Doren
William Claire, editor

Touching Base: Professional Baseball and American Culture in the
Progressive Era
Steven A. Riess

Late Harvest: Essays and Addresses in American Literature and Culture
Robert E. Spiller

Steppin' Out

NEW YORK NIGHTLIFE AND THE TRANSFORMATION OF AMERICAN CULTURE, 1890–1930

Lewis A. Erenberg

Contributions in American Studies, Number 50

GREENWOOD PRESS
WESTPORT, CONNECTICUT   •   LONDON, ENGLAND

Library of Congress Cataloging in Publication Data

Erenberg, Lewis A   1944–
   Steppin' out.

   (Contributions in American studies; no. 50 ISSN
0084–9227)
   Bibliography: p.
   Includes index.
   1. New York (City)—Popular culture.   2. New York
(City)—Social life and customs.   3. Music-halls (Vari-
ety theaters, cabarets, etc.)—New York (City).   4. Res-
taurants, lunch rooms, etc.—New York (City)—History.
I. Title.
F128.5.E65   974.7'1041   80–930
ISBN 0–313–21342–9 (lib. bdg.)

Library of Congress Catalog Card Number: 80–930
ISBN: 0–313–21342–9
ISSN: 0084–9227

First published in 1981

Greenwood Press
A division of Congressional Information Service, Inc.
88 Post Road West, Westport, Connecticut 06881

Printed in the United States of America

10   9   8   7   6   5   4   3   2   1

To my parents,
Elie and Shirley Erenberg

CONTENTS

ILLUSTRATIONS AND TABLE

FIGURES

TABLE

PREFACE

Writing in the fledgling *New Yorker* in 1925, Ellin Mackay, daughter of a powerful Long Island family and future wife of popular song-writer Irving Berlin, provided an analysis of her generation's penchant for cabarets: "We go because we prefer rubbing elbows in a cabaret to dancing at an exclusive party with all sorts and kinds of people." Reacting to the inundation of society by new money and new people, she found the cabaret a realm of public privacy, removed from the institutional demands of her social group, community opinion, and family constraints. To Mackay, public nightlife offered new, more personal choices and an informal social life. She was not alone. For the well-to-do (the professional and business classes, the wealthy, the fashionable, theatrical figures, and tourists), nightlife in the first years of the twentieth century came to include more than entertainment; it became a public social life outside the cloistered walls of home and business, and it brought diverse elements of the urban landscape into the same social arena.

The evolution of the cabaret forms the critical element in the growth of public nightlife in the years from 1890 through 1930. According to a New York Department of Licenses Report of 1927, a cabaret "shall mean any room, place or space in the city in which any musical entertainment, singing, dancing or other similar amusement is permitted in connection with the restaurant business or the business of directly or indirectly selling the public food or drink." Prior to the 1910s, cabarets were little known or were considered backroom joints or dives. They were associated with illicit saloons, red-light districts, and male culture. The transformation of this institution into a respectable one for both sexes provides a concrete example of the changing standards of social and sexual life and the gradual decline of those values commonly associated with Victorianism.

While other cities had numerous cafés, New York City served larger than local interests. As the nation's financial, commercial, and theatrical center, New York attracted businessmen and dignitaries from all parts of the country. Looking after their serious matters during the day, visitors enjoyed the city's pleasures during the evening. When they returned home, they took part of the city with them. New York also acted as an entrepôt for new trends in other ways. Many forms of entertainment originated elsewhere but received prominent notice only after passing through Manhattan. New York took rough and ready styles of music and dancing and legitimized them, making them fit standards that respectable groups could accept.

The fact that Mackay wrote in the mid-1920s should not obscure the cabaret's origins in the early years of the century. Partly because the nightclub has become symbolic for the "era of wonderful nonsense" image of the twenties, most historians have little understanding of the long history of this entertainment institution. Too, most historians only reluctantly accept that the twenties were a culmination rather than a beginning, and many still view the new consumption, entertainment, sexuality, and social styles as frills rather than the substance of cultural reorientation. The growth of public nightlife starting in the 1890s accompanied the decline of Victorianism. The changes in nightlife institutions and entertainments over the course of the first forty years of this century are a window to the process of transformation of social and cultural attitudes and behavior.

The opposition to the cabarets in the 1910s suggests how greatly they challenged contemporary mores. Progressive and conservative critics toiled to uplift the cabaret along with a host of new-style amusements, which were being adapted from the disreputable elements of city life into the mainstream. To their tastes, the cabaret was too informal and too relaxed, exercising little control over the personality

and what they considered the lower nature of human beings. They
wanted public life to mirror an ideal conception of private, individual
character. The shift from entertainment in a private, formal setting to
a more informal, public arena marks a movement away from
Victorian gentility, from what John Higham has called "the absolu-
tization of social identities," which "may have reached their apogee in
the late nineteenth and early twentieth centuries."[1] Scholars have
recognized that the period from 1890 to 1930 marked a profound
reorientation in American culture, one that broke from older forms of
gentility in which individuals were to subordinate themselves volun-
tarily to a social code. But starting in the 1890s, values became more
informal, and the restrictions placed on the individual's personal
desires and impulses were lessened. Greater emphasis was placed on
self-fulfillment, self-expression, and the development of "personality."[2] The social reformers who witnessed the growth of the cabaret
were quite correct in their assessment. In the cabaret audiences
sought to move out of their private roles into a search for a wider life;
the cabaret relaxed boundaries between the sexes, between audiences
and performers, between ethnic groups and Protestants, between
black culture and whites. Commercial popular culture in the cabarets
achieved a new importance for all classes.

The new social informality defined the setting and the structure of
the cabaret. Perhaps Marshall McLuhan said it best: "The medium is
the message." I extended this to indicate that the form conveys meaning. The relaxation of social and personal boundaries and identities in
the twentieth century is clearly revealed in the particular setting and
style of the cabaret and its entertainments. Through their appreciation of the cabaret's dances, revues, songs, and structure, moreover,
patrons themselves expressed the deep tensions of a culture in transition. In describing the cabaret, thus, we are in fact analyzing the transformation in the image and reality of male and female character and
the Protestant approach to passion in public life.

In visiting the urban institutions of the night, men and women pursued a vital and experiential life, the flux and weave of movement
and action that had been considered disreputable for the best people in
the Victorian era. As they entered public life, different groups underwent change. Society members began to compete openly for public
acceptance; theatrical personages found they need not be relegated to

the lower orders of status but instead might become models for a generation undergoing change; and ethnic entertainers, long viewed below notice, found a degree of acceptance by a culture looking for life and vitality. While providing the latter, they would also have to become more American and more accessible to their audiences. Moreover, whites began to reevaluate the role of blacks in entertainment, adapting more of black music and dance for their own. How these elements fit together and helped create a twentieth-century popular culture with norms acceptable for a large and diverse audience is the subject of this book.

In the past, nightlife has remained in the hands of gossip columnists and popular historians primarily interested in the anecdotal nature of the subject. A number of sociologists, rooted in the Chicago School of Sociology and Progressive Culture, have viewed the bright light zones, taxi dance halls, roadhouses, and nightclubs as part of cultural decline and urban pathology. The anonymity of city life, in their estimation, produced cultural decay. My approach differs from both of these. The night is a time for dreaming. Fantasies and hidden desires seek realization in an urban world whose very anonymity permits them. Dreams of success, power, social advance, self-fulfillment, and sexual love find currency more readily than in the hard-working and normal run of everyday affairs, yet are in dynamic tension with a person's daytime identity. In nightlife, people from varied social worlds found outlet for their desires, found representations of themselves with which they could identify. In the 1910s and 1920s, they helped create a new-style public dream, one concerned with vitality rather than gentility, consumption rather than production, mutuality rather than sexual separation, personality rather than character, all contained by a degree of social selectivity.

While audiences rarely articulated what they sought in nightclubs and cabarets, the structure, designs, entertainers and entertainments, scandals and reform crusades reveal much about the personal and social aspirations of the patrons. People in the past made choices about their lives; the birth of the cabaret reveals some of those choices. The changing relationship between men and women receives much emphasis, because men and women put much energy into the search for new styles of sexuality in the early decades of this century. Unlike the entertainments of the Victorian era, various forms of popular culture in the twentieth century sought to bring men and women together. The search for new sexual and social styles formed an adventurous undertaking, and we have the opportunity to view what people wanted, how far they were able to go, and what has been the legacy they left us.

NOTES

1. John Higham, "Another American Dilemma," *The Center Magazine* (July–August 1974), p. 73.

2. Warren Susman, "Personality and the Making of Twentieth Century Culture," in *New Directions in American Intellectual History*, ed. John Higham and Paul K. Conkin (Baltimore: Johns Hopkins University Press, 1979), pp. 212–26.

ACKNOWLEDGMENTS

As this study has grown, I have received aid and encouragement from many friends and colleagues. Two stand out. I owe special debt to John Higham, my adviser at the University of Michigan, in whose seminar this project began to take shape. His invaluable suggestions and insights helped form this study, and from him I have learned the importance of periodization and empathy toward people in the past. Donald B. Meyer originally inspired my interest in history and helped introduce me to the role of sexuality in history. Over the years, his criticism has forced me to reexamine my own ideas and the framework for this work. The historical ideas of both men have stimulated my thinking and have become part of my approach to the past.

A number of other people have read and commented on various drafts and pieces of this manuscript. Among them are Josef Barton, Marvin Felheim, Michael Frisch, Shaw Livermore, Jr., Elaine May, Lary May, Elizabeth Pleck, Robert Sklar, Jane Mulligan Van Buren, and Phyllis Vine. Lary May also offered innumerable sparkling insights, helpful conversation, unpublished drafts of his own manuscript, and close friendship along the way. Susan Hirsch, Charles Radding, and Janette Simms read every draft of the manuscript, helped me create order out of chaos, stopped me from my own worst excesses, and argued me out of my tendency to hold onto this manuscript forever.

In researching this manuscript, a number of people connected with the cabaret business gave freely of their time in advice, files, and interviews. The staffs of the Reference Division of the Graduate Library of the University of Michigan, the Restaurant Management School Library of Cornell University, the Local and Genealogy Division of the New York Public Library, and the Municipal Archives Center of New York City have provided kind aid and assistance. I would like to mention especially Paul Myer, Monte Arnold, and the rest of the staff of the New York Library of the Performing Arts, Lincoln Center, for their kind assistance. Karen O'Hara investigated *Town Topics* for me when I was unable to get back to New York, and my two research assistants at Loyola University of Chicago, Donald McKay and Susan Gaspar, admirably put up with my last-minute requests for new material, rechecking of footnotes, the securing of photographs and releases, and the detailed work without which a project like this could not have been written during a school year. The Office of Research Services at Loyola University of Chicago was most kind in its assistance and support. Barbara Hughett did an admirable job of deciphering my early drafts and transforming them into a finished typed product.

MCMXXXVII by Shelton Brooks. Copyright assigned to Jerry Vogel Music Co., Inc., 58 West 45th Street, New York, New York 10036. Used by permission of copyright owner. Reproduction prohibited.

Two lines of poetry by e.e. cummings from *six nonlectures*. Copyright by e. e. cummings in 1953. Reprinted with permission of Harvard University Press, Cambridge, Mass.

The quotation from *Along This Way* by James Weldon Johnson. Copyright by James Weldon Johnson. Reprinted with the permission of Viking Penguin Inc., New York, N.Y.

Steppin' Out

Part One A VICTORIAN WORLD

I VICTORIAN CULTURE AND AMUSEMENTS

> I should explain that the idea of home is
> the idea of privacy.
>
> e.e. cummings
> *six nonlectures*

In the second half of the nineteenth century, the boundless individualism of American life underwent a process of consolidation and refinement. This was an age of gentility, combining a moral fastidiousness and cultural refinement to discipline the will, replacing a waning evangelical faith. As part of a desire for greater rational order, urbanites attempted to exercise restraint in their personal lives, and they also conceived of a society based on their conception of morality.[1] Distinguishing themselves from the lower orders by their refined moral standards, hard work, and elevated leisure pursuits, the urban bourgeoisie created public and private amusements that fit their hierarchical conception of culture. Respectable men and women established categories of what was appropriate for them to attend together. Certain types of amusements were considered too fast, and hence too lower class, for well-to-do women, while others of a higher and more refined stamp fit more securely into a set of familial and class values. Great restrictions existed on what women might do for amusement, but men had a greater run of public life. Each sex, class, and race had its specialized attributes and amusements, and each was expected to occupy its exclusive sphere. Public life was increasingly divided, and the private realm of home diverged from the values of public life. By the 1890s, however, this Victorian cultural style would disintegrate as both sexes were drawn to a popular culture rooted in the lower orders.

We can glimpse the genteel culture of Protestant America through the memoirs of Henry Seidel Canby, editor of the *Saturday Review* from 1924 to 1936. Determined to rescue his Victorian youth from the ridicule of modern, less genteel, critics, Canby reconstructed the values by which most upper and upper middle-class families lived in his home town of Wilmington, Delaware, in the 1890s. As he put it in *Age of Confidence*, the better classes lived a life bound together by faith, hard work, self-sufficiency, and a belief in moral progress grounded in the refined woman and the autonomous family. These values were important in an economically and ethnically heterogeneous society for they helped differentiate the better people from those below them on the social scale. The "difference was a subtle one of manners and traditions," noted Canby, "for our manners were not always good. You lived according to a tradition of customs most conscious when breached; or you lived unconscious of a family past."[2] Unlike the plain people—the workers, Irish, and blacks—the native-born American bourgeoisie identified American progress with their families, for those alone possessed a sense of what they ought to do and a concern for the future. The bourgeoise had self-discipline, and in their minds self-discipline and social progress went together. For them, life was a unity, "indissoluble and unchangeable, like the union. It was a culture with mores, it was a life in which one quickly knew one's place."[3]

At the heart of the code lay the virtue of business success. Organized around independent entrepreneurs in individual firms and small partnerships, business in Wilmington "was the dominating occupation and chief subject of thought in our community." For men, it was more than a job; "it was a philosophy, a morality, and an atmosphere."[4] In family and schoolroom, the young male learned that his path to success lay in his "pioneer's training in self dependence, his sense of room at the top, and his certainty that work can get him there." For Protestants, the economy represented a moral frontier, where individuals who practiced self-discipline and willpower while husbanding their scarce energy would be rewarded by mobility and ordered progress. "In the ominous future which was held like a big stick over every boy's head," the young learned that "only obedience and accuracy and neatness and a contempt for the pleasures of idleness, could give a leg up to success."[5] To progress as an individual, then a young man had to master the fires of his body. In such a society, fathers set a concrete model for boys to follow: they were "called before daylight, went to work at seven, came home at six and slept Sunday afternoons and many a week day evening. They did it by code."[6]

While men staked out the public domain of politics and the economy, women played a separate role in the private world of the home. "In our town, and I think in the American nineties generally," Canby recalled, "home was the most impressive experience in life."[7] In the home, mothers reigned. It was they, moreover, who taught their children the sense of duty and "ought," which held the society together. "The woman who could not make a home," he recalled, "like the man who could not support one, was condemned, and not tacitly."[8] In this milieu, the ever-present wall placque, "God Bless Our Home," never meant "God make our home a happy one." Rather, declared Canby, "the blessing was asked upon virtues which were often more conducive to moral conduct and material success than happiness."[9] Increasingly powerful in their own homes, women rarely entered the public world of men. When they did, it was in the service of extending their familial role in "an attempt to make that world our American home."[10]

In the privacy of the domestic sphere, women taught men duty and the channeling of their passions through willpower. Passion was one element that could distract men from success, weaken their resolve, and ultimately destroy their will. It was thus considered bad for business, and businessmen's wives and daughters were expected to conform to the "kind of sexual relationship that made the least trouble."[11] Women had to be what men were not—refined, controlled, nurturing, self-effacing, and stable—so as to provide the one noncompetitive and nurturing environment in the anarchic and hostile world of nineteenth-century economic competition. Canby's generation understood the delights of sensuality but kept them outside their own culture. Placing stock in the purity of women, they practiced a double standard, which set their own women above the demands of the body and above the sexual status of men. For both men and women, sexuality was separate from romance. "We had our code," and central to it was a woman who "carried with her the sanctions and refusals of society."[12] Women provided the order in life and the social order to men's identities, and for that reason they had to live in their own private world above the temptations of the town.

The refined woman also had a social role to play in distinguishing the business classes from their inferiors. No parent, according to Canby, ever "spoke of class in society to her children," but rather let the feelings of superiority and apartness be felt implicitly. By extinguishing erotic play, mothers instilled "standards of conduct stiffer than the manners of the plain people and far more rigorous than the creed of the hated 'micks.' "[13] To Canby's parents, social hierarchy was not artificial. It resulted from superior efforts at refinement, which their subordinates had not the willpower or desire to master:

They [Irish] represented the anarchy and lawlessness that ever since the Civil War the country had been trying to subdue. . . . They were the evil, the disorganizing principle, which roused the opposite in us, and made us believe that there was something real in the precepts of our elders which usually droned above our heads.[14]

The working people "let themselves go," and thus lived a life with too great a freedom. "These indeed were our barbarians."[15]

The main social event for the best people in Wilmington was the annual ball, an occasion that reflected their concern for female morality, class status, and privacy. Formal balls marked a young woman's debut, and they also marked her proper sexual character. "A girl at a ball was still a woman on show, a custodian of honor and the home." The ball symbolized her chastity. "Wiles were allowed her, but only to advertise her charms. She could flirt and be gay and tease and be teased, but one hint of the sexual made her 'common,' which was only one word above vulgar." This was her apotheosis, the crowning glory of her character and fitness for the duties of motherhood. "At the first utter opening of her petals," she had to be more than "a lovely creature of seductive flesh"; she had to be a "goddess manifest."[16]

To shift from Wilmington to New York is to move from a provincial center to the financial and social capital of the United States. New York attracted monied individuals from all regions, including those who made their fortunes in mercantile and banking pursuits and those whose success was based on newer, industrial enterprises built after the Civil War. This elite, largely freed from daily interactions with underlings, had more time and money to experiment with social forms than did the families of Wilmington. They also had more incentive. New York social life was brilliant and competitive; members of the elite, and those who aspired to that position, put their pretensions to the test of an incessant round of activities.[17] Underlying this sparkling facade of New York society, however, we can perceive the same concerns with decorum, social distinction, and self-control that Canby found in Wilmington and that were equally evident in other noncosmopolitan communities from Brooklyn to Pittsburgh and Chicago.

There is no better access to New York high life in the later nineteenth century than through its greatest restaurant and gathering place: Delmonico's. In its early years in the 1820s and 1830s, Delmonico's differed slightly from other eating houses that fed the harried exchange men, merchants, and lawyers in lower Manhattan. Most eating houses had dark, uncomfortable rooms with simple and undemanding daytime fare suitable for men anxious to return to their businesses. Because of the all-male atmosphere, women were generally advised against entering. Delmonico's originally opened as a wine and pastry shop, but by 1848 the *New York Weekly Herald* noted its growing distinction as an "expensive and aristocratic restaurant, of which Delmonico's is the only complete specimen in the United States." This transformation was the work of Lorenzo Delmonico, who took over in 1848 and turned the restaurant into a civilized and orderly culinary institution. Under his tutelage, waiters learned deferential service, and the restaurant staff learned orderly procedures and efficient administration, two hallmarks of this genteel age. His menus, reflecting system and sophistication, introduced elegant dishes little known outside Europe. Lorenzo's special project, the Delmonico Hotel, was the first big New York City hotel to break away from the homogeneous simplicity of the American plan, which required everyone to eat at fixed times in the jumbled "ordinary." His hotel, and then all of the branches under the Delmonico name, offered a wider variety of meals and infinitely greater choices in food, all served in more elegant formal dining rooms.[18]

In successive moves up Broadway and then Fifth Avenue, Delmonico's introduced an unheard-of cosmopolitanism in atmosphere and food. By 1860, located at Fifth Avenue and Fourteenth Street, Delmonico's inaugurated a feature destined to make its mark in restaurant history: the addition of a great French chef, Charles Ranhoffer, whom it hired from the Maison Dorée, its only serious rival until the end of the century. According to the restaurant's chronicler, Ranhoffer was the first gourmet chef worthy of the name, and in his tenure from 1863 to 1895 he helped elevate the standards of American dining.[19] As a French chef, Ranhoffer brought to postwar generations European culture and mannerisms that acted as leaven for rough democratic habits. Enthusiasm for elegant French dining signified an appreciation by the better classes of the higher standards of the older, more aristocratic civilization of Europe. Rather than being a sign of decadence, European cultivation was rapidly becoming the basis for the identities of fashionable urbanites. Between the first dinner for Charles Dickens in 1842 at the City Hotel and the second at Delmonico's in 1868, American tastes had changed. They showed less emphasis on abundance of courses and a greater delight in "economy, order, balance, and smooth progression of courses."[20] Quality became a watchword at Delmonico's, and civilized manners had come to the public dining room.

The Fifth Avenue location also marked Delmonico's emergence as a social institution. With a prestigious address, an esteemed chef, and the resources to serve the tastes of even the most cultivated gourmet, Delmonico's assumed its position as the premier place for fashionable dining. The choice of its ballroom in the 1870s as the home of the exclusive Patriarch Balls, where older wealth attempted to guard its position and regulate potential applicants, heightened its image of elegance and exclusiveness. In this same period, local and national officials settled on this one superb restaurant the honor of hosting major state and business banquets, modeled after the ornate official hospitality of Paris in the Second Empire. While society reigned in the private ballroom, masculine accomplishment and power presided over the banquet hall.[21] At the center of national political, social, and business life, Delmonico's had clearly risen above the eating houses. Dining amid such elegance and prosperity, the patrons could well muse that here in the United States, politics, business, and social life were all representative of order, progress, and stability. Aristocracy and democracy could reside together in ultimate harmony. When in 1876 the restaurant moved to Twenty-sixth Street across from Madison Square between Broadway and Fifth Avenue, it had reached its height. Until the 1890s, Delmonico's reigned as a symbol of elegant nightlife, bringing wealth and dining under greater social control in the urban scene. As the *Herald* declared, the "appointments in every respect are the finest, combining a due regard for the enjoyment of the *otium cum dignitate* (leisure with dignity), and totally disregarding that excess which sometimes characterizes the surroundings of wealth."[22]

Delmonico's built its reputation on its eminent respectability. As one commentator noted of its last branch, "No tramps or beggars or bunco steerers or stool pigeons infest Delmonico's. It is as if the house were a club which none but gentlemen were allowed to enter. There is always the peace, order, comfort and elegance for which Delmonico's is famous."[23] Nowhere else did this respectability surface as with its policy on women. Here it was impeccably conservative. Perhaps it was because Delmonico's was a social center and thus a gathering place for the wealthy, but, by the 1860s, Delmonico's welcomed women and made them feel comfortable. It was this policy that signaled Delmonico's departure from the eating-house ranks. Women were made to feel comfortable because no unescorted women were permitted. Probably management wanted to prevent women from being accosted and also sought to discourage traffic from women who welcomed being accosted. The dining room thus became a respectable place for even the most refined, an orderly extension of the proper private dining room. The men's café, however, kept the double standard alive. There men took their drinks, cigars, and heartier sociability, all removed from the more elevated and formal public world inhabited by respectable women. By the 1890s, Delmonico's even eased its rules regarding escorts. Before dinner women might enter alone, but afterward, when the crowd became more mixed, male accompaniment remained a prerequisite. The presence of women ensured high standards of male decorum and an air of civilization and social formality.[24]

This late nineteenth-century trend toward elegant civility is evident also in fashionable social life. Among the patrons of Delmonico's, the wealthy, professional classes, merchants, and businessmen, there was an increased appreciation of rules imposing formalized order on social gatherings. Only under these conditions, safely removed from the urban rabble, could one enjoy the benefits of growing urban cosmopolitanism and sophistication. After the Civil War, urbanites increasingly turned to etiquette books for advice on proper behavior and social usage, and they put these dictates into practice in a formal social life. The New York elite families turned to proper modes of behavior to display their cultivation and breeding and to distinguish themselves from the populace and other less well-bred monied clans. The guides to behavior were less concerned with inner morality than with outer display of cultivation, but in both cases the purpose was to discipline the will. In the impersonal urban setting, however, more emphasis was put on the individual's behavior than upon his inner life. The etiquette books themselves were representative of a shift toward an urban culture.[25]

With the rise of industrial wealth after the Civil War, society everywhere entered a period of forceful competition. Because New York was the economic capital of a vast and growing empire and because of the high turnover of wealth within the city, one had less assurance of social status here than in other more provincial urban centers like Wilmington. "From an unofficial oligarchy of aristocrats," said Mrs. John King Van Rensselaer, "society was transformed into an extravagant body that set increasing store by fashion and display."[26] The process of self-definition in such a high-powered setting quickly became an all-encompassing profession whose goal was the maintenance of status and order. Within the scrambling social world of New York, then, there was a concomitant desire for consolidation of social position. Because one's social position was not fixed, "activities which are known as social functions" came to dominate society. To be a member of society, one had to act as society decreed and attend events that defined society. One's social status came not from one's rank but from acceptance by others into a private round of balls, dinners, and parties that distinguished the rich from everyone else. To select the elect, these functions had an elaborate set of rules to fix proper behavior and define the minor hierarchies in social life. Such questions as places at dinners and balls, the proper subjects of conversation, who led the cotillion, and the proper decorum for young ladies gave a form to one's actions and empowered the group to make the choices over one's behavior. Social ritual decreed that girls had to sit with their chaperones at balls, they could not speak to other girls, and they had to wait for a man to ask them to dance.[27] Under the formidable Mrs. Astor, and her chamberlain Ward McAllister, this process lasted until the 1890s, when the old families lost their ability to control the new industrial money and the admission into elite circles. By then, however, this elaboration of rules had consolidated, limited, and set the social circle. The notion of there being four hundred select individuals comprising the social elite of New York, while inexact, was perhaps the highest expression of this desire to consolidate society and place its members under formal rules of behavior.[28]

In elite New York, as well as in Canby's Wilmington, women dominated social life. On all levels, men devoted themselves to business, leaving the field of culture, social affairs, and leisure to women. Women quickly filled the vacuum. As one commentator put it, the tycoons were "too nerve-racked by the strain of building a fortune to be able to relax. They were prepared to spend their last cent in gratifying the whims of their womenfolk, but they were incapable of amusing them themselves."[29] European travelers often commented on the absence of men from the inner workings of American society, and Henry James considered it the characteristic fact of American social life.[30] This phenomenon increased after the 1870s as the chief social leaders became the wives of powerful men, who were too busy consolidating their business empires to spend time in leisure. As their husbands labored mightily to bring order and stability to the economic sphere, wives of big businessmen sought to consolidate their social position by devoting themselves to society as an all-encompassing occupation. In the rarefied sphere of society, women found an outlet for their vast energies within the genteel synthesis. With few economic or political roles open to them and with the highly unsure social scene, these women could achieve self-importance through society. Like their middle-class counterparts, big businessmen made enough money to provide women with leisure. Wives had servants for housework and select schools for their children. While the upper middle-class woman slowly saw her productive role evaporate in an industrial economy as outside agencies (especially education) took over her domestic role, the upper-class woman already had an outlet for her energies in society. Women of both classes found their deepest emotional and social lives with other women. Society mirrored the middle-class split between the sexes. Women dominated society, and men found little solace there. Although they attended the events and supplied the money, men still felt more at home in the library during the ball. Women ruled society as a sign of a man's power over other men, but at its core their role was hollow. The business society that produced them also deprived them of their raison d'être. They were symbols of a man's power, but they themselves exercised vast power in a private world that men considered secondary.[31]

The women who dominated New York society also taught a sexual code similar to the one Canby found in Wilmington. In 1904, for example, Mrs. Burton Harrison, a respected social authority, noted that in order to enter the formal entertainments of society, a young girl had to "equip herself in a shining armor of conventionality." By limiting herself to the private functions of teas, balls, and debuts and by staying under the watchful eye of her chaperone, the young girl could meet the elevated standards of society. Little leeway was given for public experimentation by the young. In the larger world, she was not expected to dine unchaperoned in a restaurant or enter a theatre, without falling in caste. "What young men really expect in a girl of their own condition in society is first the possession of that fine moral fibre, purely womanly, and yet stout as tempered steel, that makes them realize in her presence the gulf that divides her from the unworthy of her sex." In Victorian culture, even among the upper class, the gap between the good and bad woman was wide, for all men expected women to be better than themselves. "It is a sad moment . . . when a young, innocent girl . . . nurtured with all the sheltering tenderness that keeps evil from women's lives," declared Mrs. Harrison, makes a false slip, which ranks her "henceforth in their estimation far lower than the angels men dream of domesticating in their homes."[32]

The careful segregation of passion from respectable amusements in favor of formal, self-controlled behavior was not characteristic of the genteel classes alone. Amusements of the middle and lower middle classes reflected a commitment to this same social code. Men could be happy members of society only if they were productive respecters of the social order, while respectable women had to be carefully sheltered from more raucous, openly sexual environments. Passion could be publicly expressed only in the special establishments catering to loose men of all classes, where the anarchic traditions of male life were, in some small way, preserved.

Amusements in the early nineteenth century paralleled contemporary social life and were part of an informal, heterogeneous public life with little segregation by class or sex. Richmond, Virginia, for example, reflected the relative social homogeneity of preindustrial cities. Taverns near the capitol served all classes except blacks, and exhibitions, circuses, and theatres enjoyed the patronage of heterogeneous groups. After 1830, however, and increasingly after 1850, this pattern began to change. Taverns became more exclusively lower class and foreign, and women and the upper classes in general visited them less frequently. In Richmond, an informal street life and mixed amusement scene, characteristic of the preindustrial city, gave way to the increasing complexity and specialization of the industrial city. Amusements stratified along the lines of class, sex, and race.[33] As the middle and upper classes became preoccupied with womanly restraint and decorum, good women were increasingly insulated from a more rowdy public life. At the same time, men might still pursue an egalitarian round of informal pleasures in the semipublic milieu of the saloon, dance hall, and red-light district.

We can see the growing complexity and diversification in urban amusements in the theatres of New York City. There the relatively informal, mixed-class theatre soon gave way to one differentiated by class and function. The early melodramatic stage produced a variety of dramas for a wide audience. All kinds of performances were housed under one roof, so that audiences in the 1830s might see drama, circus, opera, and dance on the same bill. New York's Park Theater, despite a reputation as the elite house, had a relatively large room that permitted the masses to govern the stage. Each class had its own part of the theatre, but all attended: mechanics in the pit, upper classes and women in the boxes, and prostitutes, lower-class men, and blacks in the gallery. The rowdy audiences often yelled, stamped, drank, and smoked during the performance. The prostitutes occupied a special section, the third tier, because respectable women refused to attend institutions where they came into contact with the prostitutes.[34] The general unruliness culminated in the Astor Place riot of 1849, where the lower-class partisans of the American actor Edwin Forrest created a massive disturbance against Charles Macready, the British actor. The troops were called, lives were lost, and as a result, the middle and upper classes despaired of a democratic theatre. After 1850 theatres were increasingly differentiated by class and function, and the legitimate theatre divorced itself from the popular stage of minstrelsy, variety, and burlesque. The legitimate drama was made fit for respectable women by leaving the masses to their own amusements, eliminating the male anarchy and drinking of the pit and gallery, and removing the prostitutes from the third tier. Comfort was increased, order restored, and soon gentility distinguished the legitimate theatre from a popular stage, which continued to have deep roots in lower-class and male culture.[35] The former soon earned the stamp of approval from fashionable urban ministers.[36]

Some forms of theatre continued to draw a mixed audience. In the late nineteenth century, the most popular of these was the circus. Pioneered in modern form by P. T. Barnum, the circus portrayed the deeply rooted rural origins of American life. Dramatic encounters between beasts and courageous animal trainers, together with the derring-do of equestrian artists, supplied the main attraction. In subduing the wild beasts, the trainer showed that wild nature could be tamed and mastered by a man of moral and physical courage. The circus pitted the individual against nature, and the individual male always triumphed. Circus performers demonstrated the importance of self-control, for one slip would send the trainer or the high-wire acrobat to certain death. While it is true that the circus has rural roots, as Albert F. McLean, Jr., maintains, circuses in the second half of the nineteenth century also played successfully to urban audiences. Part of their appeal lies in their glorification of values that rural and urban areas shared. In both areas, the hero was the producer male who became fit to triumph over the forces of the wilderness and untamed nature through rigorous self-discipline. In order to succeed in a producer economy, the male had to strive for success through moral self-discipline. In the circus the forces of moral and progressive civilization always triumphed. Willpower subdued the wildness of life and brought order and high civilization in its wake. The taming of anarchic nature was a Victorian preoccupation.[37]

Like the circus, melodrama also attracted both men and women because it broadcast the official values of the age within a sentimental mold. In melodrama, too, the male hero incarnated the ascetic individual who triumphed over himself and over nature in order to advance upward through the social order. In melodrama, the hero failed only if he lacked self-discipline. The hero was a natural man, but nature was interpreted as representing the true moral values of any society. Thus the individual could rebel against harsh authority and social restriction, while still maintaining the proper social morality. In every play, the job of the hero was to save the chaste, refined heroine from the evil villain who sought to take her sexual favors. To rescue and win the girl, the hero first had to demonstrate those inner moral qualities that made him a fit man for society, and a man fit enough to make his own way. On the national stage and melodrama, the chaste hero and heroine always served civilization and the family. Given such themes, it is no wonder that both men and women attended. Like the circus ritual, the hero in melodrama acted out the role of ascetic producer, bent on disciplining himself both for success and the attainment of the heroine, a symbol of a higher, more spiritual existence. Melodrama did not feature the enjoyment of the debilitating fruits of victory.[38]

Because of their gentility, melodrama and the circus fit familial values, and thus made it possible for women to attend. There were other public places of amusement besides melodrama and the circus that welcomed women. The legitimate theatre and the concert hall found women making up a large proportion of the audience. If well chaperoned, a woman would be comfortable at the new concert halls and museums built by the upper classes. In the Victorian period, aesthetics underscored the split between mind and body, dictating that good art should uplift the participant to new levels of beauty and discipline. In distinguishing themselves from the mass, respectable concert goers depended almost slavishly on European culture and frowned on America's folk culture as too common and sensual. "Instead of growing upward from the masses," said Walter Damrosch, the well-known conductor, "[music] was carefully introduced and nurtured by an aristocratic and cultural community. . . . Its original impulse sprang perhaps more strongly from the head than the heart." The Germanic musical tradition, which dominated the music profession, divided the world into matter and spirit, with music assuming the first place in the realm of the spirit. Cultured music thus was divorced from the body, while popular music was "the sensual side of the art and has more or less the devil in it."[39]

Below respectable concert halls, theatres, and private social functions lay an array of popular amusements patronized more by the lower classes and by men of all classes. Variety, burlesque, minstrelsy, and the saloon shaded down to the whorehouses and dance halls of the red-light districts. These entertainments had roots in the transience of male life in the nineteenth century and in the Victorian double standard. Most of them had ties to the saloon, a lower-class and male preserve that offered liquor, sports talk, boxing, politics, and sometimes such entertainments as singing and dancing. The omnipresence of liquor and the rowdiness of the institution made the saloon a place few respectable women would enter. Unlike taverns, saloons did not serve much in the way of meals, relying on male camaraderie along the classic long bar for patronage and atmosphere. Some saloons were nicer than others. In the nineteenth century, every hotel and major restaurant, such as Delmonico's, had its own luxuriously appointed men's café. The café and the saloon were always hospitable to the man who was alone. The general mixing, drinking, and informal camaraderie of the saloon were the opposite of delicacy and gentility, and consequently the women who frequented the saloons were considered to be prostitutes.[40]

Variety was another form of male entertainment that developed in the 1850s. Variety was a saloon-connected music hall institution, where men in mining camps, urban areas, and red-light districts went to see singing, dancing, and comedy skits. This was the forerunner of vaudeville, but the difference lay in the rowdiness and the audience-performer intimacy of the variety stage, which the legitimate stage had banned. From the 1850s to 1900, men, frequently primed with alcohol, "hissed and jeered the villain, shouted encouragement to the put-upon hero, guffawed and stamped at the clowning of the low comedian when it approved and stopped the show when it didn't." Variety remained largely male until the mid-1880s, when Tony Pastor's Theater on Fourteenth Street sought to attract a family trade by eliminating male rowdiness and drinking. Thereafter variety quickly gave way to the increased decorum of vaudeville, which after 1900 supplanted its forerunner in most urban areas.[41]

Minstrelsy also had roots in the male urban, mining, and industrial life, and it took about thirty years before women were admitted. From the 1840s on, minstrelsy was popular in urban areas, and there were several well-known minstrel theatres in New York City. Cavorting through numerous invocations of Tambo and Bones, white men blacked their faces and acted out their versions of the black race. Minstrelsy usually featured two sets of characters: the southern plantation black and the northern Jim Dandy. Jim Dandy was a creature of impulse, who got drunk, danced about wildly, got into scrapes, and put on airs. He was the overdressed urban black who stepped beyond his position and always bungled the job. Because he indulged himself, he could not share the values of the popular myth of success. He was racially incapable of self-control. Thus in the minds of northern whites the urban black was doomed to failure in the egalitarian cities and the western frontier. An alternate life-style for blacks, encouraged especially after the Civil War, was life as a happy darky, living on an idyllic plantation, protected and controlled by whites. The blacks were the opposite of whites—indulgent in body, with gross lips, eyes, and legs, which seemed to dance out of all rational control. Minstrelsy thus portrayed black men as the exact opposite of the sturdy producer values that popular audiences took as their own. If all blacks were constitutionally inferior, then all whites by definition were equal in their chance at willpower, self-control, and success.

White male actors putting on the mask had a chance to live both sides of the American dilemma. They could act out the emotions in which blacks but not themselves could indulge in real life, and they could use this stereotype as a means to success and social position. In every performance, the white actors let on that they were really just like the white audience. Minstrelsy also fit into the nineteenth-century model of sexuality. The performers were overwhelmingly male and played to largely male audiences. Without females in the cast, the depiction of sexuality was absent. On the stage, black men had to be comic types, for a serious black man could be too appealing and hurt the stereotype. There were no workable sexual relations, because given the racial and sexual codes, blacks could not have been pictured as desiring a stable emotional sexual life. Sex is an emotion tied too closely to will, and for whites, a display of black will was unacceptable. Unlike the musical comedy, the minstrel shows could not offer a mixed cast of males and females or present a humorous approach to human sexuality. The sexuality of the Negro race was too dangerous a subject to be used for white models in the nineteenth century.

Perhaps for this reason blackface minstrelsy so quickly became encased in a form. Whites in blackface performed from a seated position, answering questions from a white interlocutor. The two end men, Tambo and Bones, responded with generally humorous answers. The others in the circle chimed in. Usually there was an olio sketch of several performers, which developed into the sketches of northern and southern black life. For white audiences, blackness remained formalized, forbidden to enter in serious ways into white culture and white life. And even as it was kept outside white life as too emotional and passionate, white women were kept from it. It was not until the 1870s that women could frequent minstrelsy, and by then much of the male uproariousness was gone, and other ethnic groups were entering into the comic roles. As women entered in the late nineteenth century, the black elements were reduced,[42] sentimental elements were enhanced, and passive spectatorship was encouraged.

Public dance halls largely existed as an entertainment option for males with some attendance by lower-class women. As Russel B. Nye has speculated, "The origins of the American public dance hall lay primarily in the nineteenth century saloon." The concert saloon appeared in cities during the 1840s and 1850s and peaked in popularity between 1890 and 1910. San Francisco's Barbary Coast in 1910 had over 300 in a six-block radius, while the South Side of Chicago in the same year had over 285. New York's Tenderloin and Bowery and the French Quarter in New Orleans had similar numbers and types of dance halls. While these saloons had music and dancing, the women who frequented them, according to Nye, were considered amateur or professional prostitutes: "The association of dancing, music, liquor, and sex was well established in the public mind long before the close of the century." It was usually safer for lower-class groups to take over a hall for the use of a particular fraternity or social club. By the turn of the century, reformers noted the increasing popularity of dance halls and sought to divorce them from the tradition of vice. They worked to license dance halls, rid them of liquor and objectionable characters, and even create municipal halls, all in order to set high standards and answer the increasing demand on the part of urban populations for respectable places to dance. The upper classes did not frown so much on dancing as they did at the promiscuous mixing that they assumed occurred at the public dance halls.[43]

In most cities, and certainly in New York, the saloons, dance halls, and sporting houses of the red-light districts provided the most intimate forms of public amusement outside of the lower-class dance halls. Every major metropolitan area and even some good-sized towns had their segregated red-light districts. Here men found relief from the home and at the same time retained a commitment to the dominant social values. Segregated vice districts separated vice from the respectable woman and the respectable home from vice. The intimacy, vitality, and exuberance of these districts were deemed too inherently unladylike. In a society dedicated to progress and purity, sex was a troublesome matter. As Canby notes, men and women inhabited different worlds outside the home. In clubs, saloons, and whorehouses, men went outside their own culture to feel like men. "While only the fanatics expected to abolish prostitution," noted Canby, "public opinion everywhere united to keep it regarded (and restrained) as a sin." Going to a prostitute kept respectable women inviolate until marriage and kept passion outside the culture. "If the prostitute and the easy woman could be branded as outcasts," he continued, "then respectable society, so they thought, might be kept from salacious desire." In effect, the double standard condoned prostitution. "The higher sense of mankind says that the family is the essential unit of the state," concluded one feminist. "Our practice says that the family plus prostitution is the essential unit."[44]

From the late nineteenth century through World War I, men of all racial and class backgrounds found a lively round of entertainments and cheap amusements in the Bowery, Tenderloin, and Coney Island. In the 1850s, the vice and amusement center resided in the Bowery in lower New York, but by the 1870s and 1880s, it followed the mass of population northward to the Tenderloin along Sixth Avenue between Twenty-fourth and Fortieth streets and eastward to Coney Island in Brooklyn. Protected by police and political officials, disorderly concert saloons following the lead of the Melodeon, which opened in the Bowery in 1859, formed a large part of the vice districts, and combined dancing, drinking, and risqué "girly" entertainment with prostitution. Many featured waiter girls and lewd theatricals. In 1891 Ernst Ingersoll's *A Week in New York* described these saloons as "a class of resorts such as a respectable person would not like to be seen in." According to the guide, "Women are employed as attendants . . . are seldom good looking, vulgar as a rule, and ignorant always." In all probability, these saloons were no different from those in Chicago described by the Illinois Vice Commission. The concert saloons had a piano player and/or a singer who got a percentage from drinks and who also was involved in soliciting for prostitution. The notorious Harry Hill's on West Houston Street in New York varied the regular dancing, performances, and drinking with Punch and Judy shows and prize fights, the latter not uncommon in the days when boxing was outlawed by responsible society as too aggressive and brutal.[45]

Dance halls in the vice districts were usually connected to saloons and prostitution. The Haymarket, on Sixth Avenue just south of Thirtieth Street, was the most famous dance hall of the Tenderloin. Originally a variety theatre, the Haymarket served as a dance hall from 1878 until reformers closed its doors in 1913 after waging a long and hard-fought battle. Featuring one of the better bands in town, the hall attracted a large number of big spenders and fancy women. Slummers, visiting firemen, and men out on the town took in the Haymarket as one of their necessary stops. "You never lacked a partner to either drink or dance with," noted one reporter. "Girls are everywhere . . . and the visitor far from home with no one to report him found pleasant hours there." A man could spend fifty to one hundred dollars in a single evening for his required champagne and the watered drinks for every woman who sat down with him.[46] Along the balcony, couples could repair to boxes and tables, while behind the boxes stood special enclosed cubicles featuring sexual exhibitions or "circuses." In the French Madame's, a similar establishment on Thirty-first Street near Sixth Avenue, male customers paid one dollar to see women dance in the nude and more to watch them put on sexual exhibitions. In the red-light districts, one could find exhibitions of all kinds.[47] By 1900 Coney Island lured urban males in search of "moist-lipped, slender girls" to its free and easy saloons and dance halls.[48] The traffic in women and vice had become so extensive by 1910 that reformers began a campaign to scrutinize its saloons and pavilions closely.

Many of the early hot spots in New York were run and frequented by blacks.[49] Northern and southern cities allowed blacks to find a degree of neighborhood hegemony outside white society. For the first time, they had the opportunity to express aspects of their identities and their cultures, unmolested by white society. It was in the cities that blacks developed ragtime and jazz, for it was there that they had a degree of personal freedom and also where they underwent a process of secularization. Because of the protection that cities offered, cabarets, rookeries, and saloons devoted to the worlds of entertainment, sportingmen, and crime developed and prospered. Originally a part of the Negro community in lower New York, the rathskellers accompanied the trek up Manhattan. Perry Bradford, the early blues pioneer, traced the origins of the cabaret to Ike Hines's, a basement spot that opened in 1883 near Minetta Lane and Third Street. Run by a former entertainer with the Hicks and Sawyers Georgia Minstrels, Ike Hines's saloon became the liveliest place in Greenwich Village. Retitled Ike's Professional Club after spectacular success, the club attracted black performers and welcomed anyone with an act to help entertain.[50] In the 1890s, the club relocated to West Fifty-third Street, dubbed Black Bohemia because of the number of establishments catering to the Afro-American theatrical and sporting elites.[51] There it joined the Marshall Hotel, which opened at the turn of the century as the first major hotel where blacks could eat and congregate. This was a well-appointed place, where whites often went slumming.[52] There were also a number of saloons throughout the Tenderloin for blacks and also black and tans, so called because whites and blacks of both sexes congregated there. Under favorable political protection, these joints grew and prospered. They too would eventually find their way north to Harlem by the second decade of the twentieth century.[53]

In the world I have just described, passion was indeed a difficult business. Young women were taught that sexual control was social control, and respectable women lived up to this standard by refraining from any entertainments that required them to mix socially with members of lower classes. Men were not so constrained, though they would indulge themselves only if they left their wives at home. At the core of their lives, businessmen and their wives lived separate lives, and by the 1890s this separation between men and women, mind and body, and blacks and whites was noticeable. Backed by male expectations, class norms, and women's accommodation to and elaboration of higher demands of refinement, the genteel style produced a stifling domesticity and social formality. "It was because some salt was missing that society in maturity was hollow except in the home amidst homely things. We were restless in our genial social life because we had tacitly agreed that except in sin or in the reticence of marriage, sexual desires did not exist." Canby noted that among the prosperous classes, by the time a couple reached the mid-thirties they no longer considered each other passionate beings: "Every married woman was less than woman in mixed society because her sex was dormant, canalized, inhibited because no male present (with the faint possibility of an exception for her husband) imagined her as she was." Men too felt the weight of their cultural heritage. Every man was only a man "in his club or business or at the saloon bar."[54]

By the 1890s Canby's own generation, born in the late 1870s, felt the weight of the "conventions in social intercourse, for which we were not responsible." He and his friends who felt the stirrings of new desires were typical of an American mood, of a new generation's resolve to burst out of domestic controls and get closer to real desires. "We set free the compass needle which had been pointing too long to a false north of sexual convention and a false south of outlawed desires."[55] Feeling confined and stifled by the power of business and the cloistered home as defined by his parental culture, Canby saw in the creation of impersonal corporations the agency of his own release from following in his father's footsteps. Professional managers could take over, and he could choose a new path.

It was not just the prosperous in small cities who felt restless. Mrs. Burton Harrison held a forum of Newport women and found a general complaint: men absented themselves from fashionable society. "But what are you to do when such young men see their fathers refusing to mix with society on the ground that it is all very well for women," she asked, "but they have no time to spend on it, or are too tired when evening comes to do no more than read a newspaper?" The system had succeeded, producing "husbands and fathers [who] strain too much after success in affairs, and subordinate every other concern to that of making money." Enjoying refined homes, the best people too could not achieve mutual leisure. "We American women, who have the name of being the most indulged class upon earth, are often denied the one luxury we should prefer to all others," she exclaimed, "leisure time in the society of our husbands."[56]

Out of this questioning of sex roles and cultural precepts emerged a newer conception of the family, a redefinition of success, a new set of amusements, and a new urban culture. One prominent new amusement was the cabaret, a place where respectable men and women could gather to dine, drink, dance, and view risqué entertainment together. Before turning to the cabaret, let us first examine the luxury hotels, restaurants, and new amusements of the turn of the century from which the cabaret evolved.

NOTES

1. John Higham, *From Boundlessness to Consolidation; The Transformation of American Culture, 1848–1860* (Ann Arbor: William L. Clements Library, 1967), p. 26, notes the rise of formalism, gentility, and order in northern culture after 1848 and speculates that it rose from the convergence of industrialism and urbanization in the 1850s, along with the arrival of mass immigration to those cities and the need to impose a social control on rampant individualism in the urban context. George Frederickson, *The Inner Civil War* (New York: Harper & Row, 1967), sees the order arising out of the Civil War. Daniel Walker Howe, "American Victorianism as a Culture," *American Quarterly* 27 (December 1975): pp. 507–32, views Victorian bourgeoisie believing in rational order and control in self and society. Robert Wiebe, *The Search for Order 1877–1920* (New York: Hill & Wang, 1967), maintains much the same thesis for politics for a later period. Stephen Thernstrom, *Poverty and Progress, Social Mobility in a Nineteenth Century City* (New York: Atheneum, 1969), pp. 33–56, discusses the search for new means of social order in the 1850s. Burton J. Bledstein, *The Culture of Professionalism: The Middle Class and the Development of Higher Education in America* (New York: W. W. Norton & Co., 1976), notes the increasingly formal definitions of individuals, spaces, and qualifications at mid-century.

2. Henry Seidel Canby, *Age of Confidence, Life in the Nineties* (New York, 1934), p. 20.

3. Ibid., p. 31.

4. Ibid., p. 232. For more on this view of the self-made man as a dominant preoccupation of male identity, see Irvin Wyllie, *The Self-Made Man in America* (New Brunswick: Rutgers University Press, 1954); Donald B. Meyer, *The Positive Thinkers, A Study of the American Quest for Health, Wealth and Personal Power from Mary Baker Eddy to Norman Vincent Peale* (Garden City, N.Y.: Doubleday, 1965), pp. 29–41. G. J. Baker-Benfield, *The Horrors of the Half-Known Life, Male Attitudes Toward Women and Sexuality in Nineteenth-Century America* (New York: Harper & Row, 1976), pp. 3–57, discusses male attitudes toward business and the subsequent reliance on women for order in male identities. Alexis de Tocqueville, *Democracy in America*, ed. Phillips Bradley (New York: Alfred A. Knopf,

1945), 2: 163–67. For a view on British sexuality, see Peter T. Cominos, "Innocent Femina Sensualis in Unconscious Conflict," in *Suffer and Be Still: Women in the Victorian Age*, ed. Martha Vicinus (Bloomington: Indiana University Press, 1972), pp. 155–72.

5. Canby, *Age of Confidence*, p. 235.

6. Ibid., p. 239.

7. Ibid., p. 51.

8. Ibid., p. 52.

9. Ibid., p. 50.

10. Ibid., p. 66.

11. Ibid., p. 243. For material on the separate spheres of nineteenth-century women and men, see Barbara Welter, "The Cult of True Womanhood," *American Quarterly* 18 (Summer 1966): 151–74; Robert E. McGlone, "Suffer the Children: The Emergence of Modern Middle-Class Family Life in America, 1820–1870" (Ph.D. diss., University of California, 1971), p. 169; Meyer, *The Positive Thinkers*, pp. 29–41; Nancy Cott, *The Bonds of Womanhood, "Woman's Sphere" in New England, 1780–1835* (New Haven: Yale University Press, 1977); and Ann Douglas, *The Feminization of American Culture* (New York: Avon Books, 1978).

12. Canby, *Age of Confidence*, p. 160.

13. Ibid., p. 40.

14. Ibid., p. 45.

15. Ibid., p. 28.

16. Ibid., pp. 91–92.

17. For material on New York society, see Dixon Wecter, *The Saga of American Society* (New York: Charles Scribner's, Sons, 1937), pp. 289–97; Lloyd Morris, *Incredible New York* (New York: Random House, 1951), pp. 234–58; Lloyd Morris, *Postscript to Yesterday* (New York: Random House, 1957), pp. 13–21; Frederick Cople Jaher, "Nineteenth Century Elites in Boston and New York," *Journal of Social History* 6 (Fall 1972): 32–77, and his "Style and Status: High Society in Late Nineteenth-Century New York," in *The Rich, The Well Born, and the Powerful: Elites and Upper Classes in History*, ed. Frederick Cople Jaher (Urbana: University of Illinois Press, 1973), pp. 259–84; Carrol Hunter Quenzel, "Society in New York and Chicago, 1888–1900" (Ph.D. diss., University of Wisconsin, 1938).

18. Lately Thomas [pseud.], *Delmonico's, A Century of Splendor* (Boston: Houghton Mifflin, 1967), pp. 16, 41, 56, has material on early eating houses in New York City; p. 56 on *New York Herald*; p. 64 on the growth of a new style in Delmonico's.

19. Ibid., p. 86.

20. Ibid., p. 117.

21. Ibid., pp. 93, 108.

22. Ibid., p. 160.

23. Unidentified newspaper clipping, April 29, 1901, in Restaurant Vertical File, New York Public Library.

24. Thomas, *Delmonico's*. p. 199.

25. Arthur Schlesinger, *Learning How to Behave, A History of American Etiquette Books* (New York: Macmillan, 1947), pp. 25–55.

26. Mrs. John King Van Rennselaer, quoted in Foster Rhea Dulles, *America Learns to Play* (New York: D. Appleton-Century Company, 1940), p. 231.

27. Ralph Pulitzer, *New York Society on Parade* (New York and London: Harper & Bros., 1910), p. 3. Pulitzer has a marvelous discussion of the creation of social institutions to define status for an insecure upper class. Social cohesion, not individual pleasure, dominated social life.

28. Ward McAllister, Mrs. Astor's chamberlain, is generally considered the one who articulated the idea of a Four Hundred.

29. Elizabeth Drexel Lehr, *"King Lehr" and the Gilded Age: The Extracts from the Locked Diary of Harry Lehr* (Philadelphia: J. B. Lippincott, 1935), p. 58.

30. Henry James, *The American Scene* (New York: Horizon Press, 1967), pp. 64–65.

31. Morris, *Postscript*, pp. 14–16; the original observation comes from Thorstein Veblen, *The Theory of the Leisure Class* (New York: Mentor, 1953), pp. 68–70.

32. Mrs. Burton Harrison, *The Well-Bred Girl in Society* (New York: Doubleday, Paget & Co., 1904), pp. 5–6, 39–42, 77–79, 86–87; Elsie deWolfe, *After All* (New York: Harper & Bros., 1935), pp. 113–14, seconds Mrs. Harrison: unless engaged to a man, a young woman could not be seen out with a man in public. Young women of the upper classes were watched by chaperones, and no woman dined alone with a man in public unless he was her husband. Except for those who had been in society for several seasons, drinking was frowned upon.

33. Sam Warner, Jr., *The Private City, Philadelphia in Three Periods of Its Growth* (Philadelphia: University of Pennsylvania, 1968), pp. 19–21, has material on preindustrial cities; Patricia Click, "The High Life and the Low: A Survey of Richmond Amusements, 1810–1880" (Seminar paper, University of Virginia, 1975), pp. 6–28.

34. David Grimsted, *Melodrama Unveiled: American Theater and Culture 1800–1850* (Chicago: University of Chicago, 1968), pp. 46–75, has the best discussion of the early theaters, and pp. 103–107 views the variety of performances. See also Claudia D. Johnson, "That Guilty Third Tier: Prosti-

tution in Nineteenth-Century Theaters," *American Quarterly* 27 (December 1975): 575–84; Dulles, *America Learns to Play*, pp. 100–21.

35. Grimsted, *Melodrama*, p. 56.

36. Ibid., p. 23.

37. Dulles, *America Learns to Play*, pp. 131–35, has a good discussion of the varied origins of the circus. See also Albert F. McLean, Jr., *American Vaudeville as Ritual* (Lexington: University of Kentucky Press, 1965), pp. 27–28.

38. Grimsted, *Melodrama*, pp. 171–248 provides the best insights into the structure and vision of melodrama.

39. Walter Damrosch, *My Musical Life* (New York: Charles Scribner's, Sons, 1923), p. 334, and Theodore Thomas, *Theodore Thomas: A Musical Autobiography*, ed. George Upton (Chicago, 1905), Vol. 1, epigraph, quoted in Neil Leonard, *Jazz and the White Americans: The Acceptance of a New Art Form* (Chicago: University of Chicago Press, 1962), pp. 15–16.

40. Jon Kingsdale, "The Poor Man's Club: Social Functions of the Urban Working-Class Saloon," *American Quarterly* 25 (October 1973): 472–89.

41. Felix Isman, *Weber and Fields* (New York, 1924), pp. 22–23, quoted in McLean, *American Vaudeville*, p. 30. See also H. E. Cooper, "Variety, Vaudeville and Virtue," *Dance Magazine* 7 (December 1926): 31–32, 64; Dulles, *America Learns to Play*, pp. 98, 119–20, 217–18.

42. For material on minstrelsy, see Robert C. Toll, *Blacking Up: The Minstrel Show in Nineteenth-Century America* (New York: Oxford University Press, 1974); Alexander Saxton, "Blackface Minstrelsy and Jacksonian Ideology," *American Quarterly* 27 (March 1975): 3–28; Hans Nathan, *Dan Emmett and the Rise of Early Minstrelsy* (Norman: University of Oklahoma Press, 1962); Nathan Huggins, *Harlem Renaissance* (New York: Oxford University Press, 1971), pp. 244–301; Carl Wittke, *Tambo and Bones: A History of the American Minstrel Stage* (Durham: Duke University Press, 1930); Dailey Paskman and Sigmund Spaeth, *"Gentlemen Be Seated!" A Parade of the Old Time Minstrels* (Garden City: Doubleday, 1928); and McLean, *American Vaudeville*, pp. 26–29.

43. Russel B. Nye, "Saturday Night at the Paradise Ballroom: Or Dance Halls in the Twenties," *Journal of Popular Culture* 7 (Summer 1973): 14–15.

44. Canby, *Age of Confidence*, pp. 151, 172. The remark on family plus prostitution is quoted in Andrew Sinclair, *The Emancipation of American Women* (New York: Harper & Row, 1965), p. 134. This was brought to my attention by Robert Abrams, "The Struggle to Civilize a City: Prostitution and Moral Reform in Early Twentieth Century Chicago" (Senior thesis, University of Michigan, 1976).

45. The Melodeon is cited in Jimmy Durante and Jack Kofoed, *Night-*

clubs (New York: Alfred A. Knopf, 1931), p. 12; Ernst Ingersoll, *A Week in New York* (New York: Rand McNally, 1891), p. 212; Walter Reckless, *Vice in Chicago* (Chicago: University of Chicago, 1933), p. 99 has material on the Illinois Vice Commission's description of concert saloons in Chicago; Matthew Hale, *Sunshine and Shadow in New York* (Hartford, 1869), pp. 439–40; James McCabe, Jr., *Lights and Shadows of New York Life* (New York: Farrar Straus & Giroux, 1970), p. 594 notes that most of the concert saloons were basement places employing women as waitresses and quotes an owner who said, "A concert saloon is a gin-mill on an improved plan—that's all, my friend. I don't pay the girls any wages. They get a percentage on the drinks they sell."

46. Herbert Asbury, *The Gangs of New York* (New York: Alfred A. Knopf, 1928), pp. 177–78; Richard O'Connor, *Hell's Kitchen* (Philadelphia and New York: J. B. Lippincott, 1958), pp. 88–99, contains details about Haymarket, and the reporter's quote, pp. 88–91.

47. O'Connor, *Hell's Kitchen*, p. 91, and Asbury, *Gangs*, p. 179.

48. Oliver Pilat and Jo Ransom, *Sodom by the Sea: An Affectionate History of Coney Island* (New York: Doubleday, 1941), pp. 93–94, 98, 105, 126.

49. There is disagreement in the popular literature over whether the cabaret originated in black saloons and rathskellers or in white free and easies of the 1850s. For the first position see Perry Bradford, *Born with the Blues* (New York: Oak Publications, 1965), pp. 163–71. For the second, see Durante and Kofoed, *Nightclubs*, pp. 12–17.

50. Bradford, *Born with the Blues*, pp. 163–64.

51. Roi Ottley and William Weatherby, *The Negro in New York, An Informal Social History*, 1940 (New York: Praeger, 1967), pp. 145–64 quotes *New York Sun*, June 5, 1887, on the area being called Black Bohemia, and develops the point. For general comments, see Gilbert Osofsky, *Harlem: The Making of a Ghetto* (New York: Harper & Row, 1968), pp. 12–15; James Weldon Johnson, *Black Manhattan* (New York: Atheneum, 1969), pp. 118–19. For a fictional account, see James Weldon Johnson, *The Autobiography of an Ex-Colored Man* (New York: Avon Books, 1927), in *Three Negro Classics* (New York, 1965), pp. 441–61.

52. Willie "The Lion" Smith, with George Hoefer, *Music on My Mind* (Garden City: Doubleday, 1964), p. 54; and Ottley and Weatherby, *Negro in New York*, p. 156.

53. Edward B. Marks, *They All Sang* (New York, 1934), p. 89; Bradford, *Born with the Blues*, pp. 161–72; Smith, *Music*, pp. 51–53.

54. Canby, *Age of Confidence*, pp. 173, 175.

55. Ibid., pp. 182–83.

56. Harrison, *Well-Bred Girl*, pp. 202–204.

Part Two BREAKING
THE BONDS

The great create an atmosphere which reacts badly upon the small. This atmosphere is readily and quickly felt. Walk among the magnificent residences, the splendid equipages, the gilded shops, the restaurants, resorts of all kinds; scent the flowers, the silks, the wines; drink of the laughter springing from the soul of luxurious content, of the glances which gleam like light from defiant spears; feel the quality of the smiles which cut like glistening swords and of strides born of place, and you shall know of what is the atmosphere of the high and mighty. Little use to argue that of such is not the kingdom of greatness, but so long as the world is attracted by this and the human heart views this as the one desirable realm which it must attain, so long, to that heart will this remain the realm of greatness. So long, also, will the atmosphere of this realm work its desperate results in the soul of man. It is like a chemical reagent.   Theodore Dreiser,[1]

Sister Carrie

2 AFTER THE BALL: HOTELS AND LOBSTER PALACES, 1893–1912

In 1897, Delmonico's made its last move, to Fifth Avenue and Forty-fourth Street. Following the upward path of high life on sumptuous Fifth Avenue, Delmonico's had reached the apogee of its long and distinguished career. Yet subtle changes already were dating the restaurant as part of a passing era. In the year of its new opening, for example, the managers responded to popular demand and allowed smoking in their dining rooms for the first time. No longer were female patrons offended by cigar-puffing men, who lit up in the decorous surroundings of the main dining room. Moreover, Delmonico's was no longer the only excellent restaurant favored by the sophisticated. The Waldorf-Astoria had opened its expanded doors on Thirty-fourth Street only recently (1897), and Sherry's would open across the street from Delmonico's within a year. Delmonico's had transformed dining tastes, and now others were competing for the patronage of gourmets. While the social sets swung back and forth in their allegiance, the theatre and nightlife sets were already beginning to desert Delmonico's for the gayer, more vibrant lobster palace after-theatre restaurants along the Great White Way. A new era in nightlife was in the making, "an age of mammoth glittering hotels, restaurant parties, ragtime tunes."[2]

The expansion of fashionable nightlife started in 1893 with the opening of the Waldorf Hotel on Fifth Avenue between Thirty-third and Thirty-fourth streets. Hoping to attract the first families of the city, George C. Boldt constructed a monument of grandiose elegance and elaborate cuisine, and he inaugurated the festivities with a charity ball for Saint Mary's Free Hospital for Children. Drawn from the most select circles, the patrons of St. Mary's encouraged their equally illustrious friends to attend, making the evening a grand success both for charity and the hotel business. Because of its importance, the opening attracted representatives of elite families from other major cities as well. Afterward Boldt hosted an elaborate supper to display both the cuisine and service of his restaurant staff. Commandeering six to eight private dining rooms, described by one report as "surpassing anything of the kind yet seen in this city in tasteful elegance," he engineered the growing emergence of the wealthy from the sanctity of their private homes to the public opulence of his hotel dining rooms.[3]

The facts behind the building of the hotel suggest that all was not well in the select circles of New York. One version suggests that William Waldorf Astor, son of the venerable John Jacob Astor III, built the hotel to spite his aunt, *the* Mrs. Astor, for slighting his own wife's social pretensions. Another version portrays the hotel as William's revenge upon his fashionable district for failing to elect him to Congress. In either case, he punished his foes by tearing down his own mansion on Thirty-third Street and replacing it with an imposing hotel, thereby forcing his aunt to move in order to escape the new Waldorf going up across from her door. Four years later Mrs. Astor's son collaborated on the Waldorf-Astoria, which opened amid even greater social notice in 1897. In the building of the hotel, then, the elites of New York were in conflict, unable to act as a strong, united group. Women fought for dominance. Because of rapid elite turnover, an exclusive concern with social affairs dominated New York social life. As William Astor found, they were dispersed and porous, and the elite found it difficult to enter political or economic life as a class. With the continuous and even more rapid influx of new industrial wealth from the midwest and west in the 1880s and 1890s, the wealthy began to abandon its more formally restrictive social life for a more public one. The hotel stands as the symbol of a new openness by the late 1890s.[4]

According to Lloyd Morris, the Waldorf-Astoria symbolized New

York's "aspiration to lead an expensive, gregarious life as publicly as possible."[5] The hotel was built for public display of prominence and power. The building itself was modeled after a German Renaissance design, complete with gabled and tiled roofs. The hotel's Empire dining hall, according to guide Moses King, "is modelled after the grand *salon* in King Ludwig's Palace at Munich, with frescoes, satin hangings, upholstery and marble pillars, all of pale green."[6] Although the Waldorf was famous for its private banquet and ballrooms, its public corridors and dining rooms also played an important role in its success. These public arenas gave men and women the opportunity to display their monied and powerful position and a chance to watch others doing the same. Appropriately entitled Peacock Alley, the corridor to the main dining room featured seats from which one could watch the formally dressed men and expensively attired women on their way to dine.[7] Because of its enviable location and its glass walls and wide open doors, the main restaurant, the Palm Garden, put diners on public display and became one of the most sought-after eating places in the nation.[8] People from all over came just to sit and watch "interesting people at the other tables—famous men and handsome women," both in the evening and during luncheon.[9] Lined with floor-to-ceiling mirrors, the Palm Garden gave diners an uninterrupted view of themselves and of other refined and powerful diners. To the left of the Garden was the Men's Café, separated by only another glass wall. The café provided a place for stockbrokers and men of affairs to pick up stock tips, deliver financial advice, drink, and keep their eye on business, all within view of one of the main social dining rooms in all of New York and the nation.[10]

The Waldorf's ability to attract the wealthy to its public dining rooms marks a transition in New York upper-class life, for as Boldt recognized, "the wealthy first families were growing restless and were looking for amusement outside of their own walls."[11] Starting in the late 1890s, many hotels and restaurants began to rival elite households in the style and service of cuisine, and they joined the Waldorf in expanding the boundaries of the hotel district northward along Fifth Avenue and Broadway to Forty-second Street and beyond.[12] Writing in 1906, the *New York Times* observed that "within the past ten years many new restaurants of the first order have opened, and there are under way several new ones." On the Fifth Avenue side alone,

Martin's, Sherry's, the Holland House, the Waldorf-Astoria, the St. Regis, the Savoy, and a half-dozen others opened and prospered. Broadway housed the Astor Hotel, the new Knickerbocker, Shanley's, and Rector's. "One has now," noted the newspaper, "just as one had in the old days in Paris, as they say in French, an 'embarrassment of riches' from which to choose."[13]

One explanation of the growth of elegant public restaurants at the turn of the century lies in the increasing pull of New York on the monied class of the nation and the rapid turnover of wealth in the nation's financial center. The new industries of the latter half of the nineteenth century produced great numbers of men and women with wealth and the desire for social status. Writing in 1888, Henry Clews, a respected Wall Street banker, noted that the nation's successful men and women gravitated toward New York City after making their fortunes. "In a word," he declared, "people of wealth are apt to be drawn to New York because it is the great magnet of the country, whose attractive power is well nigh irresistible." As a national city, New York inspired the presence and the imagination of the nation's rich. "What London is to the Continent, what Rome was in its imperial day to the Empire . . . ," he observed, "New York is to the immense domain of the American Republic, a natural stage . . . for the great drama of civilization on this Continent."[14]

There is some truth to Clews's observations. In 1892, 1,368 millionaires lived in the city together with their families and relatives. Within fifteen years, 70 percent of the head offices of the nation's major corporations were located in New York, and this brought to the city a tremendous amount of business and social visitation. Of the nation's 185 trusts, 69 were headquartered there. New York led the nation in banking, insurance, shipping, and manufacturing. By 1923 it had become the tourist mecca of the United States. The increasing size of both city and wealth contributed to the development of secondary institutions, such as the Waldorf-Astoria. These institutions provided a place where the rich could meet each other socially, replacing the now-too-small private home, which had housed the social events of a more rigidly defined group. In an effort to establish their positions, new and old money adopted the behavior patterns described by cynical chronicler Thorstein Veblen. They got together to display their monetary power, and hence their industrial might, in such public places as hotels and restaurants, where the circulation of the community and human contact were greatest. The larger cities like New York served as points from which they could make themselves known. Within the city, the hotels and restaurants facilitated social mixing and provided meeting places for the members of an expanded elite.[15]

Within Mrs. Astor's Four Hundred, moreover, the younger sets expressed increasing boredom with her generation's authoritarian social formalism. In the 1880s Mrs. Astor's generation utilized etiquette and formal functions to define the private world of high society. Competition in the ritualization of the balls and dining rooms, however, was considered dull. Everyone had to be on his/her best behavior in order to demonstrate breeding and cultivation, not mere money, and this constraint made the events themselves mere formalities. Besides the high turnover and rapid circulation of money prevented the establishment of a New York upper class in politics, culture, and economic life. The world of the elite focused instead on social life, the one measurement of acceptance. In this atmosphere, the social rituals lost their inner élan and reeked with competitiveness.

Increasingly wealthy women found their roles hollow. Leisured, with little other than the social round to pursue, young women had a difficult time creating a vibrant social life to compete with male business. Men did not participate. The public hotel offered rich women a place to meet, and it also provided them with a chance to pursue social leadership on a personal basis, outside the enervating round of society's all-encompassing activities. For women and men of wealth, the public restaurants allowed for the gradual releasing of the hand of convention that tied women to the domestic circle. They could learn to live an aristocratic life above bourgeois conventions. By the 1890s, the formalism that had been created to blend money with cultivation, and to distinguish the elite from the mass, had become an empty end in itself.[16]

The questioning of this cultural synthesis by those who sought to enjoy the wealth with which they had grown up is best symbolized by the rise to social leadership of the younger Mrs. Stuyvesant Fish, and her waspish aide, Harry Lehr, around the turn of the century. Compared to Mrs. Astor and stuffy Ward McAllister, Mrs. Fish and Lehr were only two of a number of social leaders. They were social jokers, bent on bringing greater life into society. Although they were still encased within older exclusive forms, they ridiculed the sterility of these manners, rituals, and functions. Disregarding the proprieties, for example, Mrs. Fish would send her guests home when she tired, instructing the orchestra to play "Home Sweet Home" until they took the hint and departed. On other occasions, she and Lehr held elaborate, formal dinners for monkeys and dogs, and they also inspired Newport millionaires to throw ingenious parties dressed as servants. Her own dinners, which she called vaudevilles, were shorter and featured literateurs, entertainers, and interesting celebrities to liven up the evening. Mrs. Astor recognized the danger. In one of her rare newspaper interviews, she disapproved of the "undignified methods employed by certain New York women to attract a following. They have given entertainments that belong under a circus tent rather than in a gentlewoman's house." While Mrs. Astor had had the iron will to hold the line for rituals against money, Mrs. Fish was already burlesquing the very forms that held society together. Mrs. Astor's style was fast losing its hold. In 1897 she held the last of her exclusive Patriarch Balls at Sherry's, and after that, society was freer to mix and meet as individuals chose.[17]

The increased desire for liveliness also found expression in a short-lived attempt in 1893 to found the private Vaudeville Club for members of select circles. Originated by men who were somewhat bored with the usual routine of society, the club was intended "for the purpose of giving entertainments which should supplement in some sense the regular theatre, and also give the ladies and gentlemen who did not care to go to the music halls now open in New York an entertainment similar in character," but of course not so "indelicate," as the common halls. Men watched from little tables with their hats on, smoking cigars and quenching their thirst with brandy and soda. Charles Belmont Davis noted the demanding rules of admission designed to protect women, but he also noted something new. The patron had the chance to see the smart, artistic, and club world, and "he will see them not as they pose in a ballroom or on the platform, but as he might see them at their own clubs or at their homes." In such an atmosphere, "he will find them with the restraint of celebrity thrown aside, and, like himself, bent on the sole purpose of finding that sort of amusement which makes a sleep easier and the next day's work less like work after all." The experiment lasted only a short while, but soon the Waldorf Hotel and the Broadway restaurants were presenting celebrities in a late-night relaxed atmosphere.[18]

The large and glittering hotels of the 1890s and turn of the century supplied stages where the exclusive and the wealthy could mix, meet, and compete at a distance and on safe ground. The old standards were giving way to the power of money, publicly displayed. Under constant pressure from without and within, the urban rich found it difficult to maintain strong hold on their membership and to develop into a firmly defined upper class; instead they fragmented into powerful but rival cliques. The huge public hotels represented an attempt by new elites to outdo other wealthy elements in the only way they knew: socially and through public claim to leadership. In this period of flux, the wealthy classes regrouped while they transferred their competitiveness to public spheres, which connoted power, money, and an ability to lead. New York society became increasingly public and competitive. Recognizing their own social enervation as social life threatened to pass them by, members of old and new money emerged into the public social life in a grand way. And once in the public, the lines between the social elect and others continued to blur, especially as the various segments of the wealthy turned to cultivating Broadway figures to increase their now-public notice and reputation.

The Waldorf-Astoria allowed the wealthy to come together amid luxury and elegance; it also became a public palace that advertised and purveyed luxury to the masses. The great industrialists had built their empires, and their hotels testified to the ordering power of businessmen. It was the power of money that made this the largest and most grandiose hotel in the world, and its public nature, grand design, and increased mixing made it different from the substantial comforts of Delmonico's. Here was display. The increase in size of the hotel dining room, occasioned by the opening of the Astoria annex in 1897, forced even the exclusive-minded Boldt to alter his approach to the hotel business, for to keep the dining and living rooms full, he had to create a brisker turnover. In the dining room, Oscar, the maitre d'hôtel, recognized that the policy of exclusive snobbery no longer could be maintained. Although trained in the old distinctions, he greeted parvenu and elect with equal aplomb.[19] A consummate host, Oscar welcomed by name whomever he thought important, making all equally at home in the public world of the Palm Garden. In public, the old barriers were waning; now money, not background, predominated.

In providing a public stage for the monied, the Waldorf, with its Peacock Alley promenade, soon became too public for the most exclusive families. They continued to patronize the Waldorf-Astoria, but they found themselves torn between their desire for public social leadership and recognition and exclusivity. They began turning to newer, smaller hotels farther along Fifth Avenue, such as Sherry's and the St. Regis, once their dominance in the new Waldorf-Astoria was no longer assured.[20] In these smaller hotels of elegant surroundings and cuisine, the rich could enjoy greater publicity while still remaining dominant in their rooms. While the elite withdrew their main patronage from the Waldorf-Astoria, they still enjoyed it as an important part of New York nightlife. The Waldorf-Astoria thus continued to offer those with money the association with wealth and power, and opened the door of the private mansion to a wider, less exclusive, city life. Anyone with money could bathe in the hotel's reflected light.

FROM THE WALDORF TO THE LOBSTER PALACE

The late 1890s also saw the beginnings of the rapid growth of nightlife along Broadway. From the late 1890s through 1910, a number of new and spectacularly designed restaurants opened above and in the vicinity of Broadway and Forty-second Street, later to be known as Times Square. These restaurants catered to the theatrical crowds that nightly surged out of limousines, taxis, and theatres in search of dinner or an after-theatre supper. While the Waldorf-Astoria represented a far more public life among the wealthy than had Delmonico's, it still had its roots in Fifth Avenue reserve and social prestige. From 1899 to 1912 on Broadway, however, new restaurants—Bustanoby's, Churchill's, Martin's, Maxim's, Murray's Roman Gardens, Rector's, Reisenweber's, and Shanley's—were pioneering a style that was even showier than the Waldorf's. Broadway was the place to celebrate, and theatrical success or sporting wins were often toasted with popping champagne corks. The lobster palaces, as they were called because of their gilded interiors and gay late-night lobster suppers, merchandised an opulent experience of material pleasure and hoped-for naughtiness for prosperous urban dwellers of varied backgrounds, many of whom lived in the luxurious but not exclusive apartments of the upper West Side. As George Rector noted, Sherry's and Delmonico's served the Four Hundred, but "Rector's not only attracted the Four Hundred, but also most of O. Henry's Four Million."[21] These restaurants were showplaces that glorified material pleasures and revealed an urban nightlife moving beyond the formalism of a Victorian world.

While Fifth Avenue and new wealth remained the core of the Waldorf's patronage, Broadway catered to the theatrical and sporting worlds' new money and the vast urban populace who wanted a good time. Consequently the lobster palace world was much more varied than the Waldorf's. Indeed the lobster palaces seemed to have grown apace with the prestige and prosperity of the theatrical profession. From the 1890s, the star system had come to replace the repertory company or the star who played the same role exclusively in his or her career. In the hands of such producers as David Belasco and Charles Frohman, for example, this new star system drew wider audiences to see new-style plays. This was the age of the drawing-room drama, the naughty French farce, drawing-room comedies, and the musical stage filled with chorus girls such as the Floradora Girls. A number of popular stars such as John Drew, Maude Adams, Mrs. Fiske, and Lillian Russell brought to the public stage stirring portrayals of the life led by the wealthy. In the hands of the great playwright Clyde Fitch, the drama indulged in examinations of wealthy living and the social aspirations and difficulties of women of the social set. Long before the theatre's star system reached the mass level through vaudeville and movies, it appealed to a carriage trade, featuring players who embodied the drawing room and advertised the nonascetic life possible for the rich and successful.[22] All over the theatrical district new and sumptuous theatres decorated with gilded interiors were going up. It was but a short step from the fantasy on stage to the fantasies portrayed by the restaurants themselves. Both patrons and players utilized the lobster palaces as stages of a more sumptuous and indulgent life.

The Broadway restaurants helped make the life of conspicuous consumption available to a wider portion of the city and the nation. As the numbers of the wealthy increased, the merely well-to-do were overshadowed, and in response they too adopted a more materialistic style of life. Theodore Dreiser expressed his understanding of this problem when comparing New York to Chicago in *Sister Carrie*. In the Windy City, "the rich had not become so conspicuously rich as to drown all moderate incomes in obscurity." Local celebrities in the "dramatic, artistic, social and religious fields" did not distract the inhabitants so as "to shut the well-positioned man from view." In New York, however, "the roads were any one of a half-hundred, and each had been diligently pursued by hundreds, so that celebrities were numerous. The sea was already full of whales." In Dreiser's estimation, "a common fish must needs disappear wholly from view— remain unseen." Such a well-positioned man was Drouet, the salesman in *Sister Carrie* who was bent on making her his mistress and success his goal. Drouet was just the type of man to see in Broadway-style restaurants the opportunity to stylize himself according to an urban model of success. Drouet often visited Chicago's Rector's, a dining place with a more successful Broadway counterpart: "Rector's, with its polished marble walls and floors, its profusion of lights, its show of china and silverware, and above all, its reputation as a resort for actors and professional men, seemed the proper place for a successful man to go." The urban vision of success was different from the old Horatio Alger myth, for the latter had glorified the man of will-power, self-discipline, and perseverance—the classic Protestant virtues. Drouet, a salesman for others, on the other hand, enjoyed indulging his love of fine clothes, good eating, "and particularly the company and acquaintanceship of successful men." In the lobster palaces of Broadway, what was important was money and the gratification it could buy, not disciplined self-denial. As Drouet looked about the room at the actors, brokers, and rich young rounders of the town, he contemplated his own future: "He would be able to flash a roll of greenbacks too some day. As it was, he could eat where *they* did."[23] Having lived with the wealthy's style of conspicuous consumption, men and women from New York and around the nation were now more accustomed to the enjoyment of money. A rising standard of living had changed the nature of status and success. The restraints surrounding individual pleasure were becoming loosened.

While the Astors, Goelets, and other families of established wealth were behind the hotel building on Fifth Avenue, newcomers, often of Irish, Swiss, and French restaurant backgrounds, catered to the crowds of Broadway. The Rectors, for example, father Charles and son George, came from a long line of restaurateurs, but their own success was relatively recent. In 1825 Charles's father had built the Frontier House in Lewiston, New York, and it was in the 1890s that Charles opened a branch of Rector's in Chicago. Charles had been a conductor on the Second Avenue line in New York and then ran the first Pullman hotel dining car. In 1899 he moved to New York after word of mouth had spread from the theatrical profession about his food, and he opened his restaurant at Broadway and Forty-fourth Street. Charles himself had a career that went up and down, and he had experience catering to the theatrical profession, just coming into its own. Jacques Bustanoby, son of a cook in Pau, France, followed his four brothers to the United States in 1897. He garnered employment at Martin's Restaurant and worked his way up from busboy to waiter to captain and to headwaiter. In 1901 he opened the Café Beaux Arts. The Shanley brothers and Julius Keller of Maxim's had similar backgrounds. While the former worked in restaurants throughout the city, the latter, who had arrived from Switzerland at the age of ten, served a term at Delmonico's before opening first a bar in the Tenderloin and then his own restaurant on Thirty-eighth and Broadway. Most of the restaurateurs started at the bottom of the restaurant business and then became fabulously successful. They were at home with people who had achieved material prosperity and took obvious pleasure in their acquaintance with successful and prominent New Yorkers.[24]

Men like Julius Keller had started out in the old oyster saloons or chophouses, which catered largely to men. As they moved up in clientele, the proprietors created luxurious environments for a mixed-sex patronage bent on taking their pleasures lavishly with a touch of refinement. Discussing the rise of elegant restaurants in this period, Eugene Dorval of the Casino in the Park remarked that patrons invariably selected "beautiful" and well-patronized restaurants over those with merely "a little better cuisine," a conclusion that Oscar of the Waldorf seconded: "They must have large and beautiful rooms in which to sit, the service must be perfect and everything must have the air of elegance about it."[25] The decor, perhaps even more than the food, marked the peculiar nature of the lobster palace and testified to patrons' willingness and ability to consume conspicuously and well.

As the *American Architect* noted in a review of the Hotel Rector, which opened in 1910, "We all know of less ostentatious examples of decorations, but not of any more suited to the majority of the patrons who must be depended on for the success of a Longacre restaurant." The review could not help but notice that "a Broadway restaurant must necessarily be magnificently gorgeous at any cost."[26]

To heighten the impression that their patrons were part of the world of wealth and opulence, the Broadway restaurants borrowed their decor from aristocratic Fifth Avenue and foreign homes. From the elaborate exteriors to the gilded interiors, the restaurants removed their patrons from the humdrum business activity of Broadway and brought them fantasies of Europe and the past. Up the elaborate and hand-carved stairways of a Shanley's or a Lorber's, women and men trod away from the business world to the visions of aristocratic enjoyment awaiting them inside. Every Broadway restaurant prided itself on its carvings, its fixtures, and especially its glittering crystal chandeliers, which shone on all as they ate in the elegance of a private dining room. In Lorber's, for example, diners entered up a hand-carved stairway to a horseshoe balcony under a crystal chandelier, which was surrounded by carved panels in an oak ceiling.[27]

The Broadway restaurants offered visions of comfort and enjoyment that had been the privilege of the world's greatest civilizations. Their architecture and design imitated the regal and imperial eras of European and ancient history. A special issue of *New York Plaisance* detailed the direction taken by Murray's Roman Gardens, which opened on Forty-second Street in 1906. Once leaving the busy street, the journal noted, the visitor was "transported as though on the famous carpet of Mahomet, back into ancient Rome." There, in this American-created foreign world, the guest would "feast his eyes on artistic and authentically beautiful features of Rome's most ornate homes, of the palaces, villas and pleasure resorts of her wealthiest and most cultured citizens." While the interior was Roman, the exterior was French, reproducing for the lower two stories the ancient hotel of Cardinal de Rohan of Paris in Caen stone. A hugh doorway marked the entrance, over which rested a copy of "Les chevaux du soleil" from the cardinal's stables. This regal imagery was not limited to Murray's. The Rectors decorated their restaurant in green and gold furnishings of the Sun King. The Hotel Martinique on Broadway and

Thirty-second Street featured a main dining room modeled after the Apollo Room of the Louvre, with panels depicting Maurice de Saxe, Ronsard, Voltaire, Louis XV, the ladies of the court, and other great figures of the eighteenth century. Up two streets, the Hotel McAlpin had a Sun King Room while the Knickerbocker bar on Forty-second Street sported a Louis XIV design.[28]

The regal and aristocratic imagery testified to patrons' ability to consume. The restaurants provided the opportunity to enjoy the best of Europe (from artwork to decor and food) in semipublic institutions. Since 1870 the rich in New York had enjoyed such privileges in private, but now a greater portion of the populace shared these pleasures. In associating themselves with such exalted imagery, monied patrons differentiated themselves both from the mass and their own more ascetic backgrounds. Dining amid European splendor signaled one's ability to copy consumption patterns of the very wealthy and to break from a small-town past. Here was an urban architecture that turned its back on the cramped, small spaces of genteel institutions and the dark design of gothic structures of the past generation and identified with an urban concern for comfort, pleasure, and well-being.

Patrons, moreover, could identify with the power of their own civilization. Murray's and Louis Martin's, both built by architect Henry Erkins, went the furthest in reproducing the Imperial Roman, French, Egyptian, and other civilizations as settings for their diners. In Murray's patrons entered the main dining room through a black and gold mosiac-lined foyer. The main dining room was built to resemble the atrium of a Roman home, complete with an open court with colonnades on each side. Surrounded by trees and statues and gazing out on an ancient barge fronting a terraced fountain crowned by a classical temple rising clear to the ceiling, diners enjoyed the illusion of being in ancient Rome or at a villa in Pompeii, "the Newport of Rome, bedecked with the sculpture, statuary and various trophies of victories, such as a Roman general would build on his return from his conquests."[29] The classical porticos and temples provided a sense of restful magnificence, while the enormous height of the room and open space suggested the lofty opulence and power of the diner. Diners at Murray's enjoyed the feeling that their success enabled them to be part of the best of all earlier civilizations.

Americans could equal European civilizations because they had the technological mastery that Europe did not. Indeed the restaurants of Broadway gloried in the power that technology had wrought, a power to bring comfort not just through the creation of luxurious settings but through the different methods and new discoveries that characterized the technological society. In Murray's, for example, the luxury was balanced by practicality in the kitchen and the service. The restaurants modeled themselves after Delmonico's and featured a complex organizational hierarchy, with the maitre d'hôtel at the top, captains, waiters, and busboys in descending order, all to bring comfort to the patrons. The very designs themselves mirrored the fascination with technology that characterized this period. All of the restaurants used electric lights for artistic effects; for example, electric chandeliers and electric colored lights on every table were used to create a subdued and romantic atmosphere. Restaurant designers extended the theme and technological dominance into the gardens as well. In Murray's there were "festoons of vines with flowers and foliage on the wall in this room, while the ceiling is decorated and lighted to represent the deep blue eastern sky with interstices through which twinkle electric stars."[30] American civilization was the technological showplace, and it was this mastery over nature that made America surpass the powerful civilizations of the past.

This fascination with imperial imagery bespoke a cultural confidence and paradoxically a fear of social weakness among captains of industry and prosperous urban groups in the period following the Spanish American War. Like the dispossessed during the depression of the 1890s, the well-to-do found their positions and social identities uncertain. Their fears of Populists, Socialists, labor strikes, class strife, and immigrant city dwellers led urbanites to worry lest the United States emulate Europe in its class hatreds and individual weaknesses. The well-to-do wavered in their belief in the certainty of progress because the society seemed weakened by corruption and ripe for a revolution. The development of great industrial enterprises also contributed to a general sense of individual helplessness. However, the grandiose hotels and restaurants symbolized a renewed belief in the power of the American businessman and in the ability of the business community to overcome social problems. Indeed, business men and their wives gloried in the industrial empire they had built. Rooting themselves in the past, they showed that change and dissension could not rock a democracy fixed in timeless perpetuity. They heralded American civilization as equal to or better than European. They trumpeted the power of the business system that permitted them to indulge in greater leisure and affluence and to adopt aristocratic and imperial ways, the fruits of a powerful economic empire.

The service and food echoed the themes of refinement and conspicuous consumption found in the decor. The dining room and food service of the Broadway restaurants extended the privileges of the fashionable private home. All was intended for the comfort of the patron, but decorum had to be maintained. The introduction of music in the restaurants after the turn of the century illustrates this concern with balancing comfort and decorum. A number of commentators viewed the small orchestras as inimical to the peaceful enjoyment of one's meal. According to the *Hotel Monthly*, public dining rooms should expunge emotional excitement and be like "the most elegant of private homes," in which every "effort is made to preserve quiet in the dining room."[31] Although the restaurants began featuring small orchestras, the management adhered to the dominant values by placing the musicians behind screens or palms and demanding that they play soft music appropriate to the dignified ambience. This arrangement demonstrated that the public world still had to mirror the private world of the home.

Because everyone was to be courteously served, proprietors demanded a uniform and efficient service, which made guests comfortable and treated them like ladies and gentlemen. Proprietors, for example, demanded the separation between guest and servant necessary for a genteel dining experience. "It was the training of restaurants of our type to feel that you were a public servant and to act the role throughout," George Rector wrote. "Not one of our patrons ever had to remind one of our waiters that he was a waiter or myself that I was there to look after his comfort." Essential to this system was a staff that could take orders and efficiently carry them out. For this reason, American boys did not make good waiters because in Oscar's opinion they considered themselves "as good as the guests." Whenever possible, restaurateurs "obtained their help from Europe," for "they were polished, subservient, and of handsome appearance." Immigrants, because they looked different and were more subservient, made better servants. To ensure smooth service, the staff was generally dressed in uniform appearance, and managers instructed them on how to act. Julius Keller of Maxim's outfitted his help in the cutaway coats, ruffled shirts, black satin breeches, silk stockings, silver buckled pumps, and powdered wigs that he imagined were part of Louis XIV's livery. Others followed the more usual pattern of full evening dress and regulations regarding personal cleanliness and appearance. In all areas, waiters, captains, and busboys sought to make diners feel well treated and courteously received. "We had one slogan," George Rector observed. "That motto was: The guest is Right, Right or Wrong."[32]

Both Oscar and Rector noted that "there was a snobbishness in those days which demanded a foreign land on its packages." In emphasizing exotic delights, Rector's eliminated such standards as ham and eggs, welsh rarebit, and the club sandwich from the dinner service. "Personally I liked all three," wrote George, "but we were striving to increase the aura of exclusiveness emanating from Rector's, so we were forced to drop three faithful favorites into the Bosporus." Beefsteak dinners were still fashionable and available, but the desire to express one's wealth or to imitate the consumption patterns of the rich favored the foreign and exotic dishes available along Broadway. Rector's owed much of its fame to its ability to recreate the delicate French sauces, such as mornay and marguery, or the dish George just "picked up in Paris," canapé of crab meat Rector. Oscar saw the social aspects in the penchant for foreign delicacies. "A wholesome and quite commonplace an article of diet as soup is made to serve as a subject for display," he noted. "Instead of the simple stock properly seasoned and flavored with vegetables, we mix it with flour until it becomes a sort of flour paste and call it bisque de creme." Food in the Waldorf had to make a visual display. According to Oscar, this grand display was vulgar, and "only a failure to discriminate between the appearance and the substance, and serving food to please the eye rather than the stomach shows both sorts of bad taste." Fancy cooking, he continued, "is quite as bad as wearing loud clothes." The unreadable French menus, moreover, also seemed "only one of the many silly affectations by which we try to out-swagger each other." As much a part of his age as the people he decried, Oscar justified retaining the French menus on the basis that his cooks were French.[33] Food was another way to compete socially.

The lobster palaces and Fifth Avenue hotels were part of an era characterized by large meals. Jerome, the maitre d'hôtel of Sherry's, noted that "people dined in those days. Now [1940] they just eat." Oscar became a celebrity because of his ability to cater large private and public meals. His rules for dining, which he laid out in 1899, emphasized the sensual indulgence of food, but within the proper forms. Oysters, he maintained, always started a meal. When not in season, littleneck clams could be substituted. Soup, the second course, required careful selection. "If two soups are to be served," he cautioned, "select one clear and one thick, but if only one is to be used, give the preference to the clear soup." Hors d'oeuvres, consisting of timbales, croustades, palmettes, mousselines, and bouchées, followed. Along with this course, Oscar advised cold dishes such as olives, canapés, caviar, and anchovies. After these preliminaries came the fish: "The fish, if it is boiled or fried, should have potatoes served with it; if broiled or cooked in any fancy manner, serve cucumber salad with it." The entrées also presented a choice, but Oscar had the rational answer: "If two entrées are chosen in a dinner, the first entrée should be made the lighter of the two, and they should be made in a fancy way, so as to avoid carving." Terrapin, oysters, crabs, lobsters, shrimps, and frogs were quite proper for the entrée. After this, the main course—roasts, solid joints, and vegetables—made its appearance, with the game following, interspersed with punch or sherbet. The meal then went on to a conclusion through dessert and coffee.[34]

In an age of food, a number of lobster palace habitués, including Evander Berry Wall, the King of the Dudes, and Diamond Jim Brady, were famous for their dining habits. Each in his distinct manner showed an emphasis on oral pleasures. Wall was fastidious and exacting, making of eating something beyond material and animal pleasure. Food was the epitome of style, and whether ordering the food with descriptive gestures or lovingly mixing his own salad ingredients in Rector's, he treated dining as a gourmet experience. Like Ward McAllister and other gourmets, he raised the cultivated palate to an ideal. Brady, on the other hand, was probably closer in style to other well-to-do men of the age. He ate to indulge himself as much as he could. He was a gourmand rather than a gourmet. The son of a New York saloon keeper, Brady made his fortune by selling railroad materials. A celebrated exponent of the expense account and personal advertising, he consciously used his huge body, his diamonds, and his actress acquaintances to advertise his prosperous position in the community. Few could match his ability to consume rich and varied foods. Just as much interested in foreign delicacies as Wall, only in larger amounts, Diamond Jim stood as a symbol of the man who could conspicuously consume more than others. To start a meal, he drank three or four of the largest of Rector's carafes of orange juice. Then he would eat two or three dozen of the Lynnhaven variety of oysters at a sitting, before moving on to a dozen hard-shelled crabs. Often he would follow this with six or seven lobsters, the specialty at Rector's, and then toy with steaks and chops. He finished off with coffee, cakes, pastry, and bonbons. After the theatre, he returned to Rector's for a midnight supper.[35]

In their separate ways, these men mastered dining as if they were mastering nature. In this age of consolidation, nature was controlled and conquered in the name of progress and civilization. For Wall and Brady, the anarchic power of sensuality was channeled into eating. This sublimation was a perfect symbol for the age, because it represented an oral pregenital stage of existence, in which sensuality produced self-gratification. Eating was a way of storing up gratification, mastering it. It was self-contained. Unlike the next generation, which pursued a social life of greater mutual expressiveness in cabarets, this generation gloried in sedentary behavior and eating, which in its consuming quality was isolating in its pursuit. Although enjoying the glories of food represented a step away from the asceticism of the past, it provided gratification only for the individual, not the pleasure of mutuality.

THE BIRD AND BOTTLE SUPPER

While the lobster palaces maintained a reputation for good food and luxurious atmosphere, they also barely contained the sensuality that was bursting the boundaries of the old order. Unlike the Fifth Avenue hotels, Broadway restaurants were always open to the "fast" crowd, made up of actors, actresses, those in the music business, chorus girls, wealthy stockbrokers and businessmen, and men seeking escape from the stifling formality of the exclusive circles. A decidedly masculine atmosphere, overlaid with civilization, reigned. As a theatrical entertainment and sporting center (for both sportsmen and gamblers), Broadway allowed its patrons a greater variety of experience. Broadway also openly purveyed its artificial environments as fantasies for hire. Looking back over the elaborate presentation of food, decor, and service borrowed from ages past, one cannot help but see that the Broadway restaurants placed their guests on show. The patrons played at spending large sums of money, and at being big men and women, creatures of will and appetite, therefore of being removed from the restraints of time, place, and circumstance. They could buy anything they wanted. If the 1890s were part of a growing revolt against the formalism of the Victorian age and an opting for greater experience, then the lobster palaces were part of that revolt, at least under the surface of their overwhelming refinement. And nowhere better do we see the new fastness and barely contained sensuality than in the bird and bottle supper: late-night champagne and lobster dinners between the wealthy males and the Broadway chorus girls.

After the evening's performance, theatregoers would often return to the Waldorf for a few hours or, for those who desired to stay up a bit later than one o'clock amid a less sedate crowd, to Broadway restaurants. Rector's small room downstairs and Louis Martin's downstairs were the places to be for the in crowd of theatrical celebrities, but most of the other lobster palaces in the area received the patronage of theatrical figures relaxing after a show, as well as that of ordinary folks with money to spend. Prominent among the revelers were a group of people that the *New York Tribune* considered a new phenomenon in 1903, a "prominent fixture of night life, the 'man about town,'" who consistently stayed up past one o'clock. These bachelors of society or single men for the evening enjoyed the traditional male privilege of staying out late at night in public places of enjoyment. For them, "the theater is just an incident, and the real fun comes afterward." Prominent in these circles, E. Berry Wall visited Delmonico's, the Brunswick Hotel, Sherry's, the Waldorf, Shanley's, and Jack's. He and other prosperous young and not-so-young bachelors, however, considered Rector's the great bohemian place for meeting the charming musical comedy actresses and actors of the theater. Especially prized were the vivacious chorus girls of the musical comedy stage.[36] Of an evening, for example, one might see

Lillian Russell with Jesse Lewisohn, Edna McCauley with Diamond Jim Brady, and the current toast of the town.

Most of the dining would occur in the restaurants' public spaces. Although behavior was still within the boundaries of propriety, gaiety and frivolity reigned. For the ordinary professional or businessman out with his wife, the after-theatre suppers allowed him to observe the theatrical figures at play. Because of the late-night character of the restaurants, less food was served and the atmosphere was much more of a drinking kind. The symbol of the late-night supper was a hot bird and a cold bottle.[37] The double entendre referred to a good-looking "chicken," as chorus girls or actresses were called, and not only to a good-tasting squab. The cold bottle often as not meant champagne, for with its bubbly effervescence, it was the very spirit of bubbling good fun and giddiness. So much champagne was sold to celebrate the public's various successes, moreover, that wine merchants would reward those who had opened a larger number of their bottles than those of a rival's. Amid the gentle popping of the corks, celebration and good cheer were the order of the night.

While much of the celebrating along Broadway was public, advertising the ability of big spenders to buy, much also was hidden away in the private dining rooms and apartments that all of the restaurants maintained. Here wealthy men wined and dined actresses or their mistresses away from the prying eyes of the public and their own social strata. Unlike the very respectable Delmonico's, Bustanoby's, Café de l'Opera, Murray's, and Rector's maintained these private dining rooms, whose activities caused quite a stir in the tabloids and, often as not, in the bedrooms of the best Fifth Avenue homes. Reserving their most passionate activities for the private sphere, just barely removed from the public eye, and with lower women from outside their own group, these men emphasized the split between their elevated and sensual lives, which also corresponded to the separation between the women of Fifth Avenue and Broadway. They showed that these private desires for a more exciting sensual life lay close to the surface, though still contained, in this period.

It was a double standard that both Broadway and Fifth Avenue figures confirmed, and that gave an air of naughtiness to the lobster palaces and the period. Although E. Berry Wall prided himself on his associations with Broadway, he made sharp distinctions between

Broadway and his own social group. "Fifth Avenue to us was sacred," he said, but "Broadway was its comic relief. Across that invisible but guarded threshold which defined Fifth Avenue and Broadway, in my time, only Lester Wallack [a distinguished actor and theater entrepreneur] stepped." Wall retained ties to a tightly knit social network. "A similarity in birth and breeding, in race and idea, knit us into the same social fabric," he stated. "There we pulled and held together. We helped our own people and kept outsiders out, but we recognized who belonged to us from however far away he came."[38]

As the famous Stanford White murder case attests, however, much stepping occurred the other way. Evelyn Nesbit Thaw, a chorus girl in the Floradora Girls, wife of Pittsburgh steel heir Harry K. Thaw, and the former paramour of married society architect Stanford White, was the central personage in a scandalous murder case. The deranged Thaw shot and killed White for seducing his wife several years before their marriage. As it turned out, White had been intimate with a number of actresses, whom he often met in the lobster palaces, while his own wife lived on Long Island. He separated the Broadway world distinctly from his own home life. White was apparently not unique, for in her autobiography, Evelyn Thaw described how members of exclusive Fifth Avenue men's clubs took her and other chorus girls to the lobster palaces but showed a distinct unwillingness to introduce them to the more refined women of their own society background. This fast set, thus, was party to the double standard.[39] The double standard also permitted men to utilize the restaurants as their province for late-night card playing and drinking. The main dining room of Rector's had a special Yacht Club table for rich sportsmen, among them Howard Gould, Commodore Cornelius Vanderbilt, Colonel James Emerson, Lloyd Phoenix, Harry Harkness, and Commodore Mills. Upstairs the management provided food and service for the private and exclusive male gambling parties. Young and old might visit Broadway, but because of the lobster palaces' questionable character, wealthy women went only in guarded fashion. If a fashionable woman visited Rector's after theatre, she went incognito, having first returned home to change her low-cut dress. It was not considered proper to be seen in such a place in revealing clothing. Her escort sequestered her in a distant part of the room so that she would not be mistaken for a woman of the town.[40]

Despite these disturbing and more giddy elements, the late-night suppers still managed to keep the new values of consumption and sensuality within bounds for most patrons. In the public rooms, the managements generally forbade smoking by women. And despite the presence of bohemian women, even Evelyn Nesbit Thaw observed the dictates of propriety and refrained from imbibing too generously in public.[41] Henry Collins Brown's memory of a visit to Churchill's after the theatre in the 1890s suggests an atmosphere of order and elegance. Swelling with pride to be in such rarefied atmosphere, "we trod the softly carpeted floor, the ladies of our party, properly impressed with our importance, trailing their long silken gowns in our wake down the aisle of tables until, with just the right adjustment of their draperies" and a dainty pat to their elbow-length sleeves, "they smiled happily at us under the rose-tinted table lights as the string orchestra struck into 'Violets.' "[42]

Stopping in after the theatre, Brown might have witnessed the elite of Broadway, or if he went to the Waldorf, he might have gazed upon a wealthier crowd "seeing and being seen." This " 'looking on' game," as Oscar called this primary feature of the late-night suppers, ". . . has crossed the ocean, and I see it here every day. In this hotel, in all hotels, the same amusement exists for many, probably the majority of those who frequent them."[43] After the theatre, "the restaurant fills again, with an even more brilliant and a decidedly more heterogeneous assemblage than at the dinner hour." According to *Harper's Bazaar*, the actress just come from work has the chance to "critically considers *[sic]* the society people who are pointed out to her by her escort," and in turn is so considered by the very people she is watching.[44]

Across town in an even more mixed crowd, patrons also engaged in this practice, which Oscar termed "Unsocial Sociability." "It is not the sociability of friends, the intercourse of congenial people," remarked the maitre d'hôtel of the Waldorf, "but the looking on as it were at a *pageant*." Instead of intimate participation through entertainment or a joyous group atmosphere, the visitor "dines in silence, broken only by the whispered communications of his friends respecting the identity of some fresh arrival."[45] Here was the epitome of the new style: to display one's women and to learn and communicate new social skills and prestige. Various decorative features of the hotels and restaurants enhanced the process of looking on. Peacock Alley in the Waldorf, for example, was a place to see the prominent display their power, wealth, and elegance. The Knickerbocker Hotel had a large stairway with a landing where men and women could stop until all eyes were upon them. At the Café des Beaux Arts and Rector's, musical comedy actresses found ready environments for making an entrance. According to Lloyd Morris, a liberal tip in advance persuaded the gypsy fiddler to meet the couple at the door and to play for and to the lady while the couple slowly made their way to the table, in time to the music.[46] The mirrors that lined the walls in the Palm Garden, Murray's, Rector's, and other places permitted guests to watch discreetly what went on at other tables. In this atmosphere of decorum, cut off from the celebrities they were learning to emulate, and with the same public style, the social projections were beginning to merge. But for the moment they remained distinct. There was an urban state of mind: a sense of sharing a community and a set of behaviors without the need for intimacy and actual experience.

By 1913 Harrison Rhodes found that New York was the restaurant capital of the United States. "The country's heart may be—we hope it is—where the home is, but the national stomach is not far from where Forty-Second Street crosses Broadway and Fifth Avenue."[47] On both sides of New York, prosperous New Yorkers of all definitions found arenas for the consumption of fine food and the display of status and refinement. In a corporate and highly urbanized age, the restaurants initiated those with money into a public style that formerly had been exclusively for the ultrarich. On Fifth Avenue, the hotels allowed a large number of widely dispersed wealthy people to meet and mix at a distance, while on Broadway, the restaurants with their imperial architecture, elaborate service, and cosmopolitan traditions of eating and drinking gave prosperous citizens the experiences that helped them remove themselves from a more ascetic identity. They established their social place by incorporating newer, more consumption-oriented values onto an older sexual division and style. Women and men could participate in new activities that would severely weaken restraint, but they would do so in a formal, hierarchical, and restrained world. In the pursuit of civilized status, the wealthy were far along a road that had loosened internalized restraint but had not yet replaced that restraint with a new pattern for the sexes. The next generation would begin to include respectable women in more vital environments. The worlds of "them" and "us" would begin to merge.

NOTES

1. Theodore Dreiser, *Sister Carrie* (New York: Holt, Rinehart and Winston, 1960), p. 265.

2. Elizabeth Drexel Lehr, *King Lehr and the Gilded Age: Extracts from the Locked Diary of Harry Lehr* (Philadelphia: J. B. Lippincott, 1935), p. 198. For details on Delmonico's, see Lately Thomas [pseud.], *Delmonico's, A Century of Splendor* (Boston: Houghton Mifflin, 1967), pp. 266–67.

3. Albert Stevens Crockett, *Peacocks on Parade* (New York: Sears Publishing Co., 1931), p. 48, estimates that fifteen hundred people attended. The reporter's remarks are on p. 50.

4. Lloyd Morris, *Incredible New York* (New York: Random House, 1951), pp. 234–58, supports the idea of political revenge, while Crockett, *Peacocks on Parade*, pp. 42–43, suggests the social-rivalry explanation. For a more detailed history of the Waldorf-Astoria Hotel see James Remington, *Peacock Alley* (New York: Harper & Bros., 1931).

5. Morris, *Incredible*, p. 236.

6. Moses King, *Moses King's New York* (New York, 1893), 1: 218.

7. Morris, *Incredible*, p. 236.

8. Crockett, *Peacocks*, p. 54.

9. Oscar Tschirky, "Unsociable Sociability," *New York Daily News*, September 13, 1902, in Oscar Tschirky Scrapbooks, Hotel and Restaurant Management School, Cornell University, Ithaca, N.Y.

10. Crockett, *Peacocks*, p. 54.

11. Oscar Tschirky, "Lives of Great Men Remind Us . . . George Boldt, 1853–1916," *Contact* 1 (December 1939), in Tschirky Scrapbooks.

12. Ernst Ingersoll, *A Week in New York* (New York: Rand McNally, 1891), p. 48.

13. "Covers for 2: A Gastronomic Study," *New York Times*, September 2, 1906, IV, p. 2.

14. Henry Clews, *Fifty Years in Wall Street* (New York: Irving Publishing Co., 1908), pp. 448–49.

15. Mary C. Henderson, *The City and the Theatre; New York Playhouses from Bowling Green to Times Square* (Clifton, 1973), p. 184, has statistics on the growth of wealth in New York. On public display of conspicuous consumption, see Thorstein Veblen, *The Theory of the Leisure Class* (1899; reprint, New York: Mentor Books, 1953), pp. 70–72. The number of millionaires is from Frederick Cople Jaher, "Style and Status: High

Society in Late Nineteenth Century New York," in *The Rich, the Well Born and the Powerful: Elites and Upper Classes in History*, ed. Jaher (Urbana: University of Illinois Press, 1973), p. 266.

16. The restlessness, competition, and turnover among the rich in New York City have been chronicled by many historians. Morris, *Incredible*, pp. 234–58; Crockett, *Peacocks*, pp. 12–14; Lucius Beebe, *The Big Spenders* (Garden City, N.Y.: Doubleday, 1966), p. 108. For more scholarly studies see Frederick Cople Jaher, "Nineteenth Century Elites in Boston and New York," *Journal of Social History* 6 (Fall 1972): 32–77, and his "Style and Status," pp. 259–84.

17. Mrs. Astor's response is quoted in Morris, *Incredible*, p. 253. See also Jaher, "Style and Status," p. 277, and Lehr, *King Lehr*, pp. 226–27.

18. "The Vaudeville Club," *Harper's Weekly* 36 (December 1892): 1243, and Charles Belmont Davis, "The Vaudeville Club," *Harper's Weekly* 37 (February 1893): 116.

19. Morris, *Incredible*, pp. 238–39.

20. Material on Louis Sherry can be found in Crockett, *Peacocks*, pp. 170, 271.

21. George Rector, *The Girl from Rector's* (Garden City, N.Y.: Doubleday, 1927), p. 60. Churchill's illustrates the usual experience for the lobster palaces, which realized their most magnificent period in the years 1908–1912. The first Churchill's opened at 1420 Broadway; the second at Forty-Sixth Street and Broadway, and the third, its greatest, at Forty-Ninth Street and Broadway in 1909. The latter had 300 employees, could seat 1400 customers, and was rumored to cost $3 million to build. Numerous others opened in the Forty-Ninth Street area around 1909–1910.

22. For material on Broadway and the lobster palaces see Allen Churchill, *The Great White Way, A Re-Creation of Broadway's Golden Era of Theatrical Entertainment* (New York: E. P. Dutton, 1962), pp. 4–25, 53–92, and Lary May, "Screening Out the Past: The Birth of Mass Culture and the Motion Picture Industry, 1896–1929" (Ph.D. diss., University of California at Los Angeles, 1977), pp. 64, 210–11; and Henderson, *The City and the Theatre*, pp. 130–31 for apartment living on the West side.

23. Dreiser, *Sister Carrie*, pp. 273, 41.

24. "Obituary—George Rector," *New York Herald Tribune*, November 27, 1947, clipping in Rector File, New York Public Library Theatre Collection, Lincoln Center; Louis Sobol, "Bustanoby, Papa of Cafe Society," *American Weekly*, May 5, 1952, p. 4; Julius Keller, *Inns and Outs* (New York: G. P. Putnam's Sons, 1939), pp. 52–53; John Walker Harrington, "Where Foreign Chefs Influenced American Taste in Food," *New York Herald Tribune*, December 31, 1933, clipping in Restaurant File, New York Public Library.

25. "Epicurean New York Is Safe," *New York Herald*, December 28, 1902, clipping in Tschirky Scrapbooks.

26. "The Hotel Rector, New York," *American Architect*, January 18, 1911, pp. 25, 28.

27. "Obituary—Adolph Lorder," *New York Times*, April 18, 1953, clipping in Restaurant File.

28. *New York Plaisance* (New York, 1908), 1: 47–48; see plate 17 for the exterior. Rector, *Girl from Rector's*, p. 28; Fremont Rider, *Rider's New York City* (New York: Henry Holt & Co., 1916), pp. 20, 168.

29. *New York Plaisance*, p. 54; "Murray's Roman Gardens," *Architect and Builder's Magazine* 39 (September 1907): 575.

30. "Murray's," p. 574.

31. "Music Misplaced," *Hotel Monthly* 21 (April 1913): 73.

32. "Old Timers Feast at Waldorf," *New York Evening Post*, March 14, 1923, clipping in Tschirky Scrapbooks; Rector, *Girl from Rector's*, pp. 92–93, 133, 132.

33. Rector, *Girl from Rector's*, pp. 156, 123, 37; Oscar's remarks in "How We Show Vulgarity in Cooking," *Boston Post*, December 18, 1898, clipping in Tschirky Scrapbooks.

34. Wallace, "Jerome at Sherry's Sighs for Old Days," *New York World Telegram*, January 8, 1940, clipping in Restaurant File. Rector had similar observations; see *Girl from Rector's*, p. 127; Oscar's elaborate meal is described in Oscar Tschirky, "Menus, or Bills of Fare," *What to Eat*, January 1899, clipping in Tschirky Scrapbooks.

35. Wall is described in Rector, *Girl from Rector's*, pp. 83–86. On gourmets in general, see A. H. Gourand, "The Cultivated Palate," *Current Literature* 32 (October 1900): 452. Brady is described in Beebe, *Big Spenders*, pp. 72–80; Rector, *Girl from Rector's*, pp. 14–20; and in Parker Morrell, *Diamond Jim: The Life and Times of James Buchanan Brady* (New York: AMS Press, 1934), and in his *Lillian Russell: The Era of Plush* (New York: Random House, 1940).

36. *New York Tribune*, May 3, 1903, p. 5; Evander Berry Wall, *Neither Pest nor Puritan* (New York: The Dial Press, 1940), pp. 33–35.

37. Beebe, *Big Spenders*, pp. 103–09; Julian Street, "Lobster Palace Society," *Everybody's Magazine* 22 (May 1910): 649.

38. Wall, *Neither Pest*, pp. 107, 109.

39. Details of the Thaw-White murder case in Evelyn Nesbit Thaw, *Prodigal Days, The Untold Story* (New York: Julian Messner, 1934), p. 62; Harry K. Thaw, *The Traitor: Being the Untampered with Unrevised Account of the Trial and All That Led to It* (Philadelphia: Dorance & Co., 1926); Gerald Langford, *The Murder of Stanford White* (Indianapolis-New York: Bobbs-Merrill, 1962); Michael Macdonald Mooney, *Evelyn Nesbit*

and Stanford White, Love and Death in the Gilded Age (New York: William Morrow & Co., 1976); "The Exposure of Vice," *Nation*, February 21, 1907, pp. 169–70. Belle Livingstone, *Belle Out of Order* (New York: Henry Holt & Co., 1959), pp. 30–50, testifies to the luxury, success, and excitement chorus girls found in the lobster palaces dining with such tycoons as James B. Duke, Pierre Lorillard, and Diamond Jim Brady. She also notes these men would keep but not marry their chorus girl mistresses.

40. Rector, *Girl from Rector's*, pp. 67–68, 78; Crockett, *Peacocks*, p. 157.

41. Henry Collins Brown, *In the Golden Nineties* (Hastings-on-Hudson: Valentine's Manual, 1928); p. 128; Thaw, *Prodigal Days*, p. 142.

42. Brown, *Golden Nineties*, p. 126; for a similar description, see *New York Times*, September 2, 1906, p. 2.

43. Tschirky, "Unsocial Sociability."

44. "At the Waldorf," *Harper's Bazaar*, March 21, 1896, clipping in Tschirky Scrapbooks.

45. Tschirky, "Unsociable Sociability," and "At the Waldorf," clippings in Tschirky Scrapbooks.

46. Morris, *Incredible*, p. 261; Rector, *Girl from Rector's*, p. 28.

47. Harrison Rhodes, "New York Restaurants," *Harper's Weekly*, November 1, 1913, p. 12.

3 WOMEN OUT OF CONTROL: CRITICS OF THE NEW AMUSEMENTS

The ancient, steeple-hatted dame
    Has come to Gotham town,
    And lifts a fizzling chalice
    Within a lobster palace.
For Mother Goose though old in name,
    Is up to date (or down),
    And as she gobbles salad
    She sings her modern ballad:

    Trot, trot in Broadway!
      Trot in the din!
    Look out, little girl,
      Or you may tumble in!

Pale-faced beneath her paint of pink,
    A young girl fox-trots by,
And oh! her dreary laughter
    Forebodes the bad day after!
And Mother Goose bestows a wink
    Of her sardonic eye,
And lends the fiddlers' tuning
    Her new-timed nursery crooning:

    Trot, trot in Broadway!
      Trot, pale of skin!
    Look out, little girl,
      Or you may tumble in!

                    John Keefe[1]

The public and private misbehavior of the rich revealed by the Thaw-White murder case provided the most dramatic evidence that urban life was changing. The lobster palaces and Fifth Avenue hotels marked the emergence of confident, prosperous men and women bent on publicly leading society and enjoying the fruits of economic empire. It was not just the rich who were changing, however. In the 1890s American popular culture began a larger reorientation away from the confinement, restrictions, and conventions of urban industrial society and the code of gentility. In working-class, black, and immigrant cultures, new institutions of amusement and leisure were growing into general respectability, offering immigrant children and middle-class urbanites visions of a more luxurious and experiential life, one not bound by the old restrictive ways. In movies, vaudeville, ragtime, and cabarets, a popular culture was being created and transformed by new values, which, by the 1910s, would achieve a legitimacy in urban life unheard of in the Victorian age, yet which would still be subject to internal questionings by the participants.[2]

From the 1890s on, moreover, these new trends in urban life were vigorously opposed by the custodians of culture and morality. Their primary concerns centered on the changing character of the American city, which offered new freedoms to people who, the reformers thought, were ill prepared to handle them. Numerous reform groups in New York City, Chicago, and other cities decried the fate of American civilization should changing sex roles further weaken the family. It was this concern, particularly with American women, poor and rich, that marked the reforms of the Progressive period. Reformers were not the only ones preoccupied with innocence; ironically both Harry K. Thaw and Stanford White were fascinated by innocence and its trespass. White sought to deflower it and Thaw to save it, yet both kept the defiled outside their own lives: White by turning to actresses while his family resided in Long Island, and Thaw by beating his ex-chorus girl wife into renewed virginity. Finding the latter impossible, he killed White in an attempt to drive the snake forever from his door. The Thaw-White case was only one of many that appeared in the newly popular Sunday supplements, themselves products of the 1890s, and that took as their theme the defilement of innocent womanhood by pleasure-hungry men.

Even before the Thaw-White case, moralists had recognized that New York life was changing. In the 1890s, the Reverend Charles Parkhurst cried out against character weaknesses of his prosperous congregation brought on by wealth, gambling, and fornication. Josiah Strong, the general secretary of the Evangelical Alliance of the United States, denounced both the rich and the immigrants for creating an organized class society, thereby crushing out the independent man of Protestant character with luxury and vice. The moralists of the 1890s often pounded the note that the end of the producer culture was nigh, and progress based on individual restraint was in deep trouble.[3] Anthony Comstock, inspector of the post office, president of the Society for the Suppression of Vice, and the nation's chief censor, intervened in the Thaw-White case and added to the chorus of complaints that had grown since the 1890s. In 1904, two years before the shooting, Thaw had persuaded Comstock that Stanford White was a constant defiler of young maidens. After the murder Comstock declared White guilty of moral trespass, a white slaver killed by a man defending wife and home.[4]

When the Biograph movie company released *The Great Thaw Trial* in 1908, social workers and ministers joined Comstock in pressuring New York City's mayor, George B. McClellan, to close the city's 550 movie houses.[5] The movies were still largely a lower-class institution, and reformers feared that these and other amusements would lead the poor away from the proper Protestant values that held them in check. Because of the changing mores of the very wealthy and the undisciplined mores of the very poor, reformers and critics thought that American society was changing for the worse. In the 1890s, many respectable urbanites were losing faith in their ability to control a corporate, industrial society in the midst of depression and massive immigration. The reformers who worked against city ills after the Spanish-American War, however, had confidence that their personal intervention could reform the worst excesses of urban life and urban amusements, make the city safe for democracy, and preserve proper male and female character. They too were part of a more activist era.

OLD CHARACTER, NEW STYLE

Many of those who decried the existence of urban amusements were traditional moralists, often of evangelical background, who believed that play itself was an affront against God, and genteel critics who felt that the popular culture was vulgar and lacked the cultivation and reason appropriate for a higher civilization. These two groups contributed to the preoccupation with amusements in the early twentieth century, but it was another group that often exercised actual power in urban life. These critics—social gospel ministers, elite businessmen, settlement workers—were more closely allied to progressive social welfare reform than were traditionalists. The Progressives shared the traditionalists' perception that the new amusements represented decline and anarchy, but unlike the traditionalists, they applied new solutions to the ills of their age. In New York City, for example, the major anti-vice group after 1904 was the Committee of Fourteen, an alliance of elite Republican merchants, professors, settlement workers, and religious leaders representing various reform groups in the city. The committee's primary aim was the abolition of prostitution, which they found spreading throughout the city, especially in poorer areas such as the Lower East Side, but they also attacked the problems presented by the new amusements. Worried over the increase in urban population, poverty, and the class warfare and political bossism made apparent in the 1890s, these reformers saw in the crusade against vice a means of uniting the disorganized and anarchic community under one banner of moral and civic leadership.[6] One of the primary leaders of the fight was Mrs. Belle Moskowitz, a college-educated settlement worker born in Harlem, who was head of the Committee on Amusement Resources for Working Class Girls, an organization devoted to her Jewish sisters on the Lower East Side. For her, as well as for Chicago's Jane Addams, Louise De Koven Bowen, and the Juvenile Protective Association, modern amusements symbolized the inherent lack of social or familial control in the modern industrial city. In their view, the young, and especially young women, dangerously free from the rural and immigrant family's traditions and from the controlling force of work, ran free on the anonymous city streets. These reformers, desirous of creating a wider social morality based on the tenets of the restrained family and ascetic character, saw the need for the state to create proper public amusements. According to the reformers, the state would serve as a wider family, ensuring the proper character for women and men. The state should be called in in matters of vice, social welfare, and minimum wages to protect the family because in the modern anarchic city, the family itself needed a protector.

The Committee of Fourteen agreed with numerous other agencies around the nation that prostitution arose from the nature of the city and the economy. In the *Report on the Social Evil of 1910*, the committee noted, "Youth is gravitating toward the city, away from home, religious and personal ideals, breaking the moorings of the past before the newer social ideal is grasped." The newness of the city and the alien nature of the teeming continental millions created a "freedom of thought, liberty of action, self expression."[7] As Jane Addams put it, "The social relationships in a modern city are so hastily made and often so superficial, that the old human restraints of public opinion, long sustained in smaller communities, have also broken down." Freed from the benevolent restraints of the small town, therefore, "thousands of young men and women in every great city have received none of the lessons in self-control which even savage tribes imparted to their appetites as well as their emotions."[8] In this environment, the social and parental controls inherent in community life no longer applied, and the model of character that these committees prized, for others and for themselves, was in dire danger.

Uncontrolled at home, poorly paid, and shielded by urban anonymity, the young went out to amusements for fun, adventure, and excitement. Their "lower" appetites were no longer sublimated by routine factory work or by the family, and they were lured even further along the path to prostitution by urban, mixed-sex amusements. As Mrs. Moskowitz declared, the cause of delinquency on every level lay in "those ungoverned, unlicensed, unregulated amusement resorts."[9] These reformers were not Puritans; rather they prided themselves on their scientific detachment, objectivity, and understanding of other people's, especially young people's, needs. If work in the factory no longer expressed channeled identity, then play could be structured to serve the same function. The problem was not with play, they argued, but with traditional institutions like the church and the school that refused to allow healthy impulses toward play. "We are afraid," Mrs. Moskowitz recalled, "but our friend, who runs the saloon, is not afraid of any such consequences."[10]

Settlement workers found that a three-pronged reform program was necessary to eradicate prostitution and to save the family as the basis of modern moral life. First, they called for the eradication of the worst features of amusements rather than their total abolition. They wanted to suppress prostitution, liquor in dance halls, and the salacious side to movies, and thereby disassociate the institutions from vice. Second, the city had to create clean public amusements unconnected to artificial commercial stimulants to vice. Clean, well-regulated recreations would help, in Walter Lippmann's words, to "invent something which substitutes attractive virtues for attractive vices" and channel the young's impulses toward healthier ends.[11] Freely recognizing the role of sensual emotions, reformers had faith in their ability to civilize them to foster character and morality. Consequently the Committee of Fourteen was instrumental in the creation of censorship boards for movies, the use of policewomen to work at amusement parks and dance halls, and the separation of liquor from dancing. From 1912 on they worked to license the cabarets so that curfew hours would be obeyed and the worst excesses of the cabaret would be eliminated. Third, reformers desired to eliminate abuses in the factory, the department store, and domestic service to reduce the monetary need that often led young women into a life of prostitution. Their deepest criticism, in fact, was that the modern factory produced prostitution. While calling for minimum wage and factory regulations, the reformers were least successful in criticizing the economy, largely because they were oriented toward creating harmony and not class power. They usually ended up trying to preserve character by saving the family rather than by reconstructing the economy.

The reevaluation of play was a particularly creative perception by social welfare reformers. They realized that specialized and monotonous work no longer stimulated the middle-class virtues of will power, self-control and character. If the young turned to exciting leisure pursuits to escape the deadening effect of the factory or the family, leisure itself could be made to serve older Victorian ends of character, family, and will. Leisure, not work, would now be used to teach universal moral character. Moral amusements would produce and preserve civic virtue and a unified society for everyone. Anarchy and class warfare brought about by the lack of self-control need not be so feared.[12]

THE NEW AMUSEMENTS

Concern with the fate of womanhood and the modern family in the new urban environment was sparked by the growth of urban amuse-

ments beginning in the 1890s, when both second-generation immigrants and respectable Protestants began to break away from the parental mores of their own cultures.[13] Many immigrants encountered a
conflict between their pre-industrial cultures and machine discipline,
and they sought release, as reformers constantly related, in the dance
halls, the movies, and the saloons available in the city. The new
amusements gave institutional expression to pre-industrial habits and
also gave the young a chance to mix with members of the opposite sex
beyond the eyes of their parents. In addition, the middle classes were
opening up their self-definitions of gentility. While working women in
the new corporations had some money and independence to choose
and pursue a life of their own, women of the upper classes found their
old roles disappearing. Many found their moral style undercut by
increasing leisure, the ability of the industrial society to replace their
own productive roles, and the growing segregation of cities that separated them from the lower classes they were supposed to discipline.
Some women went to colleges and settlement houses to find more
active roles for themselves, some began to work, and a number began
to ask more from marriage than duty. They called for greater spontaneity, passion, and intimacy with their husbands; leisure became the
realm for exploring these new styles. The industrial system helped
establish the stage of adolescence for young people, a period when
they were removed from the productive sphere of work, often in
school, taking time to learn technical skills for economic life and even
social skills with the opposite sex. Men, moreover, began to change
too. Raised to depend on women for emotional support and in families
that increasingly used contraception to keep up a standard of living
and to keep down the number of children, young men and women in
families such as these from the 1870s on, learned greater affection
from their parents.

In turn they began to seek affection from members of the opposite
sex, especially as contraception allowed them to separate sex from
procreation. The generation of men who came of age in the 1890s also
sought to prove their masculinity, largely in their leisure time. In the
corporate-dominated society, men could still experience social mobility, but in more routinized, organized ways, without the excitement
of building their own empires, but also without the terror of losing
their money and their male identities in economic gambles. The

new economic organizations threatened to entrap men, but enabled them to release some of their psychological energy from work, to step out of their exclusive dedication to work roles, and to enjoy time with women.

Vaudeville, for example, broke through the wall of disreputability surrounding urban amusements, expanding the formerly all-male audience of variety to include women. In 1910 vaudeville manager B. F. Keith recalled that in the 1880s, few theatrical performances outside of "high class theatre" had attracted women and children. In his view, "theatrical managers seemed to have quite ignored the wants of the average American family for theatrical amusements."[14] It was Tony Pastor, showman behind the famous Tony Pastor's Theater on Fourteenth Street, who first realized that variety could expand its audience to achieve greater respectability. Following Pastor's lead, vaudeville managers such as Keith, Albee, and Proctor refined the acts, the audiences, and theatres in order to attract respectable women into hitherto dangerous male environments. Jeering, drinking, smoking, and soliciting were all but abolished by policing. Managers also clamped down on vulgar stage language and actions, creating a strict system of censorship that outlawed the uttered "hell" and "damn." Vaudeville managers toned down offensive ethnic humor as part of their attempt to gain a wider audience. By the turn of the century, vaudeville had become an acceptable family entertainment for the middle and working classes.

In the years from 1900 to 1930, vaudeville substituted an urban vision of success based on the enjoyment of luxury and consumption for the older tradition of the ascetic, anarchic producer, which gloried in striving as a moral duty for itself. Fashioned from circus acts, minstrel performers, the star system of the theatre, and the multi-faceted turns of variety, vaudeville themes included more of the enjoyment of success and technology brought on by a corporate order. For example, vaudeville borrowed animal acts from the circus, but only as part of a much more diverse bill of entertainment. Horses, dogs, and other domesticated animals replaced lions and tigers. The animals were no longer used to symbolize fierce nature requiring superhuman efforts toward control; rather they were easily subdued and trained to duplicate human activities for the pleasure of men and women. Human beings had clearly triumphed over nature and now could enjoy its fruits. Minstrelsy provided blackface acts, but the form of minstrelsy declined because it could not present women and sexuality in its ritual without destroying its form and threatening audiences who had come to expect minstrel Negroes to be asexual buffoons.[15] Like the lobster palaces, the theatres of vaudeville rejected the rural ascetic past for a life of consumption. In palatial theatres, humble urbanites could enjoy the luxury of the rich, plush seats, well-dressed uniformed ushers, ladies' parlors, and gentlemen's washrooms. The star system also emphasized the rewards of success through the pacing of the bills. The top acts played the best houses, had the longest acts, and, most important, made the most money, a fact that was apparent from one's place on the eight-act bill and from discussions in the popular press. Vaudeville encouraged urbanites to enter a redefined race for success, transforming Horatio Alger into a consumer of material pleasure.

One particular vaudeville act stands out as a symbol of the development of new trends in cultural life: Harry Houdini, the self-liberator. The son of a Jewish rabbi in Appleton, Wisconsin, young Erich Weiss entered the field of magic as a way out of a necktie cutter's lowly job and the restricted world of his immigrant father. In the years 1900–1925, Houdini fashioned an act that ritualized the theme of individual masculine escape or self-liberation from all manner of tight or confining spots. From boxes and handcuffs, boilers and safes, Houdini escaped death, suffocation, and immobility. Often his restrictors were symbols of authority such as a jail, or in the case of crazy cribs, wet packs, and straight jackets connoted passivity and will-lessness associated with the mentally ill. He escaped death in everything he attempted and gave the impression that he overcame confinement through personal strength alone. He gloried in his muscles and his loincloth, presenting a picture of natural man overcoming restrictions and conventions of society, the corporate world, authority, and gentility. Through strength and sports the natural man could keep his will intact amid a corporate world of consumption and leisure.[16]

As with all other amusements, reformers viewed vaudeville critically, utilizing scientific surveys to bring the facts of an unbiased appraisal to the public. The evangelical critics went ignored because Americans of all kinds desired commercial play, but the findings of social scientists were harder to dismiss. Bent on creating a single familial unity in American society, reformers turned to science without seeing that their science betrayed their class background and morality. Immorality, the degradation of womanhood, sensuality, and vulgarity offended the critics because in modern society women were out in public life working and enjoying themselves, and on the fate of their character rested the fate of their social programs. Vaudeville's emphasis on purity and refinement for family audiences made it relatively immune from the controlling hands of the critics, however. The essential appeal of vaudeville was not sexual, although performers like Eva Tanguay were lively enough. Because managers wanted to attract women and children, they usually compromised on sexuality and language, while the ritual of a this-worldly, materialistic, pleasurable life went undisturbed. Although the critics influenced the nature of the performance, they did not disturb the underlying message.[17]

Like vaudeville, the movies started out with roots in urban working-class life but eventually found an audience among the middle and upper classes. The movies, however, earned more critical attention from reformers than did vaudeville. American and European inventors had long experimented with creating a film record of motion, and in 1893 the Edison Company turned out the first kinetoscope peep shows for commercial use. While Edison originally intended the films for moral and educational uplift, other businessmen soon entered the field and began showing films on larger screens, reaching out to larger audiences.[18] The natural outlet for movies should have been the vaudeville house, but vaudeville managers wanted exclusive rights to the films, which would have undercut the possibilities of mass production inherent in the new technology. Vaudeville's admission price also encouraged the separate development of the movies. Contrary to popular opinion, the high admission price of vaudeville (twenty-five cents) precluded the largest possible mass audience. Movie exhibitors and producers instead showed their films in storefront theatres, turning to a working-class market for a wider urban audience.[19] After 1900 storefront movie theatres expanded greatly, and "nickel madness" had arrived. From 1900 to 1908, for example, the number of nickelodeons in New York City rose from fifty to at least five hundred.[20] "The ideal location" for a storefront, noted a theatre operator's handbook in 1910, "is a densely populated workingmen's residence section, with a frontage on a much-traveled business street."[21]

The handbook also warned against locating in wealthy and church-going neighborhoods and made special pleas not to set up shop in small towns where religious values and a middle-class outlook would be ruinously inhospitable.

The nature and content of the movies soon challenged Victorian assumptions of sex and class. Women out shopping might drop in unchaperoned, mingling in the dark with working-class men. Couples could get away together, and often their attention focused on each other rather than on the twenty-minute program. The medium itself also challenged audiences. Thrown upon a large screen, films presented their characters and stories as larger than life, capable of transporting viewers across barriers of time, space, and class. Like Houdini escaping confinement, movie audiences were freed to experience a wider life through the power of man-made technology. Utilizing close-ups and dark rooms, movies had an immediacy that appealed to an irrational level, a level of impulse and dream. According to critics, this appeal to the passions had the power to evoke intense and dangerous emotions. The *New York Evening World* reported in 1899 that "for the first time in the history of the world it is possible to see what a kiss looks like . . . scientists say kisses are dangerous, but here everything is shown in startling directness. What the camera did not see did not exist. The real kiss is a revelation. The idea has unlimited possibilities."[22]

Moviemakers did not take long to exploit these possibilities. Increasingly after 1900, producers switched from travel and fantasy to more bawdy and risqué films. Numerous films of sexual innuendo, women in undress, and other compromising situations were soon available for a nickel. By 1907, middle-class reformers were deeply concerned about the nature of the movie message, and the fact that technology could spread it so far. Like the saloon and the theater, the movies encouraged passion, but they were even more dangerous because they brought the lessons of the red-light district to young people. As *Good Housekeeping* reported, "The pictures are more degrading than the dime novel because they represented real flesh and blood and impart their moral lessons directly through the senses."[23] Especially problematic was the movies' image of woman as plaything, for here was an attack on the basis of Victorian culture. To progressive and conservative critics, the refined woman was the bulwark of morality in an unruly society, and the movies stimulated the worst trends of urban industrial life: the freedom of young men and women from their families and public opinion and the expression of low passions. The settlement workers, genteel critics, and merchants also feared the movies' threat to their own authority over the 13 million foreigners pouring into American cities from southern and eastern Europe in the period 1900 to 1914.

For many reformers, the answer to the problems of poverty and oppression lay in the protection of the moral family and the refined woman. They believed that the movies could become a powerful force for good because they were capable, technologically, of spreading a single cultural message throughout a society divided by ethnicity and class. Rightly regulated and conducted as a municipal institution, the movies could serve as a "grand social worker" weaning viewers away from the vice and danger of the saloon, immorality, and disrupted immigrant culture toward self-control, progress, and rational democracy. In 1908, after the movies were closed for their immorality, reformers formed the National Board of Review in New York to oversee film content. The board was led by the People's Institute, a settlement house in the Italian and Jewish sections of Manhattan, which worked to bring together "the patriotic rich" and the poor to avert class warfare and to teach people "how to help themselves, not only physically and mentally, but morally and emotionally."[24] Working together with the Motion Picture Patents Company, formed in 1908 and itself worried about national censorship, the board prescreened movies and judged them according to solid Protestant American assumptions. The democratic family provided the model for community, class, factory, and nation. Individual passion and corruption could cause social disruption, and the board condemned "lechery and the decadence of pagan culture" in order to "arouse fear in the mind of the spectator who contemplated sexual misconduct."[25] Reformers thus saw in their partnership with the Motion Picture Patents Company the chance to bring society under a single moral and cultural standard based on ennobling middle-class virtues.

The National Board of Review's stamp of approval helped legitimize the product of the Motion Picture Patents Company by eliminating objectionable material, while the work of D. W. Griffith helped movies reach a new middle-class audience. Griffith raised the movies to a new social level by producing films that glorified Victorian values such as the refined woman, the man of will, and the autonomous family, in new and artistic terms; social and moral progress went together. However, with the rise of the Jews in the motion picture business, the single cultural standard embodied in the movies came to be one of mass culture rather than the high culture that Griffith portrayed. Using the nickelodeons as an entering wedge into a field dominated by trusts, the Jews eventually broke the back of the Protestant-dominated companies and reached out in even wider fashion to the middle-class audiences coming to the movies, but hungering less for evangelical themes and more for urban, consumption-oriented dramas featuring visions of a new life. The new producers kept the audiences by creating glorious palaces as theatres, bringing in a star system, and adopting longer features from Broadway plays, all designed to bring class to formerly forbidden pleasures. The movies were able by the 1910s to purvey to all classes the themes of urban life: experience, indulgence in exciting but safe amusements, new roles for men and women, and a redefinition of success as consumption.[26]

During the growth of movies and vaudeville, music publishers and composers also realized that they could market new songs like any other product, giving birth to the merchandising machinery and mass production techniques of Tin Pan Alley. By bringing to a wider respectable public music nurtured on the city streets that during the nineteenth century they had wanted to control, Tin Pan Alley also earned the attention of moral critics. The modern music business was born in 1892 when Charles K. Harris's ballad, *"After the Ball,"* sold 5 million copies. Harris's song exemplified the lachrymous ballads of the 1890s that glorified dead babies, parents, forgotten sweethearts, lost loves, and noble mothers. *"After the Ball"* projected a powerful sentiment of faded life, experience missed, and an era dying. As a young maiden climbs on "an old man's knee," for the story of "why are you single, why live alone," she hears a tale of mistaken mistrust when after the ball he saw her kissing a man whom he did not then know was her brother. Consequently the narrator remains lonely, without home, wife, and family and with hopes vanished after the ball.[27]

While the sentimental ballad appealed to the *fin de siècle* preoccupation with the death of Victorian styles, new forms of music of a livelier stamp offered Americans the sense that life was worth living and that new experiences awaited them. By the mid-1890s, popular music was ripe for an alternative to the death-inspired ballads, and it found it in the loud, nationally chauvinistic brass band march music of John Philip Sousa and in the more rousing music of black culture, which was breaking out of its own restricted shell. The first example of the new interest in blacks was the "coon" song, which hit its apogee in 1896. Minstrelsy was in decline; audiences wanted more lively urban adventures, and the "impudent coon" replaced the "happy darky" as the black stereotype in white minds. The "coon" had the characteristic "habit of fighting, stealing, and ostentatious dress and speech." In numerous songs, he exaggerated the uppity and inept Jim Dandy stereotype of the minstrel Negro and was always getting into social difficulty. The coon song also featured sexually active black people, but in a negative way. As urban whites first began to break away from the confinement of Victorianism, and as blacks began inhabiting northern cities in greater numbers, the former sought experiences vicariously in black life, projecting such frightening traits as "sexual passion and violence upon the 'inferior race' " where they could be experienced and condemned at the same time.[28]

Coon songs peaked in the 1910s just as whites began to admit their deeper interest in the new impulses as something capable of being integrated into their own culture. Ragtime then reached its height, transforming American popular music with the vitality of black folk music and paving the way for the influence of such other expressions as blues and jazz. Coming out of black culture, ragtime gradually made its way into Tin Pan Alley by the 1910s. From the 1890s black culture emerged slightly from behind the mask of minstrelsy as a new generation of blacks born in freedom, with some of them classically trained in music in black colleges, moved to the cities and there found greater protection for their cultural expression. Ragtime achieved initial popularity in brothels, though its steady two-four or four-four beat and syncopation were really a combination of black syncopation and the formal written compositions of European training. In their way, they broke from earlier Puritanical derogation of black music in black colleges and showed its equality with European forms. Dance halls, sporting houses, and black clubs at the bottom of the social order, primarily for men, continued to serve as an outlet for the more expressive entertainments. Under Tammany's favorable political protection, black saloons in the Tenderloin featured ragtime pianists, while a number of white players, such as Jimmy Durante, found room for their own musical exploration in the Tenderloin as well. Also Eddie Cantor and Irving Berlin started as singing waiters in Coney Island and Nigger Mike's in the Bowery, respectively.[29]

Staffed by songwriters of immigrant and at times black origin, Tin Pan Alley brought syncopation out of the red-light districts and into the larger society. Many of the songwriters were Jews, who, like Houdini, were moving out from a traditional familial and authoritarian culture into the greater openness and hence rootlessness of the American society. Irving Berlin was one; he was the son of an orthodox cantor who had lost much of his authority in success-oriented America. He was at home on the streets, that marginal land between his own culture and the culture of his new society. The streets presented a world of constant experience and action, where there was excitement at every turn and where the choices and sights could provide feelings of constant experiences of the self uprooted from a stable past. Working the city's dives, he took his speech and rhythm from the city streets, from Yiddish intonations, and from Italian, Yiddish, black, and Irish voices and caricatures he found around him. While his famous "Alexander's Ragtime Band" was not strictly ragtime, Berlin managed to widen the audience for black-influenced popular music. By the 1910s, respectable whites danced to this music, and critics argued its merits. Hiram K. Moderwell noted in the *New Republic* that genteel critics ignored this true American music that arose from the people on the streets and that expressed an urban and machine age, with its "jerk and rattle," and distinguished American culture from European. Critics, however, worried about the influence that African and vulgar "filthy and suggestive" music and lyrics had on the morality of respectable women and the tenor of urban cultural life. According to Ivan Narodny, it "suggested the ardor of the saloon, the smell of the backyard and subways." The fear of the music also suggests that many respectable urbanites feared the rising tide of immigrant- and black-inspired culture at a time when their own culture was in the midst of change, unable to resist these new elements in urban life actively seeking new patterns of vitality.[30]

The modern cabaret or nightclub was also part of the trend toward new amusements and values, and it met the same kinds of criticism as did the other forms. A prominent urban institution after 1911, the cabaret's early days are clouded in murky origins. The 1890s had already witnessed the beginnings of informal entertainment-drinking places for men and women, but they remained largely a province of the theatrical profession until 1911. White rathskellers, often located in basements, paralleled black in serving the fast set and men out on the town. Sophie Tucker recalled her initial singing venture at New York's German Village, which she described as three floors of women singers who often went to bed with male customers. Starting in the 1890s, moreover, Broadway hotels experimented with roof gardens, where customers could have a drink, sit outside or under a roof, and watch a light summer divertissement. While urbanites took advantage of the opportunity to get outside on hot nights, there was no dancing to enliven the atmosphere. Sometime around 1906 a few of the larger restaurants began presenting occasional impromptu entertainments. In the case of the Café des Beaux Arts, ad lib performances occurred only on designated nights for professional theatrical people. The highest salaried vaudeville performers appeared in a private, intimate atmosphere, thus giving the evening a touch of naughtiness, but for the most part the general public was not admitted.[31]

By 1911 cabaret-style entertainment had spread from the segregated vice districts and theatrical-sporting communities of the rathskellers to the Broadway restaurants. The restaurant managers followed the lead of theatre men Jesse Lasky and Henry Harris who attempted to build a theatre-restaurant with cabaret entertainment modeled after Parisian bohemian activities. Although the theatre failed, the idea lived on in the lobster palaces, which already had a European atmosphere. There is some question whether the idea of the cabaret in America came from Paris. It is clear that wealthy men and women had been visiting such places in Europe in the 1890s, as the Parisian haunts themselves began to attract tourists.[32] It is also clear that Lasky and Harris recognized the desire on the part of Americans for bohemian experiences. It was also true that one of the first major acts in a New York cabaret was the apache dance, taken from the slums of Paris and performed in Louis Martin's in 1911.

But if one of the sources was the Paris cabaret, another was the joints of American cities. "The 'joints' may fairly claim a sort of cousinship with this new-come French jade," declared Julian Street, "the sort of cousinship there is between the woman of the streets and the favorite of a king. Things change. It takes time to 'educate' the public. Moe would not go to the 'joints,' so the 'joints' are brought to Moe."[33] Moreover, many of the acts, which first appeared in the cafés, came from rathskellers and the lower rungs of vaudeville and variety. A number of rathskeller performers from the dives of San Francisco's Barbary Coast found engagements in New York City cafés, and they brought a number of new-style dances from that city as well. Broadway thus drew on the traditions of the male vice districts, the lower classes, and the rich to fashion a new-style institution for both men and women. With the expensive French and European decor of the lobster palaces, respectable and prosperous urbanites found that they could enjoy more risqué entertainment and dancing in public just as the lower classes did but without the vice associations of the early dives. An informal social life was becoming the province of the respectable classes and now included most noticeably American women, as the middle and upper classes sought to revitalize their culture and the relationship between men and women, which lay at its core. After 1911 when men and women visited a cabaret, they entered at street level or went up atop hotels or theatres. Indulging in these pleasures no longer required venturing beneath the street. That which had been permitted only in the dark now did not seem quite so wicked. The cabaret had made a symbolic evolution from a hidden aspect of life to one accepted as a phenomenon of human existence.

As with the other new amusements, men and women went together to a public environment where neither the activities of the entertainers nor the behavior of the customers could be considered entirely respectable or predictable by nineteenth-century standards. When in 1912 the cabarets went a step further and fed the demand for public places to dance new-style ragtime dances from black culture, they assumed an importance that made the reformers see them as a threat to proper urban life and Victorian values. Instead of mirroring the values of the private home, the public world represented a new openness and a new passion. In late 1912 and early 1913, for example, Mayor William J. Gaynor and other concerned citizens were deeply disturbed by this boisterous public dancing, drinking, and social mingling now creeping out of lower-class dance halls and male saloons into the haunts of respectable urbanites. Most important, these haunts were public, "open to every one," according to Gaynor, "who chooses to come up and pay the entrance fee." Angered by this early morning "roistering," the mayor charged that "the all-night licenses [for liquor in restaurants] were grossly abused. Under them, so-called respectable places were turned into places of vulgarity if not infamy."[34] In this dangerously open environment in the anonymous bright-light zones of Times Square, respectable women could mix promiscuously with people of unspecified moral character from whom they had been rigidly separated since the 1850s. The cabaret was thus one of the many new institutions that marked a departure in the relations between men and women of the prosperous classes. For the first time, they enjoyed a public, informal atmosphere together. As "people of position have taken to frequenting the restaurants where dancing is the attraction," claimed author Julian Street, they created a social mixture never before seen in the United States, "a hodge-podge of people in which respectable young married and unmarried women, and even debutantes dance, not only under the same roof, but in the same room with women of the town."[35]

All through the 1910s the Committee of Fourteen and other reform agencies attempted to bring the excesses of the cabaret under control. From Mayor Gaynor and Mayor Mitchel's attempts at curfew laws (in 1913 and 1914) to the Committee of Fourteen's attempt to eliminate prostitution, reformers saw in the cabaret a challenge to respectable amusements and their conception of the proper role of women. One well-publicized case, that of Eugenia Kelly, illustrates what lay behind their efforts. On the evening of May 21, 1915, private and city detectives converged on Pennsylvania Station in New York City to arrest nineteen-year-old Eugenia Kelly, daughter of a late banker and a former sister-in-law of Frank J. Gould. The young lady's mother procured a warrant for her arrest in the hopes of preventing her degradation at the hands of disreputable associates in the relatively new cabarets along the Great White Way. As a member of an eminent family, Eugenia assumed the central role in a much-publicized case, which blazened the evils of the cabaret and a generation of "pleasure-mad women" in New York City. Employing the themes of the abandonment of chastity and social position by someone of elevated status, participants in the case revealed in startling form the fears underlying the criticism of cabarets, public nightlife, and the new amusements.[36]

In her remarks to the court and to the press, Mrs. Kelly pictured herself as the savior of the sanctity of the home and of her daughter's chastity. Weeping as she spoke, she told of her daughter's returning home from nights of revelry at three and four in the morning. "Why, if I didn't go to at least six cabarets a night," Mrs. Kelly quoted her daughter, "I would lose my social standing."[37] Eugenia's mother blamed the cabaret for seducing her daughter into a life of modern evil. In this new urban institution, outside the controlling eye of social custom and the family, Mrs. Kelly charged, Eugenia had learned to smoke and drink. Although Eugenia had been making the rounds of night spots for several years, Mrs. Kelly felt that matters had finally hit bottom. Eugenia had been associating with Al Davis, a married dancer, upon whom she was lavishing expensive gifts of jewelry. When all else failed, Mrs. Kelly, as the defender of traditional morality against the fast set with whom her daughter associated, petitioned the court to have Eugenia declared incorrigible and remanded to her care or jailed.

The magistrate sided with Mrs. Kelly in a morality play that cast Eugenia as the rebellious daughter. In a preliminary ruling he charged that the daughter's neglect of her home would lead to moral depravity. "The issue is plain as to whether the defendant is disobedient of her mother, who is her natural and legal guardian," the judge said, and "whether she is liable to become morally depraved." Mrs. Kelly's lawyer added to the general outcry by labeling Broadway and its fast crowds the source of disintegration of this once-happy family. He laid down the terms: return home and give up the fast life. "You are breaking your mother's heart," he charged. "If you will promise me now to go home to her, to cut out this Broadway crowd, to eliminate this man Al Davis from your mind, I will drop this thing right now."[38]

The case seemingly had a happy resolution. Eugenia admitted in open court that "I was wrong and mother was right," and Mrs. Kelly dropped the charges of incorrigibility, but not before the judge lectured Eugenia on the value of traditional morality and social standing. "You come from one of the best families in the city," he reminded her. "I can remember, as a young man, that your grandfather stood so high in this community that when men passed him in the street they lifted their hats out of respect to him. Your father was a high type of man, and one of the city's best citizens." Eugenia, however, had rejected this heritage of social responsibility and leadership for the lights of Broadway. "I am afraid you have acted foolishly," he declared. "The best friend you have is your mother." To a generation attempting to come to terms with a growing gap in modes of behavior between mothers and daughters, this solution must have seemed most gratifying. Eugenia went home.[39]

To observers of the case, the interest lay not in Eugenia's particular unhappiness, but in the general decline of True Womanhood, which the cabaret symbolized.[40] In 1912 the cafés inaugurated a series of afternoon dances, called *the dansants* or tango teas. For the price of a drink or a relatively small admission fee, single and married women could dance during the afternoons as well as at night. The management hired dancing partners, or gigolos, to take the unescorted women through their paces. Al Davis, the man who took Eugenia through paces of another sort, was either a paid dancing partner or a hanger-on in both the evening and afternoon cafés. Here lay the fear: respectable women, seeking passion and excitement, would find them with men marked as disreputable by their sensuality and ethnicity, characteristics many people considered to be the same. In the heat of the dance and the informal air of the café, the old gentility, which kept women in their place, was forgotten. When they danced with swarthy, lower-class Italians and Jews, their chastity as well as class status was in danger. What is more, women could drop into the afternoon *dansants* while purportedly shopping, and unsuspecting parents and working husbands need never know.[41]

In seeking explanations for Eugenia's rejection of the traditional concept of womanhood and the restraint of the family, those connected with the case were unable to believe that she rationally chose her activities or her companions. Indeed no one was inclined to analyze the failures of traditional morality and family, or willing to blame the young woman herself. Mrs. Kelly, for example, was ill equipped to dissect her family. As the newspapers discovered, she too made a regular practice of visiting the cafés.[42] Instead of examining the changing culture of the best people, Mrs. Kelly said, "Eugenia is not innately bad. She is a good girl, but was *blinded* to a true perception of life by the white lights of Broadway." The young woman herself concurred: "I realize now that I was dazzled by the glamour of the white lights and the music and the dancing of Broadway."[43] Rollin Kirby's four-column cartoon of a young girl gazing into a brightly lit cabaret continued the imagery of the will-less innocent drawn to her degradation. Inside men in top hats mingled with young women in low-cut gowns. A devil figure, complete with tail, stared at her seductively as he said, "Come On In, Kid."[44] If she did not choose this life, the young woman, like any good Victorian, could be pictured as incapable of passion. For her sex was not a natural emotion but something that had to be artificially stimulated.

Others joined in the comment on a case that raised to a visible high point the issue of generational breakdown, disruption of domestic morality, and passion in public life. Liberal vice investigator Belle Moskowitz saw this incident as the norm for young women in the city. The only difference she saw was that the dance evil now affected the respectable, whereas earlier it had concerned only immigrants and the poor. According to Mrs. Moskowitz, "It is simply an evil condition working upward into other strata of society." She was convinced that "the Kelly case has done good if it has called attention to the danger that lurks in the path of the young woman of today." Mrs. Moskowitz joined the committee in advocating the closing of the afternoon cabarets, where young women found their greatest freedom outside public opinion and the family and fell "under the spell of the dance and their companions."[45]

In a lengthy editorial, the *New York Times* raised the question of why there "is a furor about the cabarets." The newspaper blamed the irrational hysteria on a well-trained New York imagination, which "conjures up hundreds of wealthy girls squandering their time and money on organized gangs of cabaret dancers" and contributes to "excited columns . . . printed about the 'social gangsters' who pluck checkbooks right and left from the daughters of the rich." The editorial raised important issues overlooked by the critics. If young women were so prone to give money and chastity to wastrels, they would just as likely do so in a theatre or hotel. Why then, implied the *Times*, did the critics blame the cabaret?[46]

The cabaret posed a direct challenge to the cult of domesticity. Progressive and conservative critics who based their conceptions of civilization on the idea that women were essentially pure, religious, and moral were disturbed by women's cavorting in dance in informal, drinking environments with men. As leaveners of democratic culture, women's presence in the cabaret heralded the destruction of individual and social progress and order. Yet unable to change their view of women's essential asexual nature, raised in that model of life themselves, the critics were caught in a crisis of family and social values and turned to external causes to explain deviation from the path of true womanhood. It was not women or the family of the prosperous classes who were changing; rather external, disorganized, lower-class agencies were influencing and infecting good women of the better classes.

Of all the cabaret's activities, the public character of dancing aroused the bitterest and most prolonged attacks. To reformers, the close physical contact and body expression connoted loss of self-control. The lifting of legs, the jerking of shoulders represented an unreserved demeanor on the part of youth and womanhood in general. The fact that respectable women danced forms originating among inferiors, sensual blacks and Latins, moved critics to envision the enshrinement of undisguised sexuality and lower-class behavior. "That for a moment persons of respectable antecedents have injudiciously endured their introduction in places where decorum guards chastity has not changed their nature or obscured their menace." This was a "Revolt Against Decency," as the *Literary Digest* called it, part of a revolt against the Victorian conception of woman's role. As one observer asked somewhat fearfully, had it struck "Sex O'Clock" in America?[47] Everyone seemed to be dancing the new steps, and the influence of the lower-class sensuality was spreading. "From the slum to the stage, from the stage to the restaurant," noted Roy McCardell in the *World*, "from restaurant to home, the dive dances have clutched and taken hold upon the young who know no better and the old who should."[48] Here was uncontrolled inundation by inferior peoples and the abandonment of civilized restraint. "Far from being 'new,' " a *Sun* editorial charged, "these dances are a reversion to the grossest practices of savage man." Indeed they "are based on the primitive motive of orgies enjoyed by the aboriginal inhabitants of every uncivilized land."[49]

The critics also feared the cabaret because, as an urban amusement, it was open to a widely diverse portion of the city's population, so that many kinds of people engaged in expressive behavior, and the respectable would be easily led astray toward their bodies and decay. Ethel Mumford in *Harper's Weekly*, for instance, focused her criticism on the mixing of peoples of different classes and moral styles. Young women, "many of them obviously of breeding and refinement," copied the habits of dangerous people. "Let them go from four till seven," she warned, "cheek by jowl with professionals whose repute is not even doubtful," and they will learn "the insidious habit of the early cocktail." The mixing of different classes and moral backgrounds endangered the restraint that Victorians believed young women needed for a successful home life. "The careless forming of undesirable acquaintances, the breaking down of barriers of necessary caution, make for carelessness in after life," noted Mumford. This casual attitude "develops a laxity of moral responsibility and a state of mind that is corruptive and vitiating to the last degree."[50] Others lashed out at the change in "nice" girls brought about by the cabaret. The *Nation*, for example, supported Mayor Gaynor's curfew orders "if he should deplore the fact that too many good women, if thoughtless, nowadays array themselves like *demimondaines*," and it blamed the cabaret for producing the change. By bringing diverse social worlds into the same orbit, the cabaret lowered the general tone of civilization: "The spirit of caste and convention is disappearing. Ideals are mingling in delightful promiscuity. A little bit of the underworld, a soupçon of the half-world—there you have the modern synthesis of New York as revealed in the neighborhood of Forty-second Street."[51]

Critics believed that too much expressive pleasure in a risqué environment endangered young women, for once they let go, they were easily led to prostitution and away from the traditional role of home and mother. The pleasure-loving woman would also destroy male identity. For those who adhered to the nineteenth-century conception of masculinity contained in the self-made man, passionate women would lead men away from self-control toward a life of sensual expressiveness. Men's concentration would be broken, their money lost, and their business affairs ruined. If men gave in to the demands of the body, they would lose both self-control and their identities.[52] Owen Johnson, for example, claimed to have found middle-aged women of the highest respectability "blissful with dance partners," while he "could not help conjuring up a vision of the husbands and sons slaving away in downtown offices that 'mother' might enjoy her youth again."[53] In effect, the author of *Dink Stover at Yale* noted, women had climbed down off the pedestal, and "whether rightly or wrongly, man has always wanted a woman to be better than himself."[54]

The ultimate fear was that once off the pedestal, respectable married and single women would find lower-class men in the cabaret better able to satisfy their cravings for pleasure. Invariably the women in these critiques seemed to pick lower-class men. Even the most reputable women hired dancing escorts of dubious pasts, generally from the service trades: chauffeurs, clerks, waiters, valets, chorus men, and pimps. "Every menial hanger-on at the fringe of society has found his evolution there."[55] Pleasure would ultimately force respectable men to ape the manners of these menial and sensual men to hold their own women, and this process would leave them lost and adrift, incapable of success. It was the spectre of these lower-class men, the tango pirates, that gave the Eugenia Kelly case and the other cabaret scares their distinctive and resonant power. The tango pirate or social gangster, as he was called, focused in one person the dangers to both women and men that resulted from the pursuit of pleasure and the disintegration of Victorianism. Tango pirates were pictured as lower-class men who lived off the rich women they met in the afternoon cafés. Despite their fashionable clothes and manners, "they are," noted ex-district attorney John McIntyre, Mrs. Kelly's private eye, "ignorant, ill-born fellows who have acquired a mere veneer of good manners and small talk." The veneer itself lured the unsuspecting, because this "is all the rich young girls ever see or try to see."[56]

Underneath the veneer, newspapers and reformers described the pirates as a caricature of nineteenth- and early twentieth-century repressions. The imagery associated with the tango pirate and social gangster suggests that they were social criminals, aggressors against the standards of propriety. Both "pirate" and "gangster" conjure up images of illegality and theft, as if these men took sex and money from women without their consent or knowledge. The pirate was a man who trapped and tapped the sexuality of women. The master of such passion-inducing dances as the tango and one-step, the pirate held women in a spell they could not easily break. Tightening his arms around her, dipping her, holding her, and in the tango from which he got his name, bending her over backward in a perfect picture of sexual subjugation, the tango pirate was the master of all he surveyed.

The use of drugs as part of an arsenal of entrapment heightened this lustful and aggressive portrait. Although not always part of the game, cocaine "is almost invariably a part of the equipment of the tango pirate. It is the stigma that classes him with the criminal of a lower and less alluring grade." The critics believed that the drugs helped him gain control of the wills of women. Telling them the drug was just for fun, the tango pirate was able to force young women into sexuality and into squandering their money. The tango pirate assumed the symbolic role of the lustful male who lured women to their destruction. Eliminate him, as reformers demanded, and women and the traditions of Victorian culture would remain sound.[57] Reformers and conservatives supported attacks on lascivious social gangsters, drugs, and alcohol in order to protect the harmonious refined family.[58]

The image of the tango pirate had another side, however, one that offers insights into the contemporary fears about sexual experimentation and modern life in general. If we look closely at how newspapers described him, we can see that this sensuous, willfully aggressive male was also effeminate, will-less, and dependent on women for money. Here was a man who, by nineteenth-century standards, spent too much time with women; ironically the penalty for such action was loss of manhood. Many of the objections against tango pirates were also made against all male dancers, and in stories and tales, men who danced spent so much time seducing women that they had little time for their businesses.[59] Male dancers had less than masculine identities because they engaged in expressive activities with women. *Variety*, for example, found male dancers too dependent on women, overly concerned with their grooming, and feminine in their attention to clothing. Moreover, the journal always pointed out that the male dancers acted in effeminate ways. Chastising Benne Dixon for putting his hand on his hip, *Variety* said that "this hand on the hip is awful stuff for a regular fellow to tamper with." This behavior was also spreading: "Here some of the traveling salesmen who think they should be professional dancers are doing it."[60] If they had to dance, *Variety* advised them to treat it as a business and not as either an art or a physical expression, for "America [is] not a nation of ballet dancers."[61] There are "several male dancers who dance manly, though professionals," the trade paper asserted approvingly, "and seem to say, 'We are doing this as a business.' "[62]

The tango pirate was an extension of the professional dancer, a man heavily involved in sensual expression, combining the traits of expressiveness, absence of work, love of luxury, and fascination with women. The opposite of the male business ideal of disciplined will, the pirate represented what could happen to men who directed limited bodily energies toward women. In 1914 *Variety*, usually a defender of the cabaret, charged that the afternoon dances "may be said to have caused more family disturbances in the time they have existed than happened among an equal number of people of the same calibre for five years preceding the real dancing fad." Once women had a taste of experience, "home doesn't look like it uster *[sic]*." The underlying assumption was clear: if women were allowed to mix freely without their husbands or parents present, they would ultimately leave their men and their social position. "If the cabarets could talk," noted the paper, "or the waiters tell all they know, the state would have to open a few extra courts to keep up with the rush for divorces."[63] Moreover, to keep their women, would not men have to keep up with them? Would they not have to spend time with sensual women and spend less time on business? If they did, they could see what would happen to them; they would become like the tango pirate, bereft of their former status, lower class, and in no way fulfilling the role of man the producer. As McIntyre put it, "It is hard for an old-fashioned man like me to understand [that] women can endure men who are palpably, serenely, and obviously parasites."[64]

The critics of the new amusements reacted to the rise of urban institutions that broke with nineteenth-century traditions by bringing men and women together in pleasurable, sometimes fast environments, and left behind some of the class- and sex-segregated entertainments of the nineteenth century. Both progressive and conservative critics were disturbed that these anonymous urban amusements with their lustful male aggressors were leading women down the path to destruction. Equally, as we have seen, this period is remarkable for the amount of fear expressed of men mixing with women and undercutting the nineteenth-century style of will. Both progressive and conservative critics saw female sexuality as potentially anarchic and dangerous, but they both agreed that women were inherently asexual and thus not responsible for their impulses. Moreover, the tremendous public concern with amusements and vice from the turn of the century through World War I also arose from the fear that men were changing, being corrupted by women of vice away from the path to moral sensibility and character. Perhaps the perception of the reformers was correct, for from the late 1890s, men of the middle classes as well as the upper and lower were seeking ways to move away from Victorian constraints. Unable and sometimes unwilling to repeat the path of their fathers' total drive for success to the exclusion of personal life, young men after the 1890s sought ways to enjoy the money of the corporation and the economy and take greater personal freedom in leisure, with women. As the Kelly case and numerous others suggest, young women also sought men who were more leisured, less dedicated to work, and hence capable of dedication to them. It was this turn to consumption at the core of Protestant culture that made reformers and men and women of the better classes uncomfortable. Reformers, however, tended to hold onto their concept of the viability of the Protestant family and character and see the causes for change as external. The tango pirate, white slaver, the city, the factory, the breakdown of family led women astray. And it was among immigrants that they looked for sources of breakdown since they assumed that the immigrants were in disorganization. The rise of new amusements suggested to them that new forms of vice were spreading, creating a situation that was alien and out of control. Already aware that their own roles were changing in moving outside the home to expand their genteel role, women reformers especially still held on to the concept of proper womanhood and amusements as a way to teach Victorian character to immigrant and upper class alike as the basis of a unified and improved social order.

The strategy of progressives arose out of their concept of womanhood as they attempted to extend ascetic motherhood to a motherless city. The city was to be a home, with the public world mirroring once again the model of the private home. Entering the public world these women and men did so only as agents of the traditional, of family. They defined female freedom as social duty and expected other well-to-do women to give up selfish idleness and lead the society to a higher moral level. They sought to clean up excesses in amusements—drinking, late hours, afternoon cafés, tango pirates, prostitution—to prevent the mixing of cultures so detrimental to Victorian concepts of the proper citizen and society. In banking so much on their concept of the family, the progressives and the conservatives were unable to understand that most men and women wanted something new in their private lives. The urban world was changing, moving away from being an extension of the private home. This desire did not go unnoticed; reformers could see that play needed to be reevaluated in an industrial order. The question was how different from the identities of the mothers and fathers the generation of the 1890s would be. The new amusement trends would come to the fore in the cabaret of the 1910s, where women and men worked out for themselves their attempt to choose new identities. While reformers sought to liberate the child of the city, others sought to liberate their own private playfulness. Where could they turn? Men and women of the respectable classes had cultivated the Protestant ethic too readily. "We Anglo-Saxons are the most incompetent of all the people in this respect," Joseph Lee, president of the Playground and Recreation Association, declared. If play was natural but undeveloped, where would the best people turn for new models? They had begun turning to Paris, to the lower classes, and to blacks, for as Lee put it, marginal groups, especially blacks, "never wholly [lose] hope for the future nor a sense of joy of living."[65] Yet this generation, as much as the critics, in releasing themselves from their parents' models, held onto the essential belief in success. It was the immigrants, not themselves, who were in the factories. How could the prosperous classes reconcile new forms of play with older notions of character?

NOTES

1. John Keefe, *New York World*, May 27, 1915, p. 8.

2. John Higham, "The Reorientation of American Culture in the 1890's," in *Writing American History, Essays on Modern Scholarship* (Bloomington: Indiana University Press, 1972), pp. 73–102.

3. For Josiah Strong, see *Our Country* (Cambridge, Mass.: Belknap Press, 1963), pp. 5–10, 72–90, 101–36. Reverend Charles Parkhurst, *My Forty Years in New York* (New York: Macmillan, 1923), pp. 107–11, 121, shows fear of men in danger; pp. 4–22 discuss city and women.

4. Michael Mooney, *Evelyn Nesbit and Stanford White, Love and Death in the Gilded Age* (New York: William Morrow, 1976), pp. 201–02.

5. Lary May, *Screening Out the Past* (New York: Oxford University Press, 1980).

6. Roland Richard Wagner, "Virtue Against Vice: A Study of Moral Reformers in the Progressive Era" (Ph.D. diss., University of Wisconsin, 1971), pp. 133–52, which details the work of the Committees of Fifteen and Fourteen, shows that the reformers hailed from New England roots and were often from merchant backgrounds as well. There were also college professors, German-Jewish families, and interdenominational religious leadership concerned with bringing the city under moral and scientific control through their own elite tutelage.

7. Committee of Fifteen, *Report on the Social Evil of 1910* (New York: Putnam, 1912), pp. xiv.

8. Jane Addams, *A New Conscience and an Ancient Evil* (New York: The Macmillan Co., 1912), pp. 104–06; for similar views, see her friend and coworker, head of the Juvenile Protection Association in Chicago, Louise De Koven Bowen, *Safeguards for City Youth at Work and Play* (New York: The Macmillan Co., 1914); Bowen, *The Road to Destruction Made Easy in Chicago* (Chicago: Juvenile Protective Association of Chicago, 1916); and her remarks in *Growing Up with a City* (New York: The Macmillan Co., 1926). For a less-heated statement of Addams's theme, see *The Spirit of Youth in the City Streets* (New York: The Macmillan Co., 1909).

9. Belle Israels, "The Dance Problem," *Playground* 4 (October 1910): 247. She noted that 95 percent of New York working girls go to dance halls, p. 251.

10. Ibid.

11. Walter Lippmann, *A Preface to Politics* (1914; reprint, Ann Arbor: University of Michigan, 1969), p. 40.

12. For the new approach to leisure, see Lawrence Finfer, "Leisure as Social Work in the Urban Community: The Progressive Recreation Movement, 1890–1920" (Ph.D. diss., Michigan State University, 1974); May, *Screening Out.*

13. They, of course, also expressed elements of their backgrounds in the process.

14. Albert F. McLean, Jr., *American Vaudeville as Ritual* (Lexington: University of Kentucky Press, 1965), p. 69.

15. Ibid., pp. 25–29.

16. On Houdini, see ibid., pp. 154–59; William Lindsay Gresham, *Houdini: The Man Who Walked Through Walls* (New York: Henry Holt & Co., 1959); and, of course, the portrait that emerges throughout the pages of E. L. Doctorow, *Ragtime* (New York: Random House, 1974).

17. McLean, *American Vaudeville*, pp. 77–90.

18. Lary May, *Screening Out.*

19. Robert Sklar, *Movie-Made America, A Cultural History of American Movies* (New York: Vintage, 1975), pp. 13–17.

20. May, *Screening Out.*

21. F. H. Richardson, *Motion Picture Handbook* (1910), p. 160, quoted in Sklar, *Movie-Made*, p. 16.

22. *New York World*, April 26, 1896, p. 1, quoted in May, *Screening Out.*

23. May, *Screening Out*, pp. 76–77.

24. Ibid., pp. 107–09.

25. Ibid., p. 110.

26. Sklar, *Movie-Made*, pp. 33–64; May, *Screening Out.*

27. For the tearful ballads, see David Ewen, *Tin Pan Alley* (New York: Funk and Wagnall's, 1964), pp. 37–54; Jens Lund, "American Minstrelsy on Phonograph Records," unpublished paper (Folklore Institute, Indiana University, n.d.), p. 13; Charles Harris, *After the Ball* (New York: Frank-Maurie, 1926).

28. Ewen, *Tin Pan Alley*, pp. 168–78; Lund, "American Minstrelsy," p. 13.

29. Lund, *American Minstrelsy*, p. 13.

30. Neil Leonard, *Jazz and the White Americans* (Chicago: University of Chicago Press, 1962), p. 27; Ewen, *Tin Pan Alley*, pp. 171, 177.

31. *Variety*, February 3, 1912, p. 15; Abel Green and Joe Laurie, Jr., *Show Biz: From Vaude to Video* (New York: Henry Holt & Co., 1951), pp. 77–78.

32. For a description of Americans rambling about the haunts of Paris, see Richard Harding Davis, *About Paris* (1895; reprint, Upper Saddle River, N.J.: Literature House/Gregg Press, 1969), pp. 47–97.

33. Julian Street, "Oh, You Babylon!" *Everybody's Magazine* 27 (August 1912): 177.

34. *New York Times*, April 5, 1913, p. 2; Mayor William J. Gaynor to Louis Fischer, April 9, 1913, Gaynor Papers, Municipal Archives, New York City.

35. Julian Street, *Welcome to Our City* (New York: John Lane Co., 1913), pp. 10–11.

36. For details of the case, see *New York Times*, May 23, 1915, IV, p. 5.

37. Ibid.

38. *New York World*, May 25, 1915, p. 8.

39. *New York Times*, May 26, 1915, p. 8.

40. The term "true womanhood" from Barbara Welter, "The Cult of True Womanhood," *American Quarterly* 18 (Summer 1966): 151–74. On changes in women before the 1920s, see James R. McGovern, "The Ameri-

can Woman's Pre-World War I Freedom in Manners and Morals," *Journal of American History* 55 (September 1968): 315–33; Daniel Scott Smith, "The Dating of the American Sexual Revolution: Evidence and Interpretation," in *The American Family in Social-Historical Perspective*, ed. Michael Gordon (New York: St. Martin's Press, 1973), pp. 321–35; Elaine T. May, *Great Expectations: Marriage and Divorce in Post-Victorian America* (Chicago: University of Chicago Press, 1980).

41. For material on afternoon teas, see "Dancing at Five," *Smart Styles* 2 (1914): 44–45, in Vernon Castle Scrapbooks, Locke Collection, New York Public Library Theatre Collection, Lincoln Center; *New York Times*, March 13, 1913, p. 20; *Variety*, March 28, 1913, p. 21, and October 17, 1913.

42. *New York Times*, May 25, 1915, p. 8, revealed that Mrs. Kelly was also a frequenter of the cafés. Among other things, this suggests that the new trends were not just for the young.

43. *New York World*, May 26, 1915, p. 1.

44. Ibid., p. 8.

45. *New York Times*, May 27, 1915, p. 11.

46. "The Latest Crusade," *New York Times*, May 31, 1915, p. 6.

47. "The Revolt of Decency," *New York Sun*, quoted in *Literary Digest*, April 9, 1913, p. 894.

48. Roy L. McCardell, "The City of Dreadful Dance!" *New York World*, March 30, 1913, p. 1.

49. "The Revolt of Decency," p. 894.

50. Ethel Mumford, "Where Is Your Daughter This Afternoon?" *Harper's Weekly*, January 17, 1914, p. 28.

51. "Trotting Forward," *Nation*, April 10, 1913, p. 352.

52. Graham J. Barker-Benfield, "The Spermatic Economy: A Nineteenth Century View of Sexuality," in Gordon, *American Family*, pp. 336–72.

53. Owen Johnson, *New York Times*, May 25, 1914, VI, p. 6. For the problems of men in an increasingly organized and consuming society, see James R. McGovern, "David Graham Phillips and the Virility Impulse of Progressives," *New England Quarterly* 29 (September 1966): 334–55.

54. *New York Times*, May 25, 1914, VI, p. 6.

55. Ibid.

56. Richard Barry, "Tango Pirates Infest Broadway Afternoon Dances," *New York Times*, May 30, 1915, V, p. 16.

57. Ibid.

58. The direction of the attacks differed. Jane Addams, Louise De Koven Bowen, and Mrs. Moskowitz supported the suppression of the most flagrant evils of the cabarets. They wanted to use sensuality for uplift and thus make play re-create the old Victorian character and family that they saw passing. Moreover, they wanted to make the state a moral entity that guarded the

values of the family in the city. The vision of the state as a moral entity, an extended family, also permitted women to enter public life as extensions of traditional moral styles.

Egal Feldman, "Prostitution, the Alien Woman and the Progressive Imagination, 1910–1915," *American Quarterly* 19 (1967): 196–206, and Roy Lubove, "The Progressives and the Prostitute," *Historian* 24 (1961–1962): 308–30, see prostitution reform in isolation. Lubove rarely asks why reformers were concerned with vice. Roland Richard Wagner, "Virtue Against Vice," collects much on the background on the Committee of Fourteen. David Pivar, *Purity Crusade* (Westport, Conn.: Greenwood Press, 1973), analyzes the growing concern with purity in the late nineteenth century, but stops before the issue becomes part of progressive reform in the twentieth century.

Robert E. Riegel, "Changing American Attitudes Toward Prostitution," *Journal of the History of Ideas* 29 (1968): 437–52, discusses the changing image of the prostitute. City after city, prior to World War I, fought to eliminate its redlight districts, and many were successful. Perhaps, as suggested here, the animus behind the desire to institutionalize the Victorian world view in actuality resulted from its growing breakdown. Not just the poor were feared, but respectable women and men as well. John C. Burnham, "The Progressive Era Revolution in American Attitudes Toward Sex," *Journal of American History* 59 (March 1973): 885–908, provides evidence for the growing fear about the spread of syphilis through the society.

59. See, for example, W. Carey Wonderly, "The Chorus Man," *Green Book Magazine* 12 (December 1915): 1066–86. The story ran through April 1915 when dancer Jay Adean gave up his tango life for hard work and a happy marriage. *Variety*, April 2, 1915, p. 14, describes the dance partner in the vaudeville playlet, "The Red Fox Trot," as "midway between a male hairdresser and a youth who has been reared and spoiled in a girl's convent."

60. *Variety*, June 26, 1914, p. 14.

61. Ibid., September 25, 1914, p. 8.

62. Ibid.

63. Ibid., February 20, 1914, p. 22. For actual cases citing cabaret-mad women as the basis for divorce, see Elaine Tyler May, *Great Expectations: Marriage and Divorce in Post-Victorian America* (Chicago: University of Chicago Press, 1980).

64. Barry, "Tango Pirates," p. 16.

65. Joseph Lee, "Play as an Antidote to Civilization," *Playground* 5 (July 1911): 125.

Fig. 1. The **Waldorf-Astoria**, Fifth Avenue and Thirty-Fourth Street, began as a combination of the older Waldorf Hotel, which opened in 1893, and the newer Astoria which opened in 1897. The Waldorf-Astoria is an example of German Renaissance style and of the new grandiose hotel building. Oscar presided, treating old and new money alike. (Photograph from the Bettman Archive, Inc., N.Y.)

Fig. 2. Rector's on New Year's Eve, sometime between 1905 and 1910, at Broadway and Forty-Third Street, in the heart of the theatrical district. Rector's opened in 1899 and was one of the premiere Lobster Palaces attracting wealthy men, actresses, sportsmen, and a fast crowd to its after-theatre suppers. (Photograph loaned for one use only from the Brown Brothers, Sterling, Pa.)

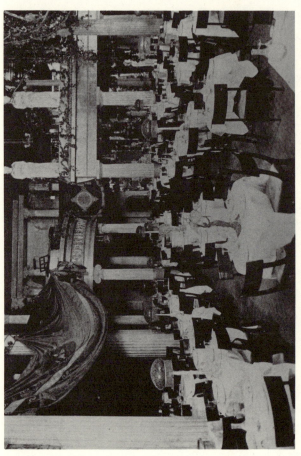

Fig. 3. The Interior of Murray's Roman Gardens, Forty-Second Street. Designed by architect Henry Erkins, Murray's was one of the most elaborate of the Lobster Palaces, featuring Egyptian rooms, Roman gardens, statues, and a French exterior. In its cabaret stage, Murray's installed a revolving dance floor. Opening in 1908, Murray's exemplified the imperial classical style. (Photograph from the *Architecture Review*, vol. 19, p. 178, April 1913, published by Bates & Guild Co., Boston, Mass.)

Detail of Staircase on First Gallery

Fig. 4. Detail of the Staircase, Louis Martin's Restaurant, originally the Café de l'Opera. The architect was Henry Erkins of Henry C. Pelton & Erkins Associates. Note the bulls' heads, columns, and other Assyrian imagery. The restaurant featured elaborate balconies that resembled the Hanging Gardens of Nebuchadnezzar. As Café de l'Opera, the restaurant opened in 1909, closing soon thereafter because of its rule of evening dress only and its high expense. (Photograph from the *Architecture Review*, vol. 19, p. 177, April 1913, published by Bates & Guild Co., Boston, Mass.)

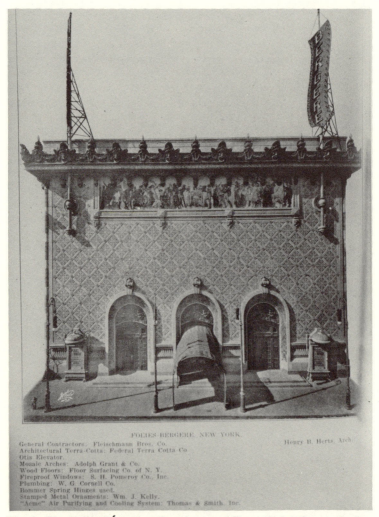

FOLIES-BERGERE, NEW YORK.

General Contractors: Fleischmann Bros. Co.
Architectural Terra-Cotta: Federal Terra Cotta Co.
Otis Elevator.
Mosaic Arches: Adolph Grant & Co.
Wood Floors: Floor Surfacing Co. of N. Y.
Fireproof Windows: S. H. Pomeroy Co., Inc.
Plumbing: W. G. Cornell Co.
Bommer Spring Hinges used.
Stamped Metal Ornaments: Wm. J. Kelly.
"Acme" Air Purifying and Cooling System: Thomas & Smith, Inc.

Henry B. Herts, Arch.

Fig. 5. The Folies Bérgere at Broadway and Forty-Eighth Street, the first cabaret in the United States. Henry B. Herts was the architect. A theater-restaurant, the Folies was the idea of movie impresario, Jesse B. Lasky, and his partner, Henry Harris. The Folies opened in May 1911 and closed soon thereafter, but the cabaret idea lived on. (Photograph from the *Architecture and Building Magazine*, vol. 43, no. 8, May 1911, p. 362, published by William T. Comstock Co., New York, N.Y.)

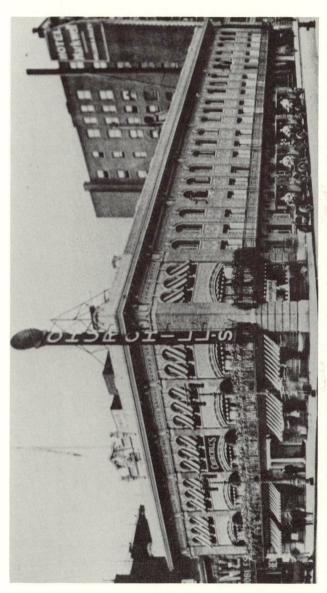

Fig. 6. The Exterior of Churchill's Restaurant, Broadway and Forty-Ninth Street, H. M. Baer, architect. Run by ex-police captain, James B. Churchill, the restaurant made the transition from the Lobster Palace era in the 1890s to the cabaret period in the 1910s. Churchill's was forced to close during Prohibition. (Photograph from *The Architecture Review*, vol. 19, April 1913, p. 173, published by Bates & Guild Co., Boston, Mass.)

Fig. 7. Bustanoby's, Thirty-Ninth Street and Broadway, about 1913 to 1914, with couples dancing, women and men seated informally, some in evening clothes and others in more informal attire. Note the position of the couple in the foreground. The mirrors around the room magnified the action of the patrons. (Photograph loaned for one use only from the Brown Brothers, Sterling, Pa.)

Fig. 8. The Hot Spell in New York, 1913, a drawing by John Sloan. The couple dancing the turkey trot at the left is Robert Henri and his wife. Note the couple to the right doing a dip. (Photograph from *Harper's Weekly*, September 6, 1913.)

Fig. 9. Irene and Vernon Castle, 1915, in one of their many poses. Dressed in the high style of the Society Dancers, both represent youthful energies and a new intimacy in the dance. (Photograph from the Dance Collection, Performing Arts Research Center, New York Public Library at Lincoln Center, Astor, Lenox, and Tilden Foundations.)

Fig. 10. Irene Castle in Riding Clothes, probably at her Long Island home, with one of her many pets. She represents an athletic, adventurous girl, capable of having fun equally with men. (Print by Roy W. Nicholson from the photograph in the Dance Collection, Performing Arts Research Center, New York Public Library at Lincoln Center, Astor, Lenox, and Tilden Foundations.)

James Reese Europe's
Clef Club Band - 1914

R.E. _____
N.Y.

Fig. 11. James Reese Europe's Clef Club Band, 1914. James Reese Europe helped organize the Clef Club, a musical agency for black musicians. He left the Clef Club later, organized the Tempo Club, and played behind Irene and Vernon Castle in cabarets and at Castle House. He went off to lead an all-black military band in World War I. Black bands played for dancing up and down Broadway during the 1910s. (Photograph from the Frank J. Driggs Collection.)

Fig. 12. Maurice and Florence (Maurice Mouvet and Florence Walton) were the chief rivals to the Castles during the pre-World War I Dance Craze. (Print by Roy W. Nicholson from a photograph in the Theatre Collection, Performing Arts Research Center, New York Public Library at Lincoln Center, Astor, Lenox, and Tilden Foundations.)

Fig. 13. Sophie Tucker, as she appeared in the Ziegfeld Follies of 1909. This is prior to Sophie's "Last of the Red Hot Mamma's" period. Because of artistic conflicts, she did not appear in the Follies on Broadway in New York. (Photograph, White Studio, New York, from the Billy Rose Theatre Collection, Performing Arts Research Center, New York Public Library at Lincoln Center, Astor, Lenox, and Tilden Foundations.)

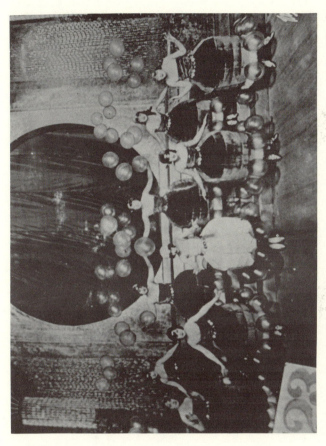

Fig. 14. Balloon Girls from Ziegfeld's Midnight Frolic, 1915, taken above the Amsterdam Theatre. The chorus girls moved among the tables, allowing men with cigars and cigarettes to pop the balloons. Note the shorter skirts, bare arms, and the slimmer forms of the chorines. (Print by Roy W. Nicholson of a White Studio Photo, from the Theatre Collection, Performing Arts Research Center, New York Public Library at Lincoln Center, Astor, Lenox, and Tilden Foundations.)

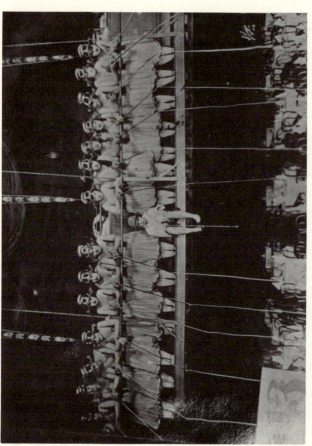

Fig. 15. Chorus Girls from Ziegfeld's Midnight Frolic, 1917. The girls made contact with the audience by fishing them. (What did they catch?) Note the girlishness of the chorus girls. (Print by Roy W. Nicholson from a White Studio Photo at the Theatre Collection, Performing Arts Research Center, New York Public Library at Lincoln Center, Astor, Lenox, and Tilden Foundations.)

Fig. 16. Gilda Gray, purveyor of exotic dances in the 1925 Ziegfeld Follies, Gilda started in Milwaukee, moved to Chicago, and then to New York. She made her name with the shimmy, had her own cabaret, the Rendezvous, in the early 1920s, appeared in the Follies doing South Sea island dances, and eventually went into films. (Photograph from the Theatre Collection, Performing Arts Research Center, New York Public Library at Lincoln Center, Astor, Lenox, and Tilden Foundations.)

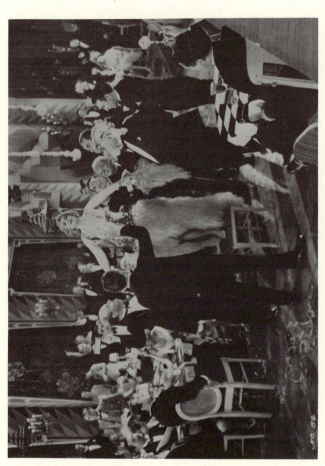

Fig. 17. Texas Guinan in a 1929 movie called *Queen of the Nightclubs*. This is a re-creation of her uproarious nightclub where she was "master of ceremonies." Note the intimacy, crowd participation, and absence of theatrical barriers. (Print by Roy W. Nicholson from a Photograph in the Theatre Collection, Performing Arts Research Center, New York Public Library at Lincoln Center, Astor Foundation.)

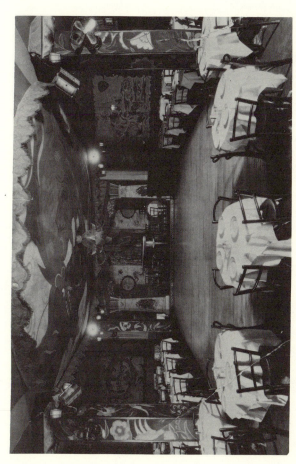

Fig. 18. The Interior of Connie's Inn, a Harlem nightclub of the 1920s, owned by Connie Immerman. Connie's presented black entertainers to white patrons and was one of the big three of Harlem nightclubs, along with Smalls' Paradise and the Cotton Club. Note how close the tables are to the stage and how few theatrical barriers exist by the 1920s. The canopy effect was a staple of nightclub decor, uniting the dancers and probably meant to be exotic and jungle-like. A number of important black performers appeared here, including Louis Armstrong and Fats Waller. (Photograph from the Schomburg Center for Research in Black Culture, New York Public Library.)

Part Three THE CABARET
AND THE
DECLINE OF
FORMALISM

4 ACTION ENVIRONMENT: THE INFORMAL STRUCTURE OF THE CABARET

Cabarets are peculiar mind you. They're not like theaters and concert halls. You don't just go to a cabaret and sit back and wait to be entertained. You get out on the floor and join the pow-wow and help entertain yourself.

Rudolf Fisher[1]

Unlike the more formal theatre and concert hall, the cabaret's setting and structure encouraged the sharing of vitality and spontaneity between patrons and performers that was once exclusively reserved for the stage and the entertainer. Transferring the performance from the stage to the floor broke down the formal barriers between the entertainer and his audience by allowing them to mingle freely. The distinctions between the respectable and the theatrical folk that existed in lobster palaces eroded after 1910 when men and women sought greater expressiveness in leisure and in each other. The emergence of a cabaret style and structure not only indicated changes in theatrical forms but also symbolized broader changes in the culture. In the pursuit of a vital and informal personality, prosperous people broke from the formal boundaries that had separated the entertainers from the respectable, men from women, and upper- from lower-class culture. The cabaret was a new public environment for the exploration of alternatives to the private character of the nineteenth century.

Reformers uncomfortably observed that women and men enjoyed pleasures equally in the open environment of the café. *Billboard* put the matter differently: "These pleasures were the peculiar perogativ [*sic*] of the male sex from the strutting gallant to the slouching plowboy," but now "romanticism is revived in the cabaret," and "the tavern has developed into the Broadway cabaret, a meeting place of the sexes in the eager pursuit of pleasure."[2] By permitting informal entertainments for respectable women, the cabaret marked a new departure in the relations between the sexes and challenged the Victorian confinements that had limited the behavior of both men and women. In an open environment, good women could mix promiscuously with people of unspecified moral character from whom they formerly had been rigidly separated. By opening up an urban, public area, the café opened up respectable culture to a wider, more spontaneous world.

For the first time, men and women were able to enjoy a public and informal social life together. Unlike vaudeville, which welcomed women and children to a family atmosphere, the cabaret made few pretenses about being for a family trade; rather it would service the fantasies and desires of adult men and women. Appealing to the image of women as a genteel, civilizing force, vaudeville policed male audiences. In the cabaret, however, men and women entered on a more equal level, and both were encouraged to participate in the entertainment. Women and men could stretch the night into hours of pleasure for themselves, away from home, business, children, and other obstructions to their own mutual enjoyment. Out in public, removed from the restrictions surrounding work and home, they were free to explore the personal dimensions of their relationships and to imbibe some of the excitement, spontaneity, and life of other people whom they met in the café. *Variety* recognized the change overtaking young and old when it asked who would have predicted in 1905 that within ten years "the soberest and most staid of New York's business men would be making the round of New York dance halls and cabarets three or four nights a week accompanied by his wife and the family friends." But, the journal remarked, "it has come to pass." At any of the better-class dance-restaurants, one can see "fathers and even grandfathers and grandmothers trotting and hesitating with the best of the youngsters."[3]

EVOLUTION OF THE SETTING

Beginning as a diversion of theatregoers and diners, the cabaret soon grew into a separate institution that became a stage for bringing intimacy and expressiveness into everyday life. The cabaret first reached beyond the vice districts to the attention of respectable New Yorkers in the spring of 1911 when Henry B. Harris and Jesse Lasky, two vaudeville entrepreneurs, opened the Folies Bergère Theater on Forty-ninth Street in the heart of the theatre district. The Folies inaugurated a specific cabaret show consisting of various singing turns added to its otherwise lavish stage revue. According to the two partners, *cabaret* meant a set of intimate entertainments, and to convey this sense of intimacy, their late show featured "an expanding stage [which] slid out over the orchestra pit and put the performers in handshaking proximity to the first-row patrons," who sat around glass-topped tables, like those used in Paris.[4] Lasky was confident that "the public would welcome a theatre-restaurant where they could dine superbly while watching a superlative show."[5] The theatre offered two shows a night: an elaborate revue from 8 P.M. to 11 P.M. and an after-theatre cabaret performance from 11:15 P.M. to 1:00 A.M. Lasky and Harris had been captivated by European music halls and cabarets, and, instead of borrowing from the indigenous rathskellers, they turned to Europe for their models. "Frankly inspired by Parisian eclat," the partners thought it fitting to make "the first cabaret in America a namesake of the original Folies Bergère."[6]

When the Folies opened, it advertised for expensive audiences the Parisian theme of fast and elegant fun as new to the United States. "Everything about the Folies Bergère was unheard of in New York," wrote Lasky, "including the prices." The two promoters introduced a champagne bar, a balcony promenade, and the first American midnight performance. Being up late was part of the appeal. "Even the word *cabaret*," according to Lasky, "was so strange that we felt obliged to specify in advertisements that it was 'pronounced cabaray'!" With a French decorative theme throughout, the Folies reproduced a continental music hall, "more Parisian than Paris."[7]

Despite the grand intentions of the founders, the cabaret acts failed to make an impact. As a setting for the cabaret, theatres quickly took a back seat to restaurants. Soon after opening, the Folies suffered financial decline. Seating only seven hundred, the theatre could not sustain its huge redecoration cost and entertainment investment. The financial difficulties paled, however, when compared to the Folies' lack of clear purpose. Designed as a theatre-restaurant, the Folies' two elements did not work well together. The Folies had 286 restaurant chairs, comprising only 41 percent of the seats. The majority of the customers in the remaining gallery and orchestra chairs were cut off from the performers, and the sale of theatre seats dropped off drastically after the first few weeks. Moreover because they were only an addition to the regular theatrical production, the cabaret acts were smothered by the longer show that preceded them. Patrons displayed a decided lack of interest, and the Folies became the "ice-house of vaudeville."[8]

The Folies' experiment may have failed, but it did not go unnoticed. By late 1911 and early 1912, a number of the lobster palaces and other restaurants in the Times Square area followed Lasky and Harris's example and began experimenting with the presentation of entertainment along with the sale of food and drink. According to reports in *Variety*, the economic depression of 1911–1912 had created a slump in the restaurant business, and any idea that might bring in new business seemed worth trying. Restaurant managers, moreover, could be convinced by the success of the restaurant portion of the Folies, which continued to make money even as the overall enterprise failed. The Folies proved that in the right setting, informal entertainment could blend nicely with the sale of food and drink.

With their European architecture, grand designs, and lavish layouts, the lobster palaces were suitable settings to adapt the cabaret for respectable people. They had the luxury and sense of class to divorce public entertainment, drinking, and dancing from its associations with the rathskellers and the vice districts. Julius Keller, proprietor of Maxim's, saw clearly that the transmission of cultural forms from the vice-ridden joints to the more respectable restaurants required a show of legitimacy and class if well-to-do patrons were to accept the cabaret. Hoping to attract a respectable clientele to his new Thirty-eighth Street establishment when he moved from his Tenderloin dive, he decorated with an explicit French theme and barred the most objectionable of his former patrons. Most important, Keller borrowed the idea for the cabaret from the singing waiters he had employed in his saloon. Noting that "if customers of that joint could derive the utmost enjoyment from hearing waiters sing," he saw no reason "why the more cultured people of 38th Street would not be similarly pleased with performances of higher quality." He discovered, however, that a smart Parisian decor and atmosphere appealed to a higher class of customer. "After all," he recalled, "the things which appeal to the various strata of society are basically pretty much the same; the differences consist mainly in the degree of embellishments."[9] To ease the transfer of social forms, Keller decorated in a showy pattern reminiscent of the classic and luxurious age of Louis XIV already familiar to habitués of Broadway restaurants and lobster palaces.

In the cabaret-lobster palaces, men and women still found themselves in replicas of the great aristocratic homes of the past. As with Maxim's representation of a Louis XIV style, the lobster palaces brought an image of grand, aristocratic living to the new cabaret environment. In making the transition from the private, restrained home to the more lively public cabaret, patrons wanted to narrow the gap between the two spheres while still retaining the legitimacy that the image of home could provide. Murray's Roman Gardens exemplifies this trend. Although Murray's adapted to the strenuous strains of the dance by installing a revolving floor, it did so in the original setting built on a model of a grandiose imperial palace.[10] Rather than merely dining in a reproduction of the atrium of a Roman home, patrons now danced and watched entertainment there. While the scope of activities broadened, these institutions of grandeur and luxury continued to signify the power and success of the patrons. Surrounded by the great ages of Louis XIII, Louis XIV, imperial Rome, and Cleopatra's Egypt, visitors to the cabarets sustained their belief that they were on par with the best that civilization had produced. The classical allusions contributed to their continuing preoccupation with order and restrained emotions and the elegance suitable to their level of success. Moving higher into the social structure, the rathskeller changed its name, according to *Variety*, to a "title befitting its most recent station in the social scale." The easiest way to achieve respectability "was to borrow 'cabaret' as the Parisian term the Folies Bergère had adopted for its $1.50 midnight novelty performance."[11] Offering French atmosphere, French names, and often French food, the cafés were able to slough off their disreputable associations and provide an image of cosmopolitan European fun. They also offered tinges of unconventional bohemianism together with respectability and success.

While Broadway restaurants had to work harder to ensure the safety and status of respectable women, they were also in a more favorable position to adapt the cabaret than were the Fifth Avenue hotels. Located along the Great White Way, the restaurants already attracted a more mixed and diverse patronage from the city and the nation. André Bustanoby of Bustanoby's, for example, noted that 75 percent of his clientele were visitors to New York, and "they come to relax and expect to find things different from their home towns, and some one has to take care of them. The night restaurants being one of the attractions of this great city, they come here, live in hotels, but go all over the city, dining and taking supper at the different restaurants, as in Paris and Berlin." Being in the theatrical district, these restaurants were more a part of the entertainment life that bubbled along in this hub of nightlife activity. While the Fifth Avenue hotels were more associated with the rich, Broadway was able to cater to the entertainment demands of a wider audience. "The average New York man and woman get no chance to dance except in rooms given over to that purpose by public restaurants."[12]

Broadway, the Great White Way, was lit by the power of godlike technology, transforming nature and making consumption and enjoyment, not just production, possible on a wide scale. Instead of the sun, "Edison has given Broadway a good substitute in the incandescent and 'neath the scintillating rays of more than a million of the little bulbs the average New Yorker and the visitor cast off the cares and woes of the business day and in the garbled worlds of the immortal punster, 'Let joy reign unrefined.' " There the dancing signs magically transformed night into day, extending human activity comfortably into the darkness and advertising a new frontier of personal joy and fun distinct from social authority, domestic drudgery, or business routine. "Barbaric is the adjective some people apply to Broadway," noted an anonymous contributor to *Atlantic*, "but it is at least a jolly barbarity." The bright lights expressed the existence of both the wherewithal and the desire to escape the everyday world into a romantic haven: "How they [lights and signs] seem to lift their radiance to the low roof of the sky above, turning it a dull glowing red! How they call to the Spirit, proclaiming crowds, proclaiming mirth and escape from care into the joyous world of make-believe of dance and song!"

Experiencing this juxtaposition of the deadness of night and the brilliance of light, viewers could not help feeling alive. "When I turn into Broadway by night and am bathed in its Babylonic radiance," our anonymous contributor exclaimed, "I want to shout with joy, it is so gay and beautiful."[13] As part of this radiance and life, the Broadway restaurants and rathskellers could better appeal to the demands for excitement than could the more sedate Fifth Avenue hotels. The restaurants could reach out to new business, cater to public demand, and spread the joys of life experienced by the rich and poor to a wider audience. As the cabaret became part of Broadway and began developing the life and vitality of the street as its public attraction, Broadway diverged more radically from Fifth Avenue. From Times Square to Columbus Circle, cabarets, ballrooms, dance palaces, and restaurants picked up the quickening and simmering pace of nightlife and the street's surging crowds, and offered man-made pleasure to an urban nation.

As Table 1 demonstrates, a large number of night spots called themselves cabarets in the 1910s. The cabarets covered a wide range of places. They differed among themselves in the cost of their entertainments and in their setting, but definite similarities united them. A number of them were expensive. The Midnight Frolic and the Century Roof (Cocoanut Grove) charged the relatively high covers of one or two dollars, plus drinks and food. Lobster palaces charged from six to eight dollars for a couple without drinks. Drinks cost twenty-five cents for cocktails and highballs, two dollars and fifty cents for a pint of champagne, five dollars for a quart. The lobster palace restaurants formed the core of the cabaret explosion on Broadway. Rector's, Maxim's, Bustanoby's, Faust's, Louis Martin's, Shanley's, Murray's, Churchill's, Reisenweber's, and Healy's all quickly entered the business of purveying entertainment, and most soon offered dancing as well. The Broadway restaurant business was highly competitive, and as soon as one hit upon a salable novelty, the others were quick to follow. All of the lobster palaces had national reputations and clientele, so they immediately had an expensive crowd from around the nation as well as from New York. At the other end of the spectrum were the rathskellers. Joe Brown's, Sweeney's, and Baron Wilkin's had been rathskellers, basement establishments that had existed before the cabaret craze and that lasted into the 1910s and early 1920s. These were less well known and remained less expensive hangouts for newspapermen, entertainers, and bohemians in the

Table 1. Cabarets, 1911–1920[a]

Origin	Location	Dates[b]	Owner
Lobster Palaces			
Café Madrid		1911–1912	George Rector
Café des Beaux Arts	80 W. 40th St.	1901	Louis Bustanoby
Bustanoby's (includes Pre-Catelan Room)	110 W. 39th St.	1911–1916	André Bustanoby
Churchill's	1603 Broadway	1911	James Churchill
Faust's	1823 Broadway	closed, 1915	Harry Salvain
Healy's Golden Glades	141–47 Columbus	1915	Thomas Healy
Knickerbocker Hotel	42nd St.	1908	James B. Regan
Louis Martin's (replaces Café de l'Opera)	42nd and Broadway	1910	Louis Martin
Maxim's	110 W. 38th St.	1909	Julius Keller
Murray's Roman Gardens	226 W. 42nd St.	1906	John Murray, later Joe Susskind
Pekin	1576 Broadway	1911	A. R. Klein
Princess Restaurant	1845 Broadway	1915 becomes Domino Rm. in Bustanoby's	Bustanoby Bros.
Rector's	48th and Broadway	1899	George Rector, Paul Salvain, George Thompson
Reisenweber's 400 Room/Sophie Tucker Room Paradise Room Doraldina's Hawaiian Room Beefsteak Grill	59th and Columbus	1911	John Steinberg and John Fisher
Shanley's	1204 Broadway	1912	Thomas Shanley
Shanley's	1493 Broadway	1912	Thomas Shanley
Tokio	143 W. 45th St.	1911	Harry Salvain, Henry Fink after 1918
Theater-Restaurant			
Folies Bergère	49th and Broadway	Spring 1911	Jesse Lasky/Henry Harris
Rathskellers			
Alamo	125th St.	1915	
Campus	900–6 Columbus Ave.	listed 1914	William H. Reicken
Garden Restaurant	Broadway and 50th St. 750 7th Ave.	at least 1913	Arthur Ellis
Fleischman's	42nd and Broadway	1913	
Joel's Hotel	207 West 41st St.	1901	Joel Rinaldo
Joe Brown's			
Kennedy's	120 W. 38th St.		
Sweeney's	125th St.	1915	
Little Savoy Club[c]	W. 35th St.	1915	Barron D. D. Wilkins
Kid Banks'[d]	Tenderloin	1917	Kid Banks
Edmond Johnsons'[c]	Midtown	1915	Edmond Johnson

Table 1. (Cont.)

Origin	Location	Dates[b]	Owner
Roof Gardens			
Strand	47th and Broadway	1914	
Cocoanut Grove	Century Theater	1917	Morris Gest
Midnight Frolic	New Amsterdam Theater 42nd St.	1915	Florenz Ziegfeld
Folies Marigny	44th St. Theater	1913–14	
Jardin de Danse	1520 Broadway	1913	G & G Catering Co.
Palais de Danse	1634 Broadway (Winter Garden)	1913	Stanley Sharpe
Castles in the Air	44th Street Theater	1915	Castles
Chez Maurice	Winter Garden Theater	1914–15	Shuberts
Cabarets			
Sans Souci (replaces rathskeller)	42nd St.	1913–14	Castles/Jules Ansaldi
Montmartre	Broadway and 50th St.	1916	Clifford Fischer
Café Madrid			George Rector
Moulin Rouge	1580 Broadway/basement	1916–17	Gil Boag, Paul Salvin, Jim Thompson
Palais Royal	1580 Broadway/2 floors above Moulin Rouge	1917	Paul Salvin, Jim Thompson
Michaud's	42nd and Broadway (replaces Fleischman's becomes Sans Souci)		
Little Club	Broadway and 50th St.	April 1917–1919	Shuberts
Bal Tabarin	Winter Garden Theater	1919	Salvin, Boag, Thompson
Other[d]			
The Parisiene Restaurant	945 8th Ave.	1914	Ferdiance Delenne
Hotel Wallick	1492 Broadway and 43rd St.	1913	
Marlborough-Blenheim	1353 Broadway	1914	
Kaiserhof Restaurant	1418 Broadway	1914	
Chez Fysher	121 W. 45th St.	1916	Clifford Fisher
Les Fleurs	45th St.	1916	V. V. Farone
Poodle Dog	1431 Broadway	1913	
Carlton Terrace	2637 Broadway	1914 at least	F. H. McCabe

[a]Refers only to Manhattan, excluding Brooklyn and Bronx, both of which had a number of cabarets.

[b]Refers to institutions which had cabarets in operation between 1911–1920; dates are earliest indication of the institution's operation and do not try to fix when the cabaret was adopted. Most opened after 1911, and the explosion occurred in 1913.

[c]Black saloon-rathskellers that moved from midtown to Harlem. Material collected from license reports and *Variety*.

[d]Refers to hotels, restaurants, saloons which were not referred to as lobster palaces.

Broadway area. A lobster palace such as Reisenweber's was somewhat unique. Instead of one or two rooms, it had at least four, including a ballroom. At various times in its history, Reisenweber's had
its large restaurant divided into the 400 Room, the Sophie Tucker
Room, and the Doraldina Hawaiian Room, all offering patrons a
choice of environments.

The Castles' Sans Souci was the first cabaret not associated with a
preexisting lobster palace. Designed after Parisian models, the Sans
Souci opened December 1913 in a basement on Forty-second Street.
The Castles and their manager moved in, taking over the seedy dive
that had been Fleischman's. Other places followed suit. The Moulin
Rouge, Montmartre, and Rendezvous opened as special cabaret establishments. Finally, theatres converted their roof gardens to cabarets and ballrooms. The Forty-fourth Street Theater did this with
Castles in the Air, as did the Midnight Frolic, the Century Roof, and
the New York Roof. All of these, however, came to employ some of
the features that were characteristic of the cabaret.

Despite their diversity in other matters, cabarets were distinguished from other forms of amusements by their combination of floor
show and tables. At first the development of the floor was almost acci-
dental, as restaurants merely followed Lasky and Harris's policy of
presenting a few entertainers as incidental diversions. Restaurant
managers would hire a few special intimate acts, such as singers and
dancers, from rathskellers or the lower rungs of vaudeville and have
them circulate among the tables as incidental attractions to the dining
and drinking. Rather than putting up stages, the restaurants cleared a
space in the dining room or installed small platforms. Close to the
tables, the floor seemed the best place for entertainment, and recon-
version expenses were limited.

Local courts, however, soon supplied legal impetus for the development of the floor show as a key element of the cabaret. In a case in-
volving whether the New York Roof Cabaret was required to have a
theatrical license for its performances, a local court ruled that a theatre license was necessary only if a stage and scenery were present. If
the New York Roof abandoned the use of scenery and stage, it would
not need to purchase a special license. Because the cabaret had not yet
proven itself financially, managers hesitated to produce attractions
that might cost them five hundred dollars extra in license fees. Con-

sequently William Morris, the manager of the Roof, chose to place his acts on the floor, dispensed with scenery, and installed his orchestra on the stage.[14] It was only in 1915, after the ragtime dance craze had made the cabarets profitable, that owners were convinced of their earning potential and began to implement more elaborate stages. By then, however, the floor had become the distinguishing feature of the cabaret and was incorporated in some form in every establishment.

The rise of public dancing in the craze of 1912–1916 also contributed to the role of the floor as a staging area in the cabaret-restaurants.[15] Jesse Lasky laid the failure of the Folies and the subsequent success of the cabaret to the booming business brought on by public dancing. "It seems to me now," he wrote in his autobiography, "that the Folies Bergère probably had all the ingredients for a smashing success, save one—a little two-by-four square of hardwood."[16] The restaurants, however, could easily adapt to the dance craze by clearing away the tables and opening the space to the dancers. Dancing not only offered diners the opportunity to participate in their own entertainment but also enshrined the dance floor as a central part of the entertainment style of the cabaret.

The seating of patrons at tables was the other distinctive feature of the cabaret, one that encouraged greater intimacy between audience and performers and among the members of the audience itself. Guests watched the entertainment from dining chairs at tables. An advertisement for Churchill's restaurant-cabaret illustrates the importance of the table. "Those who find added pleasure in artistic refined environment, and spirited cabaret when enjoying dinner," read the advertisement, "appreciate in full the atmosphere that pervades Churchill's."[17] In the accompanying picture, a well-dressed couple gazed through the palmy entranceway upon the handsomely correct diners eating at round tables in a high-ceilinged room. As this advertisement suggests, the restaurant loaned part of its structure to the setting of the café. As the basis of the cabaret in the 1910s, the lobster palaces continued to foster extensive supper and dinner fare. Through the 1920s, newspaper advertisements carried notices of special dinner rates for those who specifically wanted to dine. The size of meals declined as guests spent their time watching the acts or dancing, but the restaurant setting and the table continued as an important locus for patrons' dining, drinking, and personal interactions.

In another case concerning theatre licenses, Justice Deuel, Hoyt, and McInerny of the New York Supreme Court underscored the importance of the table in cabarets. They defined the essential ingredient that distinguished the cabaret from the theatre and made a license unnecessary as the former's requirement that tables, not just seats, be reserved in advance.[18] The serving of food and the necessity of the table required a certain fixity of place for customers, and although through the course of an evening people danced or saw entertainment during and after eating and drinking, they returned to the scene of their meal—the table. Captains aided this enterprise, for it was their function to meet customers at the door and escort them to defined areas.

Dining, drinking, talking, and flirting at their seats with members of their own party or with those at other tables, patrons were relaxed and could see the performance in a more informal way. The tables and the floor brought audience and performer into a more intimate relationship than was possible in conventional theatres. Performers started their acts on the platform and then stepped down onto the floor and appeared among the diners. Even if the act was one that could be performed on a more formal stage, the fact of appearing in this special environment altered the nature of the interaction. The dance floor, the absence of large proscenium arch stages, and the closeness of the audience seated at tables made the room a scene of expressive activity. The entire restaurant became the setting for performance, and customers themselves could not escape becoming involved in the action and spontaneity of the moment. In a theatre, expressiveness was limited primarily to hired performers. In the cabaret, audiences and performers were on the same level, and thus expressiveness spread to the audience as well. Under these conditions, the definition of the cabaret slowly and subtly expanded from a group of entertainers who worked close to an audience to being a distinctive environment different from the theatrical one. The setting became, as one columnist wrote of a particular establishment, "a friendly environment" where "there isn't a chance of feeling dull or grouchy."[19]

The layout of the cabaret also modified the formal boundaries that existed between audience and performers in the theatre. The floor, according to *Variety*, had to be located in the center of the room, to give "a good view to everyone in the place."[20] Obstructing posts and the other sight-hindering features of a theatre had to be eliminated. The closeness of the floor to the tables, moreover, placed patrons in the middle of the action rather than separating them from it. Other obstructions that had defined the formal stage were eliminated or deemphasized. Spotlights, for example, shone from above in the cabaret, eliminating the theatre's harsh footlights, which had formed a barrier between the stage and the audience and marked off the action on that theatrical stage as a magical and differentiated preserve for the actors and actresses alone. The curtains, marking off the performance in the theatre, were also removed since it was difficult to curtain off a floor that the patrons also used for dancing. Musicians no longer occupied the pit, as they did in theatres. In the cabaret, musicians were often as important as the players, for the music was an essential part of the audience's delight. To dance, one needed the band. Moreover, to have put the band in front of the small platform would have hidden it entirely. Consequently in a cabaret, the musicians either played from off to the side of the floor, on the platform, or sometimes from up on a balcony. They were out of the way, thus giving up the space between floor and seats to the patrons.

In the cabaret, performers and audiences were in much closer proximity than in theatrical presentations. Performers appeared on the floor at eye level, standing or moving amid the diners seated in a semicircle. And seated about on an equal level, patrons could glance into the entertainers' eyes and faces while the latter were at work. At this distance, the audience could easily experience the emotion—the grimaces, smiles, exultation—of performers at work. The audiences were close enough to touch the performers, and they often did so in specially designed numbers and rituals. In this way, the actors were not cardboard figures on a stage; they were personalities seen in a living, three-dimensional light. They were not just actors; they were acting out an emotionalism that could not be missed. *Variety* observed that many acts failed to appreciate the new standards of intimate performance in a floor show, thus underlining what the new standards were. Their heavily applied makeup, appropriate for the stage, took on a grotesque appearance at close range where audiences could presumably see the performers in the flesh.[21] Sophie Tucker, singer of rag songs and comedienne, also recognized the difficulty of working close to an audience. Singers who had appeared on stage often could not work at all with customers right in front of them sitting at tables eating and drinking during the performance.[22]

In removing theatrical boundaries, the cabaret modified the sacredness of the stage area and encouraged the audience to share it. Performers and patrons shared the same space in a symbiotic search for a more expressive life. In the social dancing, for example, customers trotted on the very floor upon which the entertainers did their turns, thus exchanging and sharing roles in this area. While dancing, guests performed for themselves as well as for others who chose to watch. Murray's Roman Gardens even had a revolving dance floor installed between the two rows of tables. Avid dancers invariably filled the tables on the revolving portion, while other customers spent much of their evening looking on. One commentator noted the popularity of seats closest to the floor, "from which the dancers can be seen, and this is the position for which they all contend." The *New York Times* observed that watching the dancing was part of the experience, for "those who have not yet learned to dance, seem to like the dancing of the skilled amateurs better than that of the professionals."[23] Furthermore as performers engaged patrons in asides or other interplay, the customers became the focus of attention.

Several acts exemplify this sharing of the performance area. Irene and Vernon Castle, America's premier ballroom dancers, began their numbers by coming out of the audience. Before their performance began, they could be found leisurely dining at a table near the floor. When it was time for their act, they stood up, walked onto the floor, and began to dance. According to Irene, the Castles "started the custom of performers sitting at café tables like guests." Before that time, she noted, "they had appeared from somewhere back of the kitchen." It did not take long for the custom to spread, and soon it "became general in Paris; it later spread to the United States; and now it is done everywhere." A comedy dance team at Rector's varied the routine. The host announced that a country lad needed a dance partner and then led him around the room to search each table for a girl. In the end he found his partner, dressed in country lass's clothes, hidden in a corner of the dining room, and they commenced their turn.[24] In both cases, the performers established the link between the acts and the desire of the patrons to dance on the floor.

Comedy dancers also went into the audience as part of their act, suggesting that the stage was not the sole area of performance. In a cabaret, audiences were prepared to perform themselves, to let down barriers around themselves, so that even before the dancers appeared, the former were aware that they might be presented with opportunities for play and self-expression. The dance itself was a small ritual of choice and involvement. At each stage of the lad's search for a dance partner, he went from table to table, making emotional, physical, or personal contact with other people. The question before the female spectator was whether she would be picked as the partner, whether he would pick her to stand up in front of so many others and invite her to act out a part of herself that she was there to experience. Perhaps she wondered whether she was attractive enough to be picked, and perhaps her male companion thought about the same issue.

Along the Great White Way, performers acted out some variant of this ritual every night. The comedy dancers were unusual only in their particular routine. For singers, a new style presented itself, for they could sing seated in the audience right at the patron's ear. Chorus girls, a staple of cabaret entertainment after 1915, also played an important role in the ritual. Theatre critic George Nathan described the blatant example of chorus girls mingling with the customers: "Slowly but surely, toward the table of the possible 'wine-buyers' they glided—still with their innocent eyes on the floor." Moving suggestively, they gave men the eye with "a bumping against the chairs, a teasing grin, a whispered 'Can we sit down with you after awhile? . . . all part-of-the-game!" To facilitate the interaction, choreographers in every revue created gimmick numbers to bring the audience and the chorus girl together in a shared and intimate exchange. In "Dance and Grow Thin" at the Century Roof, Blanche Ring sang the "Letter Boxes" number while the chorines moved among the tables wearing wooden or cardboard letter boxes on the front of their costumes. The management provided paper and pencils so that men seated at front-row tables could write the women personal notes and drop them easily into their costumed letter boxes.[25]

Not all manifestations of self-expression by the audience were felicitous or welcome. The Dooley Brothers, an acrobatic team appearing atop the Century Roof in 1919, were hired to perform their feats of derring-do before an assembled dining crowd. On one evening their act consisted of a mock fight, wherein one of the two brothers pretended to knock the other off the small stage onto the dance floor. The first part of the act went off smoothly. One of the brothers responded to the phantom punch and stumbled off the stage onto the floor. But trouble soon ensued. A customer seated at a nearby table, either heated by the acrobatics or more likely his drink, could no longer remain in a state of watchful waiting. Picking up a salt shaker or a toy wooden hammer provided by the management, he threw it at the prone Dooley, hitting him in the eye and causing serious injury. The act was ruined. In response, the Dooleys quit the Century Roof, but after assurances from the owners, they returned to the fold. Such incidents did not abate, however, and management was forced to place cards on the tables announcing, "The management earnestly requests patrons refrain from throwing hammers. A member of this company had an eye seriously injured by a hammer thrown by a thoughtless person."[26] This audience involvement was symptomatic of the cabaret's blurring of the lines between audience and performer. Whether it was the Dooleys or the liquor, this patron, so close to the action, felt he could interrupt the performance. Similarly one of the plagues of nightclub entertainment is the heckler, who, with or without alcohol, feels free to cross the boundary and join the show, thereby interrupting the flow of the performance and directing the room's attention toward himself.

The examples of the country lad, the chorus girls, and the attackers of the Dooleys uncover some of the underlying assumptions behind the cabaret. These acts demonstrate that the area of performance had expanded. No longer could either the audience or the performer rest secure in its place on the traditional side of the footlights. Often, indeed, managers of cabarets promoted this participation by supplying noisemakers and souvenirs. Introduced by Florenz Ziegfeld in his "Midnight Frolic" in 1915, the noisemakers created a din and encouraged patrons to join the environment. Funny hats, stuffed dolls, and other items performed the same function, for they allowed men and women to play with toys, to rediscover for at least a few minutes the prerational and emotionally expressive period of childhood when all was fun and excitement. In the supportive atmosphere of the Broadway cabaret, they recreated the childhood world of careless fun. "A Little Jazz Band of Our Own," a specialty number sung by Blanche Merrill at the Folies Bergère in 1921, acknowledged the use of hammers, bells, and other devices to keep the gatherings lively. This tune informed patrons that they need not worry about music should the band go on strike, for "they could make the jazz through their knives, forks, and plates." Hearing this invitation, the audience chimed in immediately with their musical dinnerware.[27]

A variety of contests also fostered participation in a group event that enlivened the atmosphere, breaking down the barriers among members of the audience and forming a "bright spot in the life of the city—good cheer is found there in abundance."[28] Nightclub entrepreneur Gil Boag recalled that dance contests were the rage, and everyone from socialites to sightseers took part.[29] Scheduled for slow nights during the week, contests and special nights encouraged a festive atmosphere and attracted business. The types of events varied. Healy's, a popular dancing spot at Broadway and Sixty-sixth Street, staged a series of special nights, including a Parisienne carnival and a tango contest. For the carnival, Healy's provided caps, flags, paper parasols, and other decorations to "instill the spirit of liveliness into the dancers." During the season of 1914, the Folies Marigny announced an Arabian night as part of a series of special balls. Other institutions followed the New York Roof's precedent by offering the lucky dance. For this, managements divided their floors into 198 sections, each corresponding to one marked on a large wheel. As the music finished, someone spun the wheel, and the five couples standing in the lucky spaces received souvenirs. Some cabarets promoted real contests. As a method to attract customers after the New Year's festivities tapered off, for example, the Domino Room, the club in Bustanoby's, offered a free trip to Bermuda as the main prize for its dance contest, which it ran every night at 1:00 A.M. between January 4 and January 8. The winners were decided on the basis of votes from the audience, and contestants usually brought their friends. Several places delayed decisions until the following evening, thus requiring the return of the contesting groups.[30]

The stress on sociability in the audience led to the invention of the nightclub, later to become synonymous with the term *cabaret*. Unlike the theatre, cabarets were dependent on accommodating after-theatre crowds and late-night customers still bent on enjoying themselves. In order to allow patrons to remain undisturbed by the 2:00 A.M. curfew laws and police harassment, promoters began buying charters of defunct private social organizations in the fall of 1914 and turned special rooms of their establishments into so-called clubs.

Alerted to its widespread adoption by the ever-watchful Committee of Fourteen, excise commissioner George R. Greene launched a special investigation. He found that Rector's, Healy's, Reisenweber's, Bustanoby's (Thirty-ninth Street), Broadway Bustanoby's, the Pekin, and the Garden all had secured charters dating back before 1896. When the regular portion of the restaurant closed, members adjourned to the room set aside for the club. At Reisenweber's for instance, patrons retired upstairs to the 400 Club, while at Castles in the Air they descended to the Castle Club in the rathskeller. Some establishments adhered to strict rules of membership and dues, but most merely declared those remaining after the legal closing hours as members. Writing their names on cards supplied by the management, customers henceforth had concrete proof of membership. The night "club" remained open as long as the desire for enjoyment prevailed, rather than as the law or the duration of the play demanded.[31]

The club's pretense of membership fostered the illusion that the cabaret was a friendly environment for exclusive comradeship. The size of the cabaret rooms, when compared to vaudeville houses, contributed to the sense of intimacy. In 1911, for example, a typical New York vaudeville house held approximately fourteen hundred people. Despite some exceptions, no cabaret held more than eight hundred people in any one room. Although built to hold a capacity equivalent to vaudeville, the restaurants were divided into several rooms, each holding between four hundred and six hundred persons. Because of the differences in size, the cabaret promoted the sense of sociability and personal contact, which became one of its primary attractions.[32]

The liberal use of alcohol also helped lessen audience inhibitions and contributed to the formation of an informal social group. While vaudeville and legitimate theatres were prohibited from dispensing liquor, the cabaret was defined by the courts as a drinking establishment, which permitted it to sell alcohol. *Variety* asserted that alcohol was the backbone of the café. "It's the liquor that does the business in the cabaret," it remarked. "Everything in and about the cabaret commences and stops with liquor. It starts the eating, it starts the buying, and even with the awful liquor prices, it starts everything else connected with the nightlife of Broadway."[33] Because of entertainment costs and late hours where little food was consumed, proprietors found it necessary to encourage drinking during dinner and supper hours. Without the benefit of cover charges or minimums in the early years, they demanded that customers order champagne or pay one dollar for all other drinks, a cost that was approximately four times the price of the same drink in a Broadway saloon.[34] The general ambience made the cabaret more of a drinking than an eating establishment, and the drinking helped create the friendly atmosphere beloved by patrons.[35]

The dances, contests, and alcohol produced an atmosphere of public sociability in the cabaret. People went there to interact with others, to see and be seen, and to take part in a unique form of entertainment where they helped entertain themselves. Once the prosperous began reevaluating their public respectability, they could inhabit institutions where people of different ethnic, class, and moral backgrounds were seated at roughly equal levels, close together. The barriers that had separated people were coming into question, and the cabaret symbolized that questioning. Seated among the fast crowd, women of the town, ethnic entertainers, and guests from out of town, respectable urbanites were open to the flux of public life that the city offered. The cabaret symbolized that aspect of life lived to its fullest, for in the flux and movement around the tables and in the jammed and crowded space of the dance floor, life was clearly with other people. The barriers around the privatized self were opening, and people reached beyond the self to others: to the opposite sex in new emotional intimacy, to entertainers who performed without the stage barriers, to the fast crowd that formed the nucleus of café patronage. The cabaret structure contributed to a spirit and sense of life that was closer to one's emotional nature. Instead of letting gentility define the limits of their public lives, respectable urbanites were realizing they could enter a wider world of spontaneous cosmopolitan gaiety and experience "the whirl of life" itself.[36]

Colonel William D'Alton Mann, editor of *Town Topics*, a society scandal magazine, acknowledged the importance of the removal of theatrical barriers in the cabaret. "As seen on the stage they [new ragtime dances] are not much worse than lots of other rotten and disgusting exhibitions of lewdness which we have become accustomed to seeing," complained the crusty old blackmailer, "though with the barrier of the footlights always between us and the perpetrators of the indecencies . . . no one ever dreamed of introducing them into private life until the genesis of the Cabaret in New York." The informality of the cabaret was the problem. Unlike the theatre, the café "removes the barrier and places the actors in the assemblage and this familiarity unquestionably has broken down all fortifications of conventionality."[37] The breaking of these barriers also symbolized the loosening of Victorian constraints, at least according to *Billboard*. "Let joy be unconfined," it shouted. Implicitly contrasting the vitality of the café with past public leisure, the journal noted that "the history of Puritanism proves that unduly restrained emotionalism is productiv [sic] of longing passion and vicious tendencies."[38] Self-expression was given freer rein in the cabaret and was reevaluated as healthy and necessary. Release, not restraint, was prized.

The emphasis on self-expression eventually changed the nature of the Broadway restaurants as patrons sought institutions that permitted enjoyment of all the senses. Taste, to be sure, but also smell, touch, sight, and hearing, were all jumbled together in an atmosphere of motion and institutional spontaneity. George Rector discovered that the desire for dancing, music, and excitement was replacing the penchant for sedentary eating in 1913. "All they wanted to do was dance," he remarked, "and we accommodated them." Not interested in sitting quietly and eating in restrained fashion, nor content to view the passing parade, "the diners would drop their knives and napkins the minute the orchestra broke loose, and stampede for the dancing area. It looked like an elephant dancing on a butcher's block. The couples were jammed back to back, elbow to elbow, and cheek to neck." Eating took a back seat to the expending of energy and participation. "There was a time," mused Rector, "when the old patrons of Rector's had dined to the digestive lubrication of soft string music." Now, "the only thing stringy about the [new] Rector's were the steaks and chops."[39]

ACTION ENVIRONMENT

The environment of the cabaret bears striking resemblance to what sociologist Erving Goffman calls "action." The concept of action rests on the belief that life has fateful choices, that individuals will immerse themselves in the moment and gamble their character and fate on that moment. They are willing to take risks. Commercialized action, Goffman asserts, develops when everyday life—in business, home, and community—has become too routine and organized and people turn to amusement to find new kinds of fateful activities, new forms of heightened meaning. The period between 1850 and 1890 was a period of increasing corporate, social, and personal order. This had been true for men and women in their domestic lives when marriage and family was pictured as private, comfortable, and genteel and the amusements of respectable people followed the model of the family. Beginning in the 1890s, however, the growing questioning of gentility brought about the resurgent concern with masculinity, with the breaking of barriers, and the taking of risks. Women too engaged in a new form of self-determination unhampered by the constraints and cloistered quality of Victorianism.

By the 1910s the cafés served as settings for action and vitality for both sexes, allowing them places to question limitations over their personal lives. The cabaret thus represented two major conflicting trends in twentieth-century life: an impulsive self-fostered style for individual living and an institutional and rational specialization of social roles. In the words of Robert and Helen Merrill Lynd the cabaret represented institutional spontaneity. Here in the breaking of barriers between actor and audience, men and women had the chance to risk their selves, to be expressive, to be part of a vital urban life. Moreover, the café was a commercial form of action, a "fancy milling" similar to that provided by hotel casinos, in which direct participation occurs in a commercial setting. In milling, according to Goffman, one is brought together with others, those who are famous, who appear glamorous, above the controls of social life, sometimes even above the law, who seemingly live a life of constant excitement and danger. In the café, the customers had the chance to mix with gamblers, performers, actors, gangsters, people of society, all in a luxurious setting that gave them the feeling of having risked and won. This confirmed the sense of success, occurring as it did in public in front of many other witnesses and in front of the many mirrors that lined the cabaret. In the action environment of the café, one enjoyed the feeling of living on the edge, free from the constraints of society, amid people who themselves paid little heed to society's dictates. Themselves between cultures, respectable urbanites inhabited the cabaret for the feeling of life renewing itself in each costly minute.[40]

One of the new aspects of the cabaret was that men and women were present in the same action environment. So much of the risk and adventure in the cabaret came from the public displays of private impulses. In the 1910s this occurred in a culture in which people were just beginning to experiment with opening up their private selves. Relaxation of the barriers surrounding one's expressiveness also allowed men and women to begin to play out the desire for a mutual sexual relationship. In the audience, the close seating, the intimacy, flirting, and hand holding were all made possible by the movable chairs. Men and women were bringing into public life elements of their private activities—such as drinking, dancing, smoking, and socializing—and in doing so they brought women into a faster, more risk-oriented environment.

The sense of excitement in sexual relationships arose in this period because well-to-do men and women were beginning to explore new kinds of choices. In bringing their new desires into the open, they also brought their fears; the cabaret expressed both. The Eugenia Kelly case and similar ones were never far from the minds of café proprietors, and if they ever forgot, the constant surveillance of the Committee of Fourteen's investigators was enough to remind them. In this period of bending barriers between the sexes and between cultural groups, the issue was whether the creation of informality would destroy women and, by extension, the willpower, self-control, and success orientation of men. Patrons of the cabaret also worried about the release of private impulses and the mixing of cultures. While they wanted to have women present in an environment in which they could express themselves, patrons of the cabaret also wanted to create a setting in which women and men could be open to the public world of the city without destroying their own private selves and class position. The tension between these two desires helped provide much of the excitement and naughtiness of the cabaret.

The risks inherent in the public world of the cabarets were somewhat reduced by the tables. Cabarets, for example, were the first public drinking institutions to admit well-to-do women because their approach to drinking differed from that of the male saloon. In an all-male establishment, customers moved about with relative ease, socializing with whomever they chose along the long bar that dominated the room or in the areas behind the patrons at the rail.[41] High-class cabarets followed a different policy; they allowed women to drink but in the more restrained setting of the restaurant rather than in an open mixed bar. Many cabarets maintained separate men's cafés, while women drank publicly only at the tables in the restaurant proper, away from the bar and the socializing of men. Instead of the stand-up bar, cabarets used service or cocktail bars, from which the waiters served the drinks. Perceiving this built-in control that tables gave women, *Billboard* declared "better drinks with meals than without. . . . And, as for music, better music of any kind in a Cabaret—at a table surrounded by company."[42] Thus while cabarets offered women the opportunity to drink and loosen up in public, they also provided protections to ensure the maintenance of sexual and social order.

That proprietors worried over the potential sexual dimension of female public drinking is illustrated by the Café des Beaux Arts on Fortieth Street and Sixth Avenue, which departed from the larger pattern by opening a special bar for women in late 1911 or early 1912. Recognizing that women would drink privately if not allowed to indulge openly, Louis Bustanoby decided to let them express themselves in a separate annex. "No man can buy a drink there," however, "unless chaperoned by some member of the opposite sex."[43] Because it was a ladies' bar, women could enter alone or with an escort. Prostitutes avoided it, while society women, actresses, and social climbers paid attendance. François, the stately bartender, kept order and controlled the number and kind of men who entered, and thus maintained a high quality of social interaction. Although the café permitted women to drink, it had to provide the proper atmosphere and tone to the experience so that women would not be accosted or mistaken for prostitutes.

When respectable people began dancing in public, they demanded that the activity be presented in a more controlled manner than it had been in the lower-class dance halls. Labeling the dance halls "a vicious empire contrasting unfavorably with the cabaret," *Billboard* noted that they had served lower-class and immoral youth, "before the coming of Bohemia [the cabaret]—more freely than since or now."[44] Although the good and bad attended the cabaret, they did not necessarily mix. The tables and mealtime activities of the cabaret oriented people toward their own party and a relative fixity of place rather than toward the anarchistic possibilities of the entire room. At night in the cafés, customers generally danced with partners with whom they arrived or to whom they were introduced by the management. Preferring to keep the cabaret from becoming a free-for-all, patrons and managers discouraged cutting in and the making of new contacts. When Rector's tried to introduce the Paul Jones, a party device, to liven up a small crowd one rainy Sunday evening, customers hesitated. In this particular event, dancers joined hands and whirled about until a whistle signaled them to stop. Those opposite each other then paired off and continued until the next whistle, when they once again changed partners. That night, many couples took the floor, but when it came time for the whirl-about, only six couples remained to exchange partners. Originally designed for private parties, the Paul Jones proved too dangerous for a public institution. Even *Variety* considered it risqué, suggesting that patrons desired protection from too much intimacy. This attitude ruined an event that would have been acceptable in a private home.[45]

The stress on safeguards for women in a fast environment found its apotheosis in the policy demanding that women have escorts. Fremont Rider's *Guide* of 1916 noted that single women were generally made to feel unwelcome in the cabaret. Cabarets, observed Rider, "where profit comes largely from extravagant food and wine orders, frequently bar out women unaccompanied by men." When not excluding them entirely, cabarets "reserve a less desirable room away from the dancing and the entertainment where they segregate unescorted women and allow them to give their modest orders."[46] Profits were not the only motive, although they certainly played a role. Cabarets also sought to avoid the charges leveled against low-class dance halls, rathskellers, and cafés that they permitted too much mixing of strangers and thus were dens of iniquity. After the first several years of operation, moreover, cabaret proprietors were wary of city officials and reform groups who carefully monitored the activities of the cabarets. Patrons, too, were not anxious to participate in an atmosphere where women were allowed too much public freedom. *Variety*, usually a supporter of the cafés, noted the loss of business occasioned by the publicity surrounding the Kelly case and registered the fears that the family was in danger from the activities of women out of control in an unsupervised environment. "Where the pitfalls and harm were not visible to the casual eye heretofore," exclaimed *Variety*, "the dance cabaret now looms as a bottomless pit that holds all that they and theirs should avoid."[47]

Cabaret managers had to pay careful attention to the decline of business during these scares. At night the cabaret could ensure a limit to the threat to women by keeping single women out or relegating them to rooms away from the excitement. But men and women let their fantasies and fears run wild over what the structure and public atmosphere of the afternoon cabarets could mean. By 1916, therefore, the cafés responded to public demand by closing down or more carefully controlling their afternoon programs.

The maintenance of isles of safety within an informal public atmosphere permitted the cabaret to serve as the focus for the public mixing of people of widely varying social backgrounds, a feature Goffman views as part of action. With the barriers relaxed but not destroyed, respectable men and women could frequent places where the fast set, ethnic entertainers, actors and actresses, the sporting crowd, and society runabouts added to the vicarious excitement of the evening. In general, the cabarets of the 1910s drew a wide crowd. In surveying the dancing spots of the city on Saturday night, for example, *Variety* estimated that nearly ten thousand people (five thousand couples) went out dancing in places in and around the city of New York. Popular dancing spots such as Healy's, holding eight hundred people near the dance floor, and the New York Roof with fourteen hundred, filled between 9:00 and 9:30 P.M. on this, the busiest night of the week. All kinds of people who could afford it went. This tended to eliminate anyone below the prosperous, for drinks cost four times the amount in a normal Broadway bar. However, cover charges in the 1910s were generally only twenty-five to fifty cents until larger chorus girl revues and prohibition forced up the prices, so that cabarets could serve as a dinner-dance and entertainment evening for special occasions for less wealthy patrons.[48]

The ordinary businessman and his wife often visited Broadway, but the atmosphere of "speed," an "essential of Broadway night life," came from a smaller core of regulars made up of the theatre crowd, society, and the sporting set. "To the real Broadwayite," noted *Variety*, "life does not begin until after the theaters have let out and the ordinary folk are paying their supper checks at some cabaret dining place and thinking of going home." While a number of people of the ordinary business set liked the atmosphere "clinging about the forbidden," the real action started after closing hours. "To the Salamander [flapper] and her set this is the hour that things really start and there are so many in this set that it really pays more than one place to cater exclusively to them and their wants." The fast set, or the "hectics" as Julian Street dubbed them, gave the appearance of living life quickly and to its fullest. Starting with cocktails, dinner, a show, a restaurant for a dance, and then something to eat, the members of this set went off to another place because "you're not a regular unless you are seen everywhere and see everybody every night." The regulars followed a logical route up Broadway: Murray's, Claridge's, New York Roof, Rector's, Churchill's, Reisenweber's, and then after the regular rooms closed, upstairs to the 400 Club until 4 A.M., and then on to breakfast at Ciro's or Jack's, and to bed at 6:00 A.M. Sometimes the route varied, including Healy's or the Rose Garden or the real rathskellers such as Joel's, Kennedy's, Joe Brown's, or Walter Sweeney's, but underneath it all, as they bustled into one cabaret after another, was the Broadway adage, "A short life, and a merry one." Following their own clock, moving about after every new pleasure and excitement, the fast set added immeasurably to the sense of experiential time in the cabaret.[49]

In the cabaret, entertainers, successful representatives of ethnic communities (especially Uptown Jews in the theater and a booming clothing business and the Irish who were connected to politics, entertainment, and the building trades), big-time gamblers and businessmen and their wives all could inhabit the cabaret united by little more than their common search for action. As early as the 1910s, younger members of society frequented the cafés to find some relief in public from the closed nature of societal restrictions. Young people took advantage of the opportunity to choose their own personal associations based on their morality and interest. The appeal of social dancing brought a society crowd wherever the Castles and other prominent ballroom dancers appeared. The opening of Sans Souci in late 1913, for example, brought out a crowd of socialites and Broadway luminaries, finding Vanderbilts, Burkes, and other social notables in the same room with Broadway entertainers. *Vanity Fair*, moreover, the expensive journal of society and culture, preceded the *New Yorker*'s more extensive habit of announcing the doings of the cafés, of printing pictures of dancing stars and other entertainers, and of running articles describing the personal qualities of café artists. By 1916, with the influx of so many out-of-towners, society folk even began frequenting their own special places, the Montmartre and the Midnight Frolic, for example, a practice that was to continue into the 1920s and through the 1930s. The desire for personal expression in society also brought some of them into closer proximity with more plebeian groups. The fixed boundaries between class styles of the nineteenth century narrowed as members of the social elite sought to revive their personal lives through stronger ties to popular culture.

Other representatives of the urban community made the rounds of the cabarets. Arnold Rothstein was a fixture of café nightlife, and he bridged the period from the 1910s into the 1920s. One of the most prominent gamblers in the nation, Rothstein was known as the man who fixed the World Series and brains of the underworld. Starting out as a gambler, he also made money supplying thugs to the garment district, bankrolling theatrical productions, and loaning money to a variety of illegal operations during Prohibition. From a religious Jewish family, with a father who was a well-respected businessman in the Jewish community and the garment district, the younger Rothstein married out of the faith and found his existence in the fast life of a gambler's world. As a prominent man-about-town, he visited the cabarets with other gamblers, his wife, or a number of girl friends. There he found an easy-going cosmopolitan crowd, interested in a man who lived to all outward appearances by the laws of chance rather than the laws of the clock or routine. In the cabaret and night world of New York, the gambler could easily fit into a crowd that was learning to spend impulses more freely.

The admission of respectable women and men to informal public cabarets where actors, actresses, sporting men, and prostitutes displayed themselves in a lively rather than refined atmosphere produced the bohemian image of the cabaret in the 1910s. The search for life was considered bohemian because, to respectable urbanites the informal mixing of the sexes in such an environment was a new and lingeringly sinful venture. The word *cabaret* itself, according to "the Cynic," in *Shadowland*, "suggests a certain delicious wickedness" and conjures up "visions of that delightfully naughty demimond peopled by young rakes and old roués and lively, lovely cocottes, where wine and wit flow freely, where song and dance do flourish," and where "joy is unconfined and unrefined." Seeking to loosen some of their restraints, New Yorkers and others compared the city to the fast life of Paris. *Variety*, for example, eagerly quoted an Englishman who observed that "you Americans who believe it to be the 'smart' thing to go to Paris for a 'fast' time, do not have to go out of Times Square." Writing of modern debutantes, *Vanity Fair* decreed "they are, in fact, superhumanly and preternaturally sophisticated." The smart deb knew her way to "Sherry's, or Tiffany's, or Thorleys, or—after midnight—to the Castles in the Air. To them the world is a smiling garden. New York is their oyster and they are armed, each of them, with a jewelled oyster-knife." With this view of nightlife, the publication could make comparisons only to Paris: "At last a New Yorker can look a Parisian in the face," it exclaimed exultantly. The New Yorker need no more enviously listen to the "old familiar stories of all night life in Paris, of the tango hall at the Abbaye, and of dancing at dawn in the court of the Rat Mort."[50]

George Jean Nathan understood, however, that the bohemianism was often an image. With a keen eye for what the cabaret public wanted to believe of itself, he satirically asserted that the cabaret "is free—financially and especially morally," but it was staged. "It is all as gay as a pint of uncorked domestic champagne, as unforced as a pawnbroker's smile, as devilish as deviled ham."[51] How could it be otherwise when cabaret goers wanted merely a touch of expressivism in their lives, not a complete renunciation of convention? They desired to see and be part of the theatrical, wealthy, and disreputable elements of the city; they wanted to share some values with the fast crowd, and the cabaret offered them new frontiers of experience. True intimacy with the fast crowd, however, conjured up too many images of dangerous sexuality and loss of status. Late at night, they used money, technology, and artifice to create an environment for acting out these desires in a safe and controlled manner, without having to abandon their former selves or their original social universe entirely. They used the impersonality of the public realm to enjoy and explore new values.

In New York City, the elegant cabarets were not bohemian because, rather than being a rejection of the values of success, the cabaret was pictured as its reward. Customers were not willing to abandon their status and join with groups of poets, artists, writers, and students in entertaining themselves in their own informal camaraderie. There was something new about publicly mixing with the heterogeneous crowd, in a drinking-dancing atmosphere, but the need to maintain social safety mitigated against true camaraderie. For that sense of natural intermixture, the customers of the grander cabarets would have had to go off the beaten path, to the lesser-grade rathskellers, such as Joe Brown's, Walter Sweeney's, Joel's, Kennedy's, or Baron Wilkins', all places where theatrical professionals and late-night regulars went when they wanted to enjoy life among their own. "These are the incubators of the entertainment that is finally dished up at the better class of places," claimed *Variety*. "But while they are not so much on style and you do not have to wear dress clothes before the headwaiter will deign to look at you and bow," these are the places of good fellowship "that so many of the visitors to the big town seek unsuccessfully."[52]

For the most part the cabaret provided a place for "action" and "vicarious action." The cabaret was a model of the new urban culture, where both men and women were welcome and had the chance to enter a public world where they could draw on people of impulse from whom they were no longer so rigidly separated to construct a world of personal choices and experiences removed from private convention and institutional roles. While the cabaret was not quite bohemia, it did represent a new milieu in urban social life. Seated amid the crowd with few formal distinctions separating people, visitors to the cabaret reproduced the urban mass of which they were a part. Crowded at the tables or on the small dance floor, each person's sense of uniqueness was less noticeable. One could be part of the crowd and yet desire to maintain a subjectivity by interacting with the performer or getting out on the floor and expressing oneself. It was much more difficult in modern life to preserve one's own style and uniqueness, and the table placed one in the crowd and in tension with it. Moreover, in bringing women into this world, the cabaret also dispelled the distinctions between good and bad women. The cabaret's table setting, style of drinking, and dancing allowed both women and men a comfortable testing of new definitions of self within the setting of upper class civilization. The 1910s witnessed the entrance of the most cultured women into this more informal urban institution. But first the cabaret had to divorce itself from its disreputable native roots. Then respectability could rule with bohemia and *Billboard* could shout, "Viva la cabaret! Viva two times. Young people of many nations have longed for Bohemia. Here it is within the gates."[53] The cabaret then could become a way to explore personal desires and to pursue the dreams money could buy.

NOTES

1. Rudolph Fisher, "The Caucasian Storms Harlem," *American Mercury* 11 (May 1927): 398.

2. *Billboard*, February 1, 1913, p. 17.

3. *Variety*, December 25, 1914.

4. Jesse Lasky with Don Weldon, *I Blow My Own Horn* (Garden City, N.Y.: Doubleday, 1957), p. 84.

5. Ibid., p. 81.

6. Ibid., p. 84.

7. Ibid., p. 83.

8. *Variety*, May 6, 1911, pp. 6, 23, 25, May 20, 1911, p. 24, details the life of the Folies Bergère.

9. Julius Keller, *Inns and Outs* (New York: G. P. Putnam's Sons, 1939), pp. 115–16, 122; George Jean Nathan, "The Deadly Cabaret," *Theatre* 16 (December 1912): 184, notes that the cabaret "would be a 'joint' if it weren't for the fact that there are carpets on the floor and a fine chandelier hanging from the ceiling."

10. Descriptions of Murray's are in *New York Plaisance*, 1908, pp. 13–17, and chapter 2 of this book. *Dramatic Mirror*, November 23, 1918, p. 780, notes the continuing style of Murray's: "The same elements of old Roman dignity, elegance, and swift, noiseless service have been insisted on." Edward Hungerford, "America's New York," in *The Personality of American Cities* (New York: McBride, Nast & Co., 1913), p. 50, says that "the decorations of the great dining-rooms must rival those of a Versailles palace while the so-called minor appointments—silver, linen, china and the rest must be as faultless as in any great house upon Fifth Avenue."

11. *Variety*, December 3, 1912, p. 5.

12. *New York World*, April 3, 1913, p. 2.

13. *Variety*, December 25, 1914, p. 7; "Broadway," *Atlantic* (June 1920): 855–56. For this use of "frontier," see Murray Melbin, "Night as Frontier," *American Sociological Review* 43: 3–22.

14. *Variety*, April 16, 1915, p. 7.

15. For details of the dance craze, see chapter 5.

16. Lasky, *Blow My Own Horn*, p. 86.

17. *New York American*, April 6, 1919, p. 3.

18. *Variety*, November 21, 1914, p. 23.

19. Plain Mary, "Shanley's Cabaret," *Variety*, November 28, 1913, p. 21; *New York Times*, January 10, 1915, p. 9, has an advertisement for Maxim's stating that the cabaret is "something which makes time pass more quickly and happily."

20. *Variety*, October 27, 1916, p. 12.

21. Ibid., March 23, 1912, p. 9.

22. Sophie Tucker, *Some of These Days* (Garden City, N.Y.: Doubleday, 1948), p. 136.

23. *Variety*, December 10, 1915, p. 7; Anne Rittenhouse, "Society Dances in the Costumes of To-morrow," *Vanity Fair* 1 (February 1914): 57; *New York Times*, November 13, 1913, clipping in Castles Vertical File, New York Public Library Dance Collection, Lincoln Center.

24. Brian Duryea, "Introducing the Real Mrs. Castle," *Green Book* (December 1915), Robinson Locke Collection, New York Public Library Theater Collection, Lincoln Center; also see Irene Castle, as told to Bob Duncan and Wanda Duncan, *Castles in the Air* (Garden City, N.Y.: Doubleday, 1958), pp. 66–67. *Variety*, November 28, 1914, p. 7, discussed the country lad and lass.

25. Nathan, "Deadly Cabaret," p. 183; *Variety*, January 26, 1917, p. 13.

26. *Variety*, March 21, 1919, p. 9, covers the Dooley case. More recently, comedian Larry Storch told me in conversation (July 1971) that he preferred greater differentiation between himself and the customers to prevent their attacking him.

27. *Variety*, October 13, 1916, p. 12, January 9, 1915, p. 8, December 18, 1916, p. 13, and December 16, 1921, pp. 20, 26, has material on audience participation.

28. Advertisement Shanley's for *New York Times*, May 23, 1915, X, p. 7.

29. Gil Boag, as told to Dorothy Bobbé, "When Nightclubs Were in Flower," unpublished manuscript, in Bobbé's possession, New York, p. 82.

30. *Variety*, January 30, 1914, p. 8, January 16, 1914, p. 20, July 10, 1914, p. 17, July 24, 1914, p. 13, October 31, 1914, p. 23, all have information on the contests.

31. Ibid., December 18, 1916, p. 13, comments on patrons' staying as late as they could. *New York Times*, February 28, 1916, p. 4; *Variety*, November 11, 1914, p. 7; *New York World*, n.d., Castle Scrapbooks, Robinson

Locke Collection; and *Variety*, March 26, 1915, p. 13, have information on the club.

32. For vaudeville, see Michael Davis, *The Exploitation of Pleasure* (New York, 1911), cited in Albert F. McLean, Jr., *American Vaudeville as Ritual* (Lexington: University of Kentucky Press, 1965), p. 25. My estimate of cabaret capacity is based on *Variety*'s occasional information.

33. *Variety*, February 3, 1912, p. 10, discusses the absence of liquor in theatres and vaudeville. Ibid., December 27, 1918, p. 157, discusses alcohol in the cabaret.

34. Castle, *Castles in the Air*, p. 93, discusses their policy at Sans Souci.

35. *Billboard*, February 1, 1913, p. 17.

36. "Whirl of Life" taken from the title of a cabaret revue.

37. *Town Topics*, January 18, 1912, p. 1.

38. *Billboard*, February 1, 1913, p. 17.

39. George Rector, *The Girl from Rector's* (Garden City, N.Y.: Doubleday, Page, 1927), pp. 204–05.

40. Erving Goffman, "Where the Action Is," in *Interaction Ritual* (Garden City, N.Y.: Doubleday, 1967), pp. 149–270. "Institutional spontaneity" comes from Helen Merrill Lynd, *Middletown Revisited* (New York: Harvest Books, 1965), pp. 276–77.

41. Jon M. Kingsdale, "The 'Poor Man's Club': Social Functions of the Urban Working-Class Saloon," *American Quarterly* 25 (October 1973): 472, notes that saloons were central to workingmen's leisure time: "It was a neighborhood center, an all-male establishment and a transmitter of working-class and immigrant cultures." Also Ned Polsky, *Hustlers, Beats and Others* (Garden City, N.Y.: Doubleday, 1967), pp. 1–30, discusses the pool hall, another institution that excluded women and fit the larger separation of the sexes of the nineteenth century. These institutions are unlike the cabarets and nightclubs of the twentieth century, which are for both sexes and certainly for both sexes of the middle and upper classes.

42. *Variety*, August 25, 1916, p. 8, discusses men's cafés, and *Billboard*, February 1, 1913, p. 17, noted the greater safety of drinking in a restaurant setting. See also Sherri Cavan, *Liquor License: An Ethnography of Bar Behavior* (Chicago: Aldine Publishing Co., 1966), pp. 163–65, which states that the night spot allows less sociability than the bar, especially because the tables turn people inward toward their party. She sums up the difference: "Thus, as the likelihood of contact between the unacquainted in nightspots is less than the likelihood of such contact in other public drinking places, the ranks of the nightspot patrons may be swelled by many who, as a general rule, do not frequent other types of establishments. For those who may feel repugnance toward a setting where they can expect to be subjected indiscrimi-

nately to the overtures of others and where they are accorded no rights to moral indignation in the face of such overtures, the nightspot may provide a place where they can drink with an immunity to contact that is similar in effect (if not similar in reason), to that which is available to them in other public places."

43. *New York Times*, October 12, 1913, p. 2.

44. *Billboard*, February 1, 1913, p. 17. Attempting to profit from the dance craze starting in 1912, entrepreneurs opened popular-priced dance halls, foreshadowing the cleaned-up lower-class mass halls of the 1920s. The new dance institutions tried to avoid the evils of the saloon by banning alcohol and serving only soft drinks and sandwiches. Customers danced continuously; most of the space was sacrificed for the dance and greater social intermixture. See *Variety*, February 13, 1914, p. 20.

45. *Variety*, November 21, 1914, p. 23.

46. Fremont Rider, *New York City, A Guide-Book for Travelers* (New York: Henry Holt & Co., 1916), pp. 13–14.

47. *Variety*, May 28, 1915, p. 6.

48. Ibid., November 28, 1913, p. 10, December 25, 1914, p. 8. Julian Street, *Welcome to Our City* (New York: John Lane Co., 1913), pp. 10–11, discusses how "practically any well-dressed person who is reasonably sober and will purchase supper and champagne for two, may enter." The price of six to eight dollars comes from Keller, *Inns and Outs*, p. 138. He adds that a pint of champagne cost two dollars and fifty cents and a quart five dollars.

49. *Variety*, December 25, 1914, p. 7.

50. The Cynic, "The Cabaret—An Impression," *Shadowland* 6 (August 1922): 42; *Variety*, August 22, 1913, p. 19; "In Vanity Fair," *Vanity Fair* 3 (December 1915): 33; "All-Night Life in New York," *Vanity Fair* 3 (April 1915): 50.

51. Nathan, "The Deadly Cabaret," p. 183.

52. *Variety*, December 25, 1914, p. 7.

53. *Billboard*, February 1, 1913, p. 17.

EVERYBODY'S DOIN' IT: IRENE AND VERNON CASTLE AND THE PRE-WORLD WAR I DANCE CRAZE

The afternoon was already planned; they were going dancing—for those were the great days: Maurice was tangoing in "Over the River," the Castles were doing a stiff-legged walk in the third act of the "Sunshine Girl"—a walk that gave the modern dance a social position and brought the nice girl into the café, thus beginning a profound revolution in American life. The great rich empire was feeling its oats and was out for some not too plebeian, yet not too artistic fun.

F. Scott Fitzgerald, "The Perfect Life"[1]

F. Scott Fitzgerald was not alone in estimating the importance of the nationwide dance craze sweeping through the cities from 1912 to 1916 and the central role played in the excitement by such popular ballroom teams as Irene and Vernon Castle and Maurice Mouvet and Florence Walton. "It's about th' on'y thing ye see in the pa-pers," observed Finley Peter Dunne's wizened Mr. Dooley at the height of the hysteria. "People ar-re dancin' that a few years ago wud've as soon thought 'iv lettin' their mothers or their bankers see them on a slippery flure as entrin' an opyum joint."[2] Mayors, vice commissions, and social reformers looked on in horror at what they considered the degeneration of public and private morality, but they were powerless to prevent all types of people from every class level—debutantes, staid businessmen, housewives, Lower East Side dwellers, and Upper West Side matrons—from feeling the spell cast by the dance and flocking to the dance halls, hotel ballrooms, and cabarets. Jesse Lasky recalled the important role that the renaissance of public dancing played in the growth of the cabaret. In 1911, he observed, "it was still scandalous to dance in a public place. Only a year or two later that prejudice was swept aside, and then nightclubs blossomed like magic."[3]

Having begun with exhibition dancers only, the cabarets by 1912 had almost universally installed dance floors so that patrons might partake of the novel proceedings. After an initial period of reluctance, sedate Fifth Avenue hotels followed suit to meet a demand that fluctuated but did not diminish into the 1920s. Centrally located urban institutions had come to replace the lower-class dance halls, vacation resorts, and amusement-park halls as the major places of public dancing. Dancing was becoming a regular and public urban form of entertainment.

To extend the hours of the dance even into the afternoons, cabarets and then hotels inaugurated tea dances, or as they were known in fashionable circles, *thé dansants*, in 1913. Noting the prevailing trend, the *Craftsmen* exclaimed that "suddenly in the midst of this money-getting machine-made age, we throw all our caution to the wind; we give up some of our business hours, and we do not only dance in the evening, but in the afternoon and in the morning."[4] Two general policies governed the afternoon events. The hotels charged one dollar admission, which included tea or other light refreshments, while the cabarets limited their profits to the sale of tea or liquor rather than charging an entrance fee. Lasting from two or three in the afternoon until six in the evening, *thé dansants* drew all kinds of women to public dance institutions during the formerly sedate tea hour, which was transformed into "merely an excuse for dancing." This tremendous expansion of commercial dance facilities led Troy and Margaret Kinney to wonder in amazement that "there should have been a period of sixty years in which people did not wish to dance every day."[5]

In the cabarets, special bands played for dancing before, during, and after the dinner hour. Patrons needed little encouragement to drop their forks and take a few turns around the floor, exhibiting as they did so the active hand they took in their own entertainment. The dance craze of 1912–1916 helped establish the first stars of the cabaret. Irene and Vernon Castle and Maurice Mouvet and his many partners found success and an aura of glamour in the cafés of New York City. Their relationship to the dance craze was an intimate one, for they exhibited all of the current dances and represented the deeper values desired through dance. Appearing at midnight, Irene and Vernon slipped from their table and glided ever so gracefully out onto the dance floor. The lights dimmed, the spotlights played upon them, and they stepped through a series of dances before the delighted eyes of their bewitched fans. After they had finished, patrons themselves tried to imitate what they had just witnessed. In the years of the dancing mania, the ballroom teams personalized many of the fears and dreams of urban life and offered guides as to how the dances were done and life could be lived; the upper and middle classes performed styles established by the Castles, the premier ballroom and cabaret artists of their day, and looked to them for clues on new relationships between men and women. Before examining the new dances and their stars, especially Irene Castle, "a model for the sophisticated twenties women," let us first examine the older dance patterns that changed.[6]

BACKGROUND

Prior to 1910 the well-to-do who desired to dance could do so largely in private and on irregular occasions. Small parties did not necessarily revolve around it. The upper classes valued dancing in their social life, but they generally held their balls during the winter season for a restricted group. In humbler circles a club or an organization hired a hall for a general dance and occasionally the police held a grand ball. The seclusion of dancing reflected a society bent on maintaining privacy against the intrusions of outsiders and the dangerous urban world. Women in particular, as bearers of class and culture, were to inhabit a distinct sphere. To step outside the private social network of balls, teas, and debuts was to abrogate social class and propriety. In this atmosphere, it was difficult to introduce respectable women into public, commercial dance halls associated in the public mind with concert saloons that dispensed liquor and prostitution. The fear of women mixing with all elements of urban life mitigated against widespread public dancing.[7]

Unlike those inaugurated after 1912, the favored dances of the nineteenth century exhibited control, regularity, and patterned movement. Set and figure dances—the german, cotillion, and lancers— were favorites at the exclusive Patriarch balls in New York City in the 1870s and 1880s; these dances emphasized that individual pleasure arose from participation in hierarchy, social interdependence, and group unity. Allen Dodworth, a society dancing master, considered the german "an epitome of all there is in private dancing."[8] Introduced to New York about 1844, the german was an elaborate round dance, perfect for private parties because its frequent partner exchanges during the course of the dance ensured a general acquaintanceship among members of the same social set. Its figure formations also elevated group cohesion over the pleasure of the individual. Dodworth advised fledgling steppers to remember that all "pleasure depends entirely upon the kindly cooperation of others." Each individual had a duty to the larger body, and when all united in a cooperative endeavor, "the pleasure is augmented in proportion to the number engaged."[9] Dances of this kind required practice for some time before a ball to ensure that all parts would work well together. As such, they were the ritualistic height of the evening, and the fact that they were organized and led by a society grande dame served to heighten order, refinement, and social responsibility over tendencies toward privatization between partners.

The waltz, introduced into western Europe in 1812, was also a nineteenth- and early twentieth-century favorite for the upper classes and the rest of society. The first closed couple dance, replacing the open hold of the minuet, the waltz changed the position of the feet from ballet to normal but kept an overall pattern movement. Beginning with a certain step, the dancer had to complete an entire sequence of steps until reaching the original place. Dodworth illustrates the fixity of the overall pattern. It "consists of six motions," he wrote. "The lady begins at 1, continuing with 2, 3, 4, 5, 6; then beginning again at 1, and repeating the same succession, in every direction, under all circumstances." The attraction of the waltz lay in the actual steps, which varied little from individual to individual.[10] Both the set and sequence dances, in their group and individual manifestations, required a certain unity in the steps, creating a standardized form of motion.

Initially the source of much consternation, the waltz established the close hold whereby the man held the woman at the waist in semi-embrace. The proper hold, however, established a definite distance of three to four inches at the shoulders, increasing downward.[11] The rapid turns prevented lingering embraces and cheek-to-cheek contact. Each partner looked over the other's shoulder while maintaining an erect posture. The formal distance, the courtly style, and the emphasis on a sequence of steps circumscribed the amount of expression allowed mutual body movement and contact. The waltz perhaps expressed the emphasis on disembodied love in the nineteenth century. It was a more companionate dance to be sure, but the movement of the dance, much like the mobility enshrined in the society, kept the man and woman apart. Given the correct hold, the waltz expressed a look but do not touch approach to one's partner, a distance between sexes under the guise of ideal, bodiless love contained in the face of one's partner. Moreover, the institution of the dance card mitigated against individuals fulfilling their heart's desires, since they had to dance with a number of different people to meet social obligation. Even with the waltz, individuals had to follow group norms. According to one scholar, social dancing in the second half of the nineteenth century lacked inventiveness and tended toward formality.[12]

The challenge to this formalism in the dance began in the 1890s, burst into flower in the 1910s, and continued with a good deal of creativity into the 1920s. In the 1890s, men and women began to do the more active strains of the two-step and the "Washington Post March." John Philip Sousa wrote the "Washington Post March" in 1891, and the music caught on immediately. It had a new kind of military march beat, and the two-step, the dance done to it, was not much more than a double-quick march with a skip in each step, done rapidly as a couple could go forward, backward, and turn. The actual "Washington Post" dance arrived before 1894. In it the man stood behind his partner, slightly to the left, while she raised her hands above her shoulders to take those of the man. Barely perceptible beneath the march rhythms, the dancers of the two-step and the "Washington Post" began expressing themselves to a heightened beat.[13] The Boston waltz, moreover, which reached the height of popularity around 1900, was already moving to the leisurely walk step, as dancers took a full four bars instead of two in their turns.

After 1912 social dancing changed dramatically. Several commentators estimated that "over one hundred new dances found their way, in and out of our fashionable ballrooms" from 1912 to 1914.[14] The vast increase in dances with such exuberantly unpretentious names as the turkey trot, Texas tommy, bunny hug, monkey hug, lame duck, foxtrot, and tango, together with their astonishing rapidity of discovery, gave to this regeneration of social dancing the appearance of a mania. Caught in its spell, New Yorkers picked up these new steps from around the nation and danced in new rhythms in public and private places of amusement. In dance halls, ballrooms, cabarets, and private homes, the rest of the nation was quickly bent on following suit. The dances, like the cabaret itself in the 1910s, were part of a growing social and cultural ferment as men and women turned to greater intimacy in social and sexual relations and a single standard of sexual relations. As an element lying at the core of the body, dancing's regeneration bespoke a society breaking from gentility and discovering new options and forms of behavior between the sexes.

Well-to-do New Yorkers found new forms of the dance to match their impulses in the steps borrowed from black American dance, music, and culture, rather than formal European steps. In borrowing from the more natural shuffle walk-step, in which partners moved about shuffling their feet as if walking, respectable whites sought a greater emphasis on body movement rather than patterned feet movement. In seeking new sources of vitality, respectable whites looked outside the halls of propriety to a people and a culture they had previously considered disreputable. The first attempts by whites to copy black steps for the ballroom occurred in the 1890s and early 1900s. Often in the honky-tonks of this period, an occasional white would perform the Negro cakewalk to vary the waltz and two-steps. The cakewalk soon penetrated even high society. The William K. Vanderbilts found it a unique diversion for one of their balls. The cakewalk, however, was primarily an exhibition rather than a social dance for common usage, and it was not until the 1910s that the rate of influx from lower groups increased and specifically social forms predominated. After the almost nonexistent beginning in the cakewalk, whites turned with ever-increasing frequency to the more primitive steps of black culture. The Texas tommy, turkey trot, fox-trot, charleston, and black bottom, for example, had Negro origins and were originally performed in black communities or in red-light districts.[15] Marshall and Jean Stearns, in their book *The Jazz Dance*, traced the Texas tommy, the dance acknowledged as the first one accepted by whites, to a Negro cabaret on the Barbary Coast of San Francisco. In 1910 it arrived in New York from Chicago and was first danced professionally by a black vaudevillian on the stage. It was quickly taken over by white exhibition dance teams for use in the cabarets. Because of the paucity of sources, it is difficult to tell how old these dances were within the black community, but it is clear that, under the demands of whites, they were beginning to make their way into the larger society during this period.

Ragtime, the music for the new dances, also came from black culture, and it stimulated a host of new steps. Another product of the 1890s, it too started in southern black dives and cabarets as blacks began moving in increasing numbers into the city and coming into contact with each other, minstrel show music, white march and band music, and Negro barrelhouse piano. Irving Berlin brought the music to its widest vogue after the publication of "Alexander's Ragtime Band" in 1911, when Tin Pan Alley joined in the production of the musical form. Previously intended for listening, ragtime now became an important element in the intimate movement of mainstream whites.[16] The music originally permitted blacks to laugh at white culture and behavior through the "ragging" of the host culture's cherished melodies and sentiments. According to Mark Sullivan, the surprise of hearing old melodies with new and quickened accents destroyed the original intent of the music.[17] When whites adopted ragtime, it meant that they were beginning to question some of the formal aspects of their culture. In its spirit and rhythm, rag, when combined with the dance, provided the pep that men and women sought in their music.

As purveyors of the new music, black bandsmen found jobs in the Broadway cabarets and restaurants from which they were otherwise excluded. They replaced the gypsy string orchestras intended for listening only, and their opportunities derived from the new demand and the formidable organizing job performed by James R. Europe. He helped form black musicians into the Clef Club, a place where work could be efficiently handed out and where black bands could be contacted. Europe quit the Clef Club in 1914 to play for dancers Irene and Vernon Castle. His star rose with the Castles, reaching a peak when his bands played all along Broadway in 1915, and his own Tempo Club was a mainstay of the dance craze before the war.[18] While whites to a degree could accept happy-go-lucky black music because it fit their image of the Negro, they were reluctant to accept black culture's serious music. They ignored the more complex rag compositions of Scott Joplin, just as did the Negro musicians who were afraid to acknowledge seriously their lower-class musical tradition. Black and white musicians thus wrote and played a light kind of dance music, which the white public was willing to accept.[19] The black dominance of Broadway cabarets did not outlast the war. As whites borrowed the newer musical styles after 1917, they also took over the high-paying jobs.

Along with the more natural shuffle walk-steps of black dancing and their Afro-American and Tin Pan Alley ragtime accompaniment, dancers enjoyed heightened bodily expression and intimacy with their partners. Black music, according to music historian Maud Cuney-Hare, "ignores any division of time that follows the natural pulse of a regular metrical beat," and anticipates or holds over accents beyond their expected time.[20] Emphasizing rhythm and a beat, this complex music encouraged spontaneous movement and undercut the formal conventions about moving the body that had prevailed in social dancing. As Vernon Castle remarked, "When a good orchestra plays a 'rag' one has simply *got* to move." The music emphasized rhythm rather than the vocals, redefining popular music and the music business as an extension of dancing rather than listening. It is no accident that from this period on, Tin Pan Alley decreed that a successful song had to be danceable.[21]

The simplicity of the shuffle walk and the finely accented rhythms of the music encouraged couples to interpret the beat in a wider variety of ways than had occurred previously. One couple, for example, could be dancing one dance, while others did quite another to the very same music. Styles such as the tango and the one-step contained innumerable variations from which a couple could choose the ones that most appealed to them. The new styles freed the dancers from the sequence of steps that had served to prescribe their behavior in the past. Commenting on this increase in individual interpretation, dance and art critic Troy Kinney remarked in 1914 that "the resumption of ballroom dancing with the utmost freedom of individual invention has resulted in some far from beautiful forms, as for instance, the Turkey Trot."[22] What Kinney was noticing was that dancers were adding more body expression—more arm pumping, more shaking, and more jiggling—to their movements on the floor. Bodily interpretation of the beat was achieving a place, however slight, in the modern social dance.

The major attraction of the new dances rested on the rhythm rather than on prescribed steps. By adding body movements to the steps, dancers experienced immediate pleasure in the dance—expression of the body—rather than going in a purposeful direction.[23] A number of commentators observed the boring and monotonous movements of the steps, but what they saw was the box step, which submitted to the external constraints of an urban industrial society but within those constraints subtly elevated the body as an irreducible unit of freedom. Irving Berlin's popular "Everybody's Doin' It Now" of 1911 illustrates the new-style shoulder, arm, and hip movements done to the irregularly accented ragtime beat, describing couples swaying, throwing their shoulders in the air, snapping their fingers, and hunching like bears to the phrase, "Its a bear."[24] Dancing now contained pleasure along the way; it was not just a direction to travel. Instead of using the steps alone to define the dance, women and men moved their bodies in response to the rhythm.

The acceptance of black music and dance paralleled and drew upon a reevaluation of the previous formalism between men and women. The wonderful nomenclature of the dances, taken from the barnyard, added to the general tone of exuberance, unpretentiousness, and informality between the sexes. Doing the turkey trot, grizzly bear, monkey glide, bunny hug, lame duck, or fox-trot, whites did movements that placed them closer to the natural processes of the animal kingdom than to the restrained pinnacle of the genteel hierarchy that they and well-to-do women had occupied in the Victorian era. By turning to the animal world, black culture, and the red-light district for the sources of their cultural regeneration, well-to-do urbanites were searching for a way to liberate some of the repressed wilder elements, the more natural elements, that had been contained by gentility. Their liberation found their way into dance and into social relations. The new dances were part of the rebellion against the older sexual mores.[25]

Indeed the dances fostered an unheard-of casualness between partners, permitted greater options in holds and distances, and symbolized the high value placed on mutual heterosexual intimacy and attraction. Couples often held each other very close, grasping each other firmly about the waist or about the neck as if in a hug. The one-step brought men and women into closer contact than the formal six inches decreed for the waltz. And unlike the waltz, in which couples whirled about so that they nearly lost touch with each other, the one-step, the bunny hug, and the other new dances allowed a lingering close contact.[26] "Certainly their essence is a very close proximity," emphasized Julian Street in *Welcome to Our City*. "Two persons, moving with the music, as one—much more as one than in the old time waltz or two step." Conventions had changed drastically. "The debutantes of five years since would have indignantly refused to dance with the young man who held her as he must needs hold her in the dance of today." To the dismay of moralists, men and women in the tango even brought legs and pelvic regions into intimate contact in the much feared dip portion of the dance, which placed women in a horizontal position reeking of sexual exploration and subjugation. In the new dances, men and women were taking on a sexual cast and bringing their bodies into greater affectionate contact. As one society dance instructor summed it up, "The young dancers simply take advantage of the dances to embrace."[27]

Whether these dances were done in private or public, they reflected an emphasis on the primacy of the intimate couple instead of the group. In the public cabaret, this was even more so, because a man and woman usually came together, and the chances of their dancing with someone they did not know were, if not impossible, at least remote. In the cabaret there were few mechanisms to facilitate the mixing of people who did not know each other. The dance card was not in force, and the idea that one should never dance with the same person twice in succession was forever broken.[28] The customs of the private dance did not apply in the public space, and even cutting in was frowned upon. This left the partners performing their own steps to a common music. Within the public dancing area, the desire for more life, for more fun, for more adventure, was confined to the couple. The couple carried the weight of these and other cultural changes.

The new dances bespeak a reevaluation of women of the prosperous classes and the institution of marriage. By the early twentieth century the institution of marriage among the upper and upper middle classes perhaps began shifting away from the traditional economic and childbearing functions toward more personal factors as the determinants of a relationship. Moreover, the ideal of the family oriented to duty or toward male success was in the process of transformation. What was important were the personal compatibilities of two people, their companionableness, and their mutual sexual attractiveness. The positive value placed on sexual factors extended the institution of dating for the young. They needed a certain amount of free opportunity to explore each other if the personal factors were to be found right. Sexual attractiveness could not be measured merely by talking; it had to be explored in a mutual excitement of each other's bodies. By emphasizing this in the dance and in public places like the cabaret outside the eyes of parents or friends whom one did not want to have watching, young people of well-to-do backgrounds could search for a mate who met their personal definition of a marriage partner.

The renaissance of public dancing, furthermore, provided young men and women a relatively safe place and manner of searching out the sexual factors for marriage and lifelong companionship. Private dances took place in front of such authority figures as parents and social superiors. The cabaret offered a degree of freedom from watchful eyes of people they knew. Yet while there was room to explore in some ways, the cabaret was also a public place, filled with anonymous eyes so that nothing could progress beyond a mildly intimate stage. A woman and a man might proceed by automobile to a secluded place after leaving, but if they were young, they most probably had to be home by a certain time to answer to their parents. Within these constraints, the dances themselves offered a greater realm for exploration of those indefinable qualities associated with the body. Shuffling around the floor, swaying and moving, couples could feel if the person they danced with was compatible for pleasure along the path of life and offered a chance of personal fulfillment.

Although the young made up a large bulk of the dancing crowd, they were not the only ones who danced in the public cabarets. Geared to a new mood of self-expresison, the dance craze also drew on the impulses of older people. Prior to 1910 the dance was primarily the recreation of the young, with parents in society circles joining in for an occasional figure or a set dance. As Frederick Lewis Allen noted, "Through the length and breadth of middle class America few people danced after they were married, or had reached the age of twenty-five." The keen-eyed Mark Sullivan observed that the man who danced after thirty-five was held in disesteem. He "was looked upon as one who made dancing and its associated diversions his career, and therefore not to be taken seriously in his ordinary vocation." As only the young danced, the activity was seen as a childish endeavor, to be relinquished shortly after marriage.[29]

Consequently when married and unmarried couples began to dance regularly in hotels and cabarets, it signaled their adaptation to a more youthful set of social values. While the young developed special peer styles for themselves, older men and women also tried to perpetuate a sense of youthfulness in the marriage institution. Henry Canby contrasted older hierarchical values with the newer development:

Self-expression for youth is supposed to have brought about the great change in family life which came with the new generation. It was a cause, but an equally powerful one was self-expression for parents, who determined to stay young and live their own lives, while the boys and girls were sent off to camps and schools. Fathers and mothers in the earlier time put fatherhood and motherhood first.[30]

Desiring their own self-expression and youthfulness, married members of society joined in the social activities of adolescents. Dancing became a way of affirming one's identity as a youthful individual, vital to and in society. It also meant that older people confirmed the activities of adolescents, looking to them to set the styles. The continuation of dancing after marriage also showed that sexual attractiveness was an ongoing theme.

For the older set, having public places to dance meant that dancing recaptured a spontaneity that it had missed when it was regulated by the round of society or occasional ball activities. Whenever a couple who could afford it felt like dancing, all they had to do was step out. The public atmosphere meant that parents could escape their children, and couples could escape their particular social set and concentrate on dancing and each other. The opening up of this public realm afforded greater anonymity and potentially greater personal freedom.

The reevaluation of marriage implied by the dance craze was caught in one of the many short stories that explored the dance craze, Mary Cutting's "Dance-Mad Billy." The story opens with a depiction of a young married couple mired in the genteel family of male duty and female refinement. Working as an architect in a large firm, William Stirling finds that his imagination has dried up, and as a consequence, he turns to dancing and the body as a new realm for his energies. Unfortunately his wife, Tips, insists on abjuring joy and remaining a homebody. She wants Bill to settle down, work hard, and stay away from pleasurable activities that would prevent him from achieving financial success. In her stubborn resistance to the new fashions, she symbolizes the older notion of the home and family as a place of regularity, responsibility, and sobriety. Because of her insistence on the older virtues, Bill goes alone to afternoon dances where he trots with a friend's wife. The conflict in the story derives from whether his dancing will lead his sexual impulses outside the family and thus destroy their home. Cutting resolves the issue by having Tips, through a miraculous change of heart, choose to share joy with her husband. We learn at the end that she refused to accompany him only because he did not make his desires for her presence forcefully known. She was hurt. Her new feelings resolve the dilemma: "I'm sick and tired of being a makeweight. I want—I want—I want—" her voice rises uncontrollably—"to en-*joy* myself too." The story ends as Bill proclaims, with Tips's full agreement, "Let's go out to-night and have a lark!"[31] This story demonstrates that dancing was a way for both sexes to revitalize their marriage and to legitimize joy in marriage as a positive value that both partners should expect. Marriage was to fulfill the personal expectations of both people.

WATCH YOUR STEP: SOCIETY DANCERS AND THE CASTLES

The prewar dance craze produced a host of popular ballroom dancers who became the stars of the early cabarets. Among the exhibition steppers were Maurice and Florence Walton; Joan Sawyer and several partners, including Carlos Sebastian and Rudolph Valentino; Mae Murray; Bonnie Glass and Clifton Webb; John Murray Anderson and Genevieve Lyon; and Mr. and Mrs. Douglas Crane.[32] A significant attraction for the cabarets, the ballroom dancers introduced new dances to the restaurants. As the fashionable *Vanity Fair* asserted, they "were the chiefest *[sic]* magnets for luring the public." With only a "harmonious pair who can cover their twenty miles a night in various original ways," concluded the magazine, "and abundant floor space on which their audiences may emulate them," any cabaret was sure to be a success.[33]

Irene and Vernon Castle, the well-known husband and wife team, were the premier dancers of their day. The *Dramatic Mirror* called them "our supreme ballroom artists, possessing distinction, intelligence, delicacy of the dance, and what is termed in the varieties—class."[34] Although he was considered the better dancer, she became one of the most written-about women of the period, a model for dancers and a symbol of urbane fashion and the new woman.[35] With their exceptional grace and decorum, the Castles offset the negative values associated with the early dances. As the barriers between the sexual spheres began to lessen, these performers helped to reform the steps and present acceptable ways for dealing with the questions raised by the mixing of cultures and the new roles for women and men that the dance suggested.[36]

Like others in their field, the Castles achieved success at an early age and grew up in the changing social environment of the 1890s. Born in Norwich, Great Britain, on May 2, 1887, Vernon Castle graduated from Birmingham University with an engineering degree and then traveled to the United States where he acted in musical comedies and burlesques, most notably as an eccentric comedian in Lew Fields's *Hen Pecks* company. In May 1910 he married Irene Foote, the sprightly eighteen-year-old daughter of respectable middle-class parents in New Rochelle, and in the summer of 1911 they went to Paris to reproduce a Lew Fields sketch for the French musical stage. The French were unaccustomed to his form of comedy and the act failed. Alone except for a black family servant and without money, they contracted to dance in the Café de Paris, an exclusive cabaret in the French capital. This was the first time they ever danced together. Improvising as they went along, performing the turkey trots and grizzly bears they heard were being done in New York, the Castles became huge favorites of the international crowd in Paris. Their success created a rage for American dancers in Paris and a demand for the Castles in the United States. They returned to New York in fall 1912, where Vernon appeared in the Broadway production *The Lady of the Slipper*. After each performance, he and Irene would dance at Louis Martin's café, where they quickly doubled their starting salary of three hundred dollars. From this beginning, they made their names almost synonymous with dancing. Their career alternated among musical comedies, vaudeville appearances, regional tours, and restaurant engagements. Extremely popular and well paid, they, like other exhibition dancers, opened several cabarets under their own names: the Sans Souci in late 1913, Castles in the Air in late 1914, and a summer place, Castles-by-the-Sea, in 1915. From these strongholds in New York, they ventured forth to other cities, which hailed them amid an avalanche of publicity and attention. As part of their enormous teaching function, the Castles produced dance instruction films, wrote a book, *Modern Dancing*, and proffered advice through the nation's newspapers and magazines.

Representing the freedoms of urban life as well as respectability, the Castles found favor in many circles. They not only appeared in the cabarets, they also earned the name Society Dancers because of their ties to the upper class. They instructed them in the new dances and appeared at their fetes. Society saw the Castles as more refined than the usual run of cabaret performers and invited them to entertain at soirees in their Fifth Avenue and Long Island homes. Among others, they performed for Mrs. Stuyvesant Fish, an acknowledged society figure of her day, and the equally prominent Elbert Garys.[37] Irene painted a lucrative picture of their early days. "We were being invited to more and more soirees at three hundred dollars a piece and we very often made nine hundred dollars an evening before we went to work at the Café de l'Opera," she wrote.[38] At twenty-five to one hundred dollars per hour, the ballroom performers found private instruction a path to the mansions of the rich.

The Castles developed their connections to the upper class by inaugurating an exclusive establishment for the instruction of society and its young in the intricacies of the modern steps. The fashionable Elizabeth Marbury, along with two well-placed friends, Anne Morgan and Elsie de Wolfe, proposed the idea for a Castle House in late 1913. The establishment, located across from the Ritz Carlton Hotel on Forty-sixth Street, would serve as a haven for the young heirs and heiresses of New York wealth. "The dance craze sweeping America needed regulation," Marbury noted, "an uplifting influence to bring dignity to it. Castle House would be that uplift, a place where their children could go to learn the dance without being exposed to the discredited elements."[39] Offering special dances during the holidays for the young home from the schools and colleges, Castle House taught young and old the model set by the Castles. "Refinement," explained the program, "is the key note of their method, thus it is hoped that Castle House will become the model school of modern dancing and that through its influence the spirit of beauty and art may be allied to the legitimate physical need of healthy exercise and of honest enjoyment."[40] Finding the idea sound, numerous society women agreed to act as patronesses and "pour tea during the afternoon for the dancers."[41] Mrs. Stuyvesant Fish, Mrs. T. J. Oakley, Mrs. Herman Oelrichs, Mrs. William G. Rockefeller, Mrs. Anthony Drexel, Jr., Mrs. Bourke Cochran, and Miss Elsie de Wolfe all lent their names and their time to the effort. The underlying motive of Castle House was to protect the select young from Broadway dancing cabarets to which they were already casting hopeful eyes and which they frequented at night and during the afternoons.

The refined air of the Castles and other exhibition dancers helped attract members of the most exclusive circles to the Broadway cafés. When they opened their Sans Souci on Broadway and Forty-second Street, the Castles drew a decidedly mixed crowd. Besides the usual Broadway celebrities, they attracted a gathering of society "such as a restaurant in Broadway seldom sees."[42] Many of their wealthy pupils attended, making the occasion, as one newspaper reported, "the most brilliant, at the same time cosmopolitan and best behaved, party any one ever saw."[43] The lure of the dance brought old and young society to Broadway, creating a pattern of interrelationships that broke down the rigid social and moral separations between the two worlds. Gossip columnist Plain Mary remarked that "the Avenue is invading the Broadway dance palaces and there are so many invaders in the army from 'the Avenue' that recently the society journals have taken notice of the fact."[44] Having already entered the public social realm on Fifth Avenue at the turn of the century, the wealthy were now less removed from the influences of popular and college peer culture and able to be more positively tied to them. By the early 1920s this social world had come to be known as café society.

Their social connections gave society dancers the air of upper-class refinement desired by the less exclusive cabaret audiences. In part, the Fifth Avenue image of the Castles allowed prosperous devotees to partake of the luxurious and well-publicized life of the very rich. Amid the splendor of large and well-appointed cabarets, women and men could now enjoy the symbols of economic success for the price of a meal and a drink. While this was not mass leisure, the cabaret and the dance craze extended the leisure patterns of the very wealthy to the middle class and to the Americanized children of the immigrants. The press extended the image by portraying the Castles as aristocrats, claiming that Irene came from a privileged background and that Vernon had noble forebears. Irene had had something of a fashionable small-town upbringing, but Vernon's pub-keeper father probably would have been extremely surprised at his rapid social elevation. However, just like their audiences, the Castles and other society dancers acted the part, living out in fantasy the life of the rich. Vernon, for example, had all "of the greatest personal charm and impeccable polish which made him at home on any level of society."[45] Their social graces, expensive formal evening wear, and elaborate buying habits enhanced their entrance to exclusive circles and gave them greater selling power to cabaret audiences. Others utilized the same technique. The Shuberts advertised Joan Sawyer as having "the aristocratic manner. This is one of her most potent charms, the secret of her wonderful popularity with society people. Her dancing is always exquisitely refined."[46] The cultivation of an aristocratic background and manner helped counter problems raised by the lower-class origins of the new steps and allowed the Castles to show the wealthy young how they could widen their capacities for passion and yet reconcile this letting go with traditional concepts of social responsibility and leadership, all on the level of personal style.

If status was no longer intimately associated with womanly restraint, how could dancers preserve their sense of social well-being now that women and men expressed themselves with their bodies? By connecting the dance to aristocratic imagery and performing it in expensive and luxuriously decorated cabarets, the dance public could distinguish itself from the lower classes and their women from the demeaning activities of their social inferiors. Expensive settings and glamorous dress thus compensated for the fear that sensuality would disturb their social status. Moreover, the notion of upper-class refinement precluded, by definition, an overly sensualized style of dance. The same *New York Review* that wrote of Joan Sawyer's aristocratic manner described her as one who "never allows the least suggestion of the sensual to enter into any of her dances."[47] By thus holding passion within the bounds of the genteel synthesis, these performers allowed sensuality to find an ambiguous place in the public life of the well-to-do.

In offering refinement, the cabaret dancers answered society's concern over the lower-class, hence sensual, origins of the new steps and made the dances acceptable for respectable women and men. Starting with rag steps, the Castles soon mixed European, South American, and waltz forms into their repertoire. Europe served as the source of culture; the Castles' first New York success, in fact, followed on the heels of their European popularity, and they always maintained that their tango had European, not vulgar Latin origins. Distinguishing their Parisian tango from the Argentinian, Vernon Castle had to admit that it originally came from Argentina. "Oh, it came from the Argentine. It is purely a native dance in its origins. Down there it has only three steps and is danced to just a kind of strumming." Their tango, however, came from Paris. "A man named Anchurina, who is secretary or something of the legation and the best dancer in Paris, started doing the Tango at Maxim's," and they took it from him.[48] In *Modern Dancing* Vernon noted that the tango actually originated in Spain but eventually ended up in Paris. The Argentinians adopted the dance from the Spaniards and then passed it on to the French, who toned down its sensual character, and "it bloomed forth a polished and extremely fascinating dance, which has not had its equal in rhythmical allurement since the days of the Minuet."[49]

Toward the black sources of the new dances, they were equally ambivalent and hesitant. James Reese Europe's Society Orchestra achieved a large measure of fame in white circles through its association with the Castles and the Broadway cabarets, and it is more than likely that Europe taught the Castles the fox-trot to slow down the faster one-step.[50] However, the band remained in a subordinate position to the Castles who were, after all, the stars. The Castles, not black ballroom performers, exhibited the new steps and instructed whites in the proper styles. For blacks to demonstrate the steps would have been too threatening to white audiences, just as mingling with black patrons in the cabarets in the 1910s was not even considered. It was not until the Harlem cabaret explosion of the 1920s that the relatively few black ballroom dancers appeared. The white dancers chose to intervene in the transmission of cultural forms to refine the display of passion associated with Latin and Negro dances. Writing of the shimmy, Irene described the role she had established for herself in the transmission of black dance forms:

We get our new dances from the Barbary Coast. Of course, they reach New York in a very primitive condition, and have to be considerably toned down before they can be used in the drawing-room. There is one just arrived now—

it is still very, very crude—and it is called "Shaking the Shimmy." It's a nigger dance, of course, and it appears to be a slow walk with a frequent twitching of the shoulders. The teachers may try and make something of it.[51]

Society dancers thus sought to eliminate the excesses of the new styles in creating suitable forms for their own culture. As the most notable exponents of the new steps, the Castles insisted on a dance of restrained sensuality so that it could be placed "before the public in its proper light."[52] Their success at this led Frederick Lewis Allen to remark that they "brought to the awkward and vulgar-looking dance forms of the current mode a combination of easy gayety and almost patrician fastidiousness. They sublimated the dance craze."[53]

Along with the notion of refinement in their dances, the Castles emphasized the gracefulness of dance as another means of controlling excessive bodily expression. The Castles considered grace another form of discipline, a retention of energy, and a purposeful direction of the body. "To be truly graceful in dancing," Vernon declared, "presupposes a certain stateliness, a dignity of movement that has charm rather than gymnastic skill behind it." With this in mind, it was easy to conclude that "shuffles and twists and jumps are no longer words to be used in connection with dancing." By making the dance "the poetry of motion" and the dancer "a poetical architect," the Castles followed a path common in their time. They attached to the body spiritual and ethereal values, giving the dance a noble, almost genteel purpose.[54]

The Castles followed their own prescriptions. Their numerous variations and figures for the one-step and tango allowed for the freedom of individual expression, while their overall dance style was smooth and restrained. Their one-step, a variation of the turkey trot, was shorn of much of the arm pumping and body shaking of the original. "When I say *walk*," Vernon commanded, "that is all it is. Do not shuffle, do not bob up and down or trot. Simply *walk* as softly and smoothly as possible, taking a step to every count of the music."[55] Even in the tango they envisioned grace rather than fiery passion. "It should be practiced frequently, so as to make it smooth," they said. The Castles also moderated the dips that revealed too much of the woman's leg, brought women's pelvic regions dangerously close to male bodies, and placed women in a sexually suggestive position. It "is hardly more than bending the knee," Irene and Vernon wrote, "it does not mean an exposure of silk stocking, or should not, if the dancing costume is properly cut." Most important, "it should not be done in a romping spirit."[56]

Under the tutelage of society dancers, the dancing public increased and the steps themselves began to change. The one-step replaced the more exaggerated turkey trot in early 1913, and the general excesses of the dance subsided a bit. The fox-trot, introduced in 1914, readily became the leading dance, for it allowed variations in movement and steps, with places to feel the beat without being too raucous or too expressive. Looking over the 1913–1914 season, the very height of the public renaissance of dancing, the *New York Times* observed that the earlier turkey trot had been reformed and was no longer danced. The newspaper said it was true that the turkey trot of 1912 "smacked strongly of the Dahomeny-Bowery-Barbary Coast form of revelry, but since then it has been trimmed, expurgated, and spruced up until now it is quite a different thing."[57]

CASTLES IN THE AIR: NEW WOMAN AND THE FUN HOME

Comparing the Castles to their nearest rivals, music publisher E. B. Marks explained that "the Castles were a sprite and a steel spring; Maurice and Walton were a tiger and a woman."[58] Florence Walton's beauty was more voluptuous compared to Irene's elegant girlishness, and she and Maurice were both swarthier in complexion. Maurice and Walton represented the underlying currents of sensuality that emerged as significant possibilities for the dance and for men and women during the 1910s. Although born in Brooklyn, Maurice Mouvet was often represented as either French, Belgian, or Spanish, and he was considered Latin and a romantic devil with women, a person for respectable women to desire and fear at the same time.[59] His image initially arose from the apache, a passionate lower-class French exhibition dance, which he introduced at Louis Martin's in 1910. He described its appeal as "an intensely brutal dance of realism, of primitive passion; as a picture of life in the raw it has beauty and strength."[60] Apart from this dance Maurice stood as an exponent of grace as a solution to the problems posed by the new dances. But there was always something lurking, perhaps the image of the dangerous Latin gigolo, which placed him second in public estimation to the Castles.

The clean-cut image of the Castles paralleled the tone they established for the dance and raised them to the top of the society dancer profession. Explaining their popularity, Irene concluded, "I think it was because both sides [reformers and dancers] regarded us as their champions. We were clean-cut; we were married and when we danced there was nothing suggestive about it."[61] The youthful innocence that they projected diminished much of the fearful potential of the dance and helped to form an image of the new woman that was acceptable to an upper-middle and upper-class following. "There was always something unimpassioned, cool, not cold, in their eyes," remembered Gilbert Seldes, the lively arts critic for the *New Republic*. "It was certainly the least sensual dancing in the world; the whole appeal was visual."[62] The *Dramatic Mirror* concurred: "The Castles' specialty was very, ve-e-ry informal, don't you know. Personal, chatty, yet smartly aloof—and all that sort of thing."[63] It was something more too. The Castles transformed potentially dangerous impulses into youthful fun and healthy exercise. They had, in Irene's estimation, "the sense of humor that permeated our dancing, the great sense of bubbling joy we shared when we danced." Their tango was clean fun. "If Vernon had ever looked into my eyes with smoldering passion during the tango," she recalled, "we should have both burst out laughing."[64]

Through her association with expressive social dance, Irene promoted the image of the new woman as distinctly freer than her mother's generation, yet still essentially wholesome. She and Vernon channeled these impulses into a new, expanded vision of the fun home. Reversing the nineteenth century's view of women as frail and motherly, Irene symbolized the active, free, and youthful women of the twentieth century. "Dancing is the language of the body," she wrote. "It is, as in social dancing, the exponent *par excellence*, of the joy of living. It is the natural and contagious outlet for a hilarious and youthful spirit."[65] Dancing also helped one achieve freedom, she thought, because it kept one young, beautiful, and healthy, the exact opposite of her vision of nineteenth-century women: "The woman who dances does not need other beauty aids; beauty will seek her . . . for when a woman is dancing she is happily unconscious, and therefore easily carrying out all the exercises taught by beauty experts."[66] Older women could also achieve the beauty that glorified youth. Mrs. Douglas Crane, an exhibition performer, echoed Irene in her announcement that "dancing should continue from early youth to old age. In the realm of the dance there is no old age, however, for this art is the royal road to beauty and happiness and perennial youth."[67] Whatever her age, the new woman could be healthy, slim, and attractive to men. Slim and active themselves, the Castles hoped that social reformers would agree with doctors that "dancing is not only a rejuvenator of good health and spirits, but a means of preserving youth, prolonging life, and acquiring grace, elegance and beauty."[68] Unlike the image of their mothers, who tended toward matronly heaviness and psychological enervation, modern women found a release from the physical and psychological restraints of the past through body expression. Through dancing, women, according to Irene, could recreate and expand themselves along new lines. From the image of fat women stepping their way to slenderness, Irene moved to sick women troubled by inactivity dancing their way to health and meaning. Fighting with "unnatural lines of figures and gowns," they were at the same time "warring against fat, against sickness, and against nervous troubles. For we are exercising." In the end they were making themselves "lithe and slim and healthy" and, like Houdini, stepping out from many of the old bonds of Victorianism. "These are things that all the reformers in the world could not do for us."[69] The dance was thus more than physical; it was also psychological in its appeal to women who wanted to be new.

Irene Castle embodied the paradox of this new woman's increased expressiveness and properly channeled sexual impulses. She showed audiences how to alter traditional sex roles and create a life lived emotionally closer to men. She fought the sexual double standard and helped widen the conception of women's role. She did what appeared impossible in the old culture: she merged the virgin to the vamp and validated a wider range of behavior. In the forefront of changes in fashions, Irene played out new options and set fashions that were copied by urbane women of fashion and by other professional dancers. She was the first to bob her hair, and although she did it for surgery, others chose to interpret it as a symbol of youthful winsomeness. The *Boston Traveler* commented that Mrs. Castle had "established a type of American girl." Now "girls in the United States dieted, exercised and practised to become tall, dainty, slim and willowy. They sheared their locks and called it a 'Castle Clip.' "

Breaking sexual barriers by attending boxing matches and other formerly all-male sporting events, she proclaimed, "I am most enthusiastic about all forms of sport. I really understand the finer points of our great games and believe that women should be more interested in them."[70]

Top fashion magazines featured Irene in one issue after another because of her stylish apparel and her views on women's clothing. She advocated freer fashions for women, pronouncing that modern dance "has come boldly to the front and demanded, and won, sensible styles." She believed that the power of the dance would force cruel corsets, tight shoes, hats like peach baskets, heavy petticoats, and stiff-boned collars to give way to easy-moving skirts with slits in them, collarless frocks, and subtly cut, freely falling gowns. Because of the universal addiction to the new steps, "the trained or awkwardly tight frock has been relegated to the past," and the "gowns most in vogue this year are youthfully simple, full about the ankles and short enough to show the feet." Styles should be, as the dancing frock itself, "first of all, comfortable. It should permit absolute freedom of movement." In sum, Castle reasoned that the dance was responsible for the end to clothing that "trussed them [women] like fowls for the roasting."[71]

With her freer dances, hair styles, clothing, and manner of living, Irene projected an elegantly youthful and girlish image. Her favorite frock combined youth and innocence in its "girlish little girdle with its little knot of pink baby roses that fasten it." Her dress styles matched her most treasured portrait, a picture in *Town and Country* depicting her as a winsome, boyish American girl—a pal. Instead of producing an effect of mature sensuality, her dances and her fashions created an image of an elegant American girl, forever flowing and forever free. While women of her generation differentiated themselves from their mothers, they were not to synthesize passion fully with womanhood. As reformers and social critics decried the increase of white slavery brought on by urban amusements and the city streets, the Castles offered an image of women as youthful gamins who could not possibly be subject to the tragedies the reformers feared. Even to dabble with the female sensuality that was expressed in the dance required that women become girls, safely isolated from the dangerous knowledge they were beginning to acquire. As young girls, they were still able to be subordinated by more dominant males.[72]

Irene demonstrated that women could handle the culturally and personally troublesome problems of passion associated with the new life of black dances and freedoms by retreating from womanhood with its associations with sin, to the model of the young girl, who by her very youth made dangerous activities more acceptable. By following her dictates on womanhood, women in her audience would know how far to go in attracting a man without ruining the game and losing the quarry. By restraining herself as an elegant girl, a young woman would be exciting enough to attract, yet innocent enough not to be associated with sinful lower-class sexuality, and the demanding quality that a mature woman might present. She could achieve marriage but in a recreated way. And the marriage she achieved could be much like the Castles' was said to have been, one in which leisure and work blended and the man, attracted by the qualities of the woman, spent more time with her in fun and pleasure. The Castles thus offered the vision of a more romantic conventional marriage. Women could search for meaning by expending their energies in leisure, an area that need not stand in opposition to marriage or work. In reversing the older stereotype of woman as mother, women could now devote their energies to remaking themselves, finding vitality in creating youthful selves, who could attract but would not need to demand and thus drive their men away. Their solution to the inactivity and unhappiness of their mothers' generation lay in self rather than in social reformation. Women could be youthful and vital yet still remain proper wives.

As Irene herself noted, the couple's vogue derived from their portrayal of a couple involved in a marriage of continual public romance. The *Chicago Examiner* noted, "They look more like a pair of school-children out on a frolic than like a staid man and wife in dancing as a business. And that's one of the charms of their work."[3] This reoriented family actually gave legitimacy to new freedoms for men and women and made them safely compatible with the bourgeois commitment to the home and duty. Irene conveyed images of rebellion from the social constraints of the day. She danced black dances, made fabulous sums of money, associated with the wealthy and with blacks, became a leading woman of her day, and defied the conventions to advocate that women could publicly cross the barrier of the double standard and enjoy life more equally with men. She also showed that these new freedoms could revitalize marriage without destroying it or men's and women's character. Despite her formidable business success and drive for self-achievement, Irene always depicted Vernon as the creator of their success and fame. She took a back seat to him, picturing herself as a young married woman out on a lark, enjoying herself immensely with her husband. It was toward these ends that her personal freedoms of dress, hair, and dance tended. They made her exciting to men, capable of attracting a successful man who could devote time and energy to his wife in leisure. For women, this was a change from the images they carried of their parents' lives. Part of the ability to attract men was to make oneself attractive. For this, Irene showed them how they could cross racial and cultural barriers and adopt some of the elements of both high and low life.

By interpreting the new impulses as a means to revitalize the private home rather than the public world of men, the new woman demonstrated that she would not destroy male achievement or the social order. Vernon, for example, benefited from being married to Irene in the public eye. Instead of representing the dangers of new freedoms, he too showed that success was compatible with pleasure, if one found the right type of girl. As Irene noted, Vernon was capable of conveying an interest in women, clothes, consumption, and pleasure without losing masculine character. "He wore his clothes with a distinguished flair and had the ability which few men have," she recalled, "of being able to wear jewelry without being ostentatious or looking effeminate."[74] Neither a gigolo nor an "effeminate Latin," Vernon showed that once the home was made secure, a man need not become enervated by expressive pleasure with women but instead could have fun in an expanded home and remain a business-minded dancer, a success in the entertainment world. Instead of pursuing a wasted life, he channeled his pleasures into marriage and leisure and expanded the image of the eternally romantic, personally challenging marriage, and kept his other eye on business. The fun home and the fun couple became the dream vision of the new model life, and the private home, rather than the public world, absorbed the new personal expectations.

Amid the cabaret world of luxury and sensuality, the Castles stood out as elegant and graceful figures who legitimized pleasure, sexuality, and expenditure of impulses and returned some of that legitimacy to the institution of the cabaret. They helped make social dancing legitimate and thereby expanded the activity to a public much wider than anyone had ever dreamed. Dancing became a mass leisure activity. They also showed the public how to combine personal freedom, refined eroticism, and social duty. At the height of their popularity, World War I intervened to end their professional life together. As a patriotic native of Great Britain, Vernon enlisted in the Royal Air Force in 1915 and crashed to his death two years later while teaching recruits to fly. Decorated for bravery, Vernon showed that dancing and fighting were compatible. Irene's energies also turned toward the conflict. In 1916 she entered motion pictures in *Patria*, a preparedness serial, which showed her fighting off the symbolic attacks of the Germans on womanhood, which threatened to engulf her in sensuality and waste. Throughout their career, they uplifted the low-life sensuality of the city and made it eligible for the home. In doing so, they also made possible the expansion of dancing and the exploration of body which was to come in the following years. The high-class dance teams remained atop the cabaret entertainment world into the 1930s.

NOTES

1. F. Scott Fitzgerald, "The Perfect Life," in *The Basil and Josephine Stories* (1928; reprint, New York, 1976), pp. 158–59.

2. *New York Times*, March 1, 1914, p. 5.

3. Jesse Lasky, with Don Weldon, *I Blow My Own Horn* (Garden City, N.Y.: Doubleday, 1957), p. 86.

4. "The Craftsmen, 1914," as in Ellis Loxley, "The Turkey Trot and Tango in America, 1900–1920." *Educational Dance* (December 1939): 8, in Turkey Trot Folder, New York Public Library Dance Collection, Lincoln Center.

5. Troy Kinney and Margaret Kinney, *The Dance* (New York: Frederick A. Stokes, 1914), p. 269.

6. Russel Nye, *The Unembarrassed Muse* (New York: Dial Press, 1970), p. 327.

7. Frederick Lewis Allen, "When America Learned to Dance," *Scribner's Magazine* 102 (September 1937): 13; for Britain, see Arthur H. Franks, *Social Dance, A Short History* (London: Routledge and Kegan Paul, 1963), p. 161.

8. Allen Dodworth, *Dancing and Its Relation to Education and Social Life* (New York: Harper & Bros., 1885), p. 145.

9. Ibid., p. 146.

10. Ibid., p. 35; Franks, *Social Dance*, p. 176.

11. Franks, *Social Dance*, p. 130; Dodworth, *Dancing*, p. 41.

12. Philip J. S. Richardson, *The Social Dances of the Nineteenth Century in England* (London: Herbert Jenkins, 1960), p. 113.

13. Ibid., p. 119; Frederick Lewis Allen, "When America," p. 13, and Franks, *Social Dance*, p. 165, note the importance of the Boston but provide little analysis.

14. Sylvia Dannett and Frank Rachel, as quoted in Marshall Stearns and Jean Stearns, *Jazz Dance: The Story of American Vernacular Dance* (New York: Macmillan, 1968), p. 95.

15. Mark Sullivan, *Our Times* (New York: Charles Scribner's Sons, 1932), 4: 242; Stearns and Stearns, *Jazz Dance*, p. 96. Franks, *Social Dance*, pp. 178–79, traces the origin of the tango to the tangano, an African dance transplanted to Central America and then farther south by the slaves. They grafted on European forms and developed a new style.

16. Nye, *Unembarrassed Muse*, pp. 317–38, traces ragtime to Babe Connors' Castle Club in St. Louis.

17. Sullivan, *Our Times*, 4: 242–43.

18. Samuel B. Charters and Leonard Kunstadt, *Jazz: A History of the New York Scene* (Garden City, N.Y.: Doubleday, 1962), pp. 22–37, essays the career of James R. Europe.

19. Ibid., pp. 45–46.

20. Maud Cuney-Hare, *Negro Musicians and Their Music* (Washington, D.C.: The Associated Publishers, 1936), p. 133.

21. Vernon Castle, quoted in Franks, *Social Dance*, p. 176. Nye, *Unembarrassed Muse*, p. 327, and Sigmund Spaeth, *A History of Popular Music in America* (New York: Random House, 1948), p. 369, comment on the change in music.

22. *New York Times*, May 3, 1915, VI, p. 5.

23. Franks, *Social Dance*, p. 176.

24. The words to "Everybody's Doin' It Now" can be found in Sullivan, *Our Times*, 4: 252. Irving Berlin, Inc. does not permit reproduction of lyrics.

25. The dances thus matched a larger search for primitiveness in the culture, as suggested by the interest in nature. For the latter, see Higham, "The Reorientation of American Culture in the 1890's," *Writing American History*, and Roderick Nash, *The Call of the Wild: 1900–1916* (New York: Braziller, 1971).

26. Stearns and Stearns, *Jazz Dance*, p. 96.

27. Julian Street, *Welcome to Our City* (New York: John Lane, 1913), p. 10, and George Dodworth, the society instructor, in Ellis Loxley, "The Turkey-Trot and Tango in America," p. 8.

28. Arthur Marwick, *The Deluge, British Society and the First World War* (London: Bodley Head, 1965), p. 143.

29. Allen, "When America Learned to Dance," p. 13; Sullivan, *Our Times*, 4: 234. Perhaps this explains the fascinating argument over the healthfulness of dancing by the middle-aged. The *New York Times*, December 20, 1913, p. 12, ran an editorial, "Elderly Men as Dancers," attacking the *Journal of the American Medical Association's* stand against middle-aged people doing the tango. Asking, "Are all men over fifty to give up everything to the youngsters, who in these days are such a stupid, self-satisfied lot of fellows, that all girls actually prefer seniors?" the *New York Times*, December 28, 1913, V, p. 2, produced its own expert, Dr. Luther H. Gulick, who validated youthful activity by middle-aged men as a break from their usual sedentary regimen: "But just because a man is middle aged," Gulick said, "he mustn't think it is dangerous for him to dance at all. As a rule it will do him good if he goes at it by degrees."

30. Henry Canby, *Age of Confidence* (New York: Holt, Rinehart & Winston, 1934), p. 71.

31. Mary Stewart Cutting, "Dance-Mad Billy," *McClure's* 45 (September 1915): 223. For more on the reevaluation of marriage, see Elaine Tyler May, *Great Expectations: Marriage and Divorce in Post-Victorian America* (Chicago: University of Chicago Press, 1980).

32. For material on cabaret dancers, see Maurice Mouvet, *The Art of Dancing* (New York: G. Shirmer, 1915); John Murray Anderson, as told to Hugh Abercrombie Anderson, *Out Without My Rubbers, The Memoirs of John Murray Anderson* (New York: Library Publishers, 1954), pp. 1–56; Jane Ardmore, *The Self-Enchanted, Mae Murray: Image of an Era* (New York: McGraw-Hill, 1959), pp. 2–70; Irving Shulman, *Valentino* (New York: Simon and Schuster, 1968), pp. 75–87; Ada Patterson, "A New Tango Star," *Green Book* (April 1914): 609–15.

33. "The Dance Craze—If Dying—Is a Very Healthy Invalid," *Vanity Fair* 2 (February 1915): 34.

34. *Dramatic Mirror*. June 30, 1915, untitled clipping, Vernon and Irene Castle Scrapbooks, R. Locke Collection, New York Public Library Theatre Collection, Lincoln Center. *Atlanta Journal*, March 16, 1913, p. 5, said, "Of all the cabaret dancers who have appeared on the restaurant horizon Vernon Castle is the most popular. Society has taken him up and it is no exaggeration to say that he is the most sought after dancing teacher in America. He has dozens of private pupils in the Social Register."

35. For their life story, see Irene Castle, as told to Bob and Wanda Duncan, *Castles in the Air* (Garden City, N.Y.: Doubleday, 1958), and the large collection of scrapbooks in the New York Public Library Theatre Collection, Lincoln Center.

36. Allen, "When America Learned to Dance," p. 14, makes the Castles too responsible for changing the dances rather than viewing them as fulfilling public need.

37. Castle, *Castles*, p. 72.

38. Ibid.

39. Ibid., p. 88.

40. "Program" for Castle House, approximately December 1913, Vernon Castle Scrapbooks.

41. Castle, *Castles*, p. 88.

42. *Broadway Banter*, approximately December 1913, Vernon Castle Scrapbooks.

43. *New York Herald*, December 7, 1913, p. 5; an unidentified newspaper clipping, approximately December 1913, Vernon Castle Scrapbooks, has a page list of social luminaries who attended, including the Fishes, Goulds, Harrimans, Oelrichs, Astors, Chandlers, Rhinelanders, Dukes, and Vanderbilts.

44. Plain Mary, "All for the Ladies," *Variety*, November 14, 1913, p. 13. She also reported on the infatuation of a society woman with a Latin dancer: "His fascinations are many and the latest of the fair sex to succumb to them is married and a resident of one of the ultra-exclusive hotels on the Avenue."

45. Castle, *Castles*, p. 44.

46. *New York Review*, March 7, 1914, n.p., clipping in Joan Sawyer clippings, R. Locke Collection. The *Review* was a Shubert organ, and we can see the image they tried to create.

47. Ibid.

48. "Tango According to Castles," *Metropolitan Magazine* (June 1913): 3, in Castle Scrapbooks.

49. Mr. and Mrs. Vernon Castle, *Modern Dancing* (New York: Harper & Bros., 1914), pp. 83–84.

50. Noble Sissle Interview, August 1971.

51. *Dancing Times*, untitled clipping, approximately 1918 or 1919, in Castle Scrapbooks.

52. Mr. and Mrs. Castle, *Modern Dancing*, foreword.

53. Allen, "When America Learned to Dance," p. 15.

54. Mr. and Mrs. Castle, *Modern Dancing*, pp. 38–39.

55. Ibid., p. 44.

56. Ibid., p. 136.

57. *New York Times*, January 4, 1914, V, p. 8.

58. E. B. Marks, *They All Sang* (New York: Viking Press, 1935), p. 166.

59. Maurice Mouvet, *Art of Dancing*, p. 38.

60. Ibid., p. 35.

61. Castle, *Castles*, p. 86.

62. Quoted in ibid., p. 87.

63. *Dramatic Mirror*, June 30, 1915, untitled clipping, Castle Scrapbooks.

64. Castle, *Castles*, p. 87.

65. Mr. and Mrs. Castle, *Modern Dancing*, p. 164.

66. Ibid., p. 151.

67. *New York Sun*, June 28, 1914, p. 16.

68. Mr. and Mrs. Castle, *Modern Dancing*, foreword.

69. Ibid., pp. 145–46.

70. *Boston Traveler*, October 28, 1914, *New York Review*, May 15, 1915, n.p., clippings, Castle Scrapbooks.

71. Mr. and Mrs. Castle, *Modern Dancing*, pp. 144–45; unidentified newspaper (Milwaukee, Wisconsin), March 24, 1914, and Mrs. Vernon Castle, "Mrs. Vernon Castle's Gowns," *Green Book* (June 1915), n.p., both in Castle Scrapbooks.

72. *Green Book* (June 1915), in Castle Scrapbooks.

73. *Chicago Examiner*, November 12, 1913, n.p., clipping in Castle Scrapbooks.

74. Castle, *Castles*, p. 44.

6 SOME OF THESE DAYS: SOPHIE TUCKER, THE FRIENDLY ENTERTAINER

> When you leave me,
> Ya know its gonna grieve me
> Gonna miss your big fat mamma, your fat mamma,
> Some of these days.
>
> Sophie Tucker's theme song[1]

Surveying the state of entertainment at the end of 1916, *Variety* found the cafés flourishing despite the decline in popularity of the society dancers. The prosperity of the cabaret engendered by the respectability and popularity of the dance teams convinced restaurant managers that café entertainment was firmly linked to show business and not merely an incidental attraction to dining.[2] Two factors probably helped this process. First, reformers united behind John P. Mitchel, a successful fusion candidate for mayor, who established a reasonable 2 A.M. curfew instead of Gaynor's unmanageable 1 A.M. limit, and by so doing disassociated the cafés from earlier all-night excess. Second, the Castles helped legitimize the cabaret. They heralded that personal vitality generated by contact with both the lower orders and the upper classes was compatible with the male pursuit of success and woman's secondary position in society and the home. By 1916, the cabaret public was willing to support expanded entertainment, chorus girl revues, and vaudeville headliners.

Sophie Tucker (1887–1966) was one of the first vaudeville headliners to move into the cabaret with any regularity. From a poor Hartford ethnic family, she saw in entertainment another variant on the reorientation of success and new roles for women and men. The informal world of entertainment in general, and the cabaret in particular, brought her into contact with the successful in urban life and opened up for her a wider world than was previously available for women from her social background. Conversely many ethnic entertainers found employment in the cabarets, as in vaudeville, acting out for native-born Americans and the children of immigrants, the role of vital, friendly entertainer, who was more expressive and less confined by Victorian restraints. In the informal setting of the cabaret, "vicarious action," in Goffman's words, "vicarious bohemianism," in mine, entertainers from outside the dominant classes portrayed the traditional American ideals of personal liberation from authority and the past in the realm of leisure, just at a time when social and economic life had reached peaks of rationalization and hierarchy. By the 1910s, entertainers like the Castles and Sophie Tucker were a new aristocracy, making a success connected with personal liberation accessible to much wider audiences. As part of the trend toward private rather than public liberation, performers made their private personalities part of the public performance. The cabaret raised this to new heights, and it was Sophie Tucker who mastered the art of being the personable performer, the friendly entertainer.

IDOLS OF CONSUMPTION[3]

In 1916 vaudeville headliner and ragtime singer Sophie Tucker allowed herself to be convinced of the possibilities of the cabarets by her agent, William Morris. From that date until 1922, she appeared in her own Sophie Tucker Room in Reisenweber's, alternating in a variety of vaudeville theatres in New York City and around the nation. In 1925 she opened Sophie Tucker's Playground, a midtown nightclub, and after its demise, until the end of her career, she remained a major nightclub attraction. Her success in both arenas signals parallels between vaudeville and the cabaret. Although both portrayed a vision of urban life of consumption and pleasure with the star as the personal embodiment of this new myth of success, the cabarets could feature fewer performers and bring out in fact the myth presented on the stage. While the cabaret borrowed many vaude-villians, it presented them in closer proximity to the audience, and thus in a manner more conducive to highlighting their personalities. When reviewing the "Brazilian Nut," a comedy dancer, *Variety* observed that she failed in vaudeville because she could not use her bubbling personality to breach the barriers to the audience. Atop the Century Roof, however, the story was different. There she could actually mix with customers and display her infectious traits.[4] In the cabaret, audiences demanded more of the performer than of their performance. Tucker always greeted people with the "big hello," said a few words to them, and circulated about the room. The illusion fostered by the café was that the entertainers lived there, and the public was invited to drop in to see how they lived, offstage as well as on, sitting at a table, dancing, or talking to friends.[5] This well-exploited feature of the cabaret made it a prominent place to enjoy celebrities at their leisure, removed from the more formal and differentiating apparatus of the stage and the demands of playing a theatrical role. Personality triumphed over organization, and the private became much more accessible to the public world, in fact, often became the public role.

Seated at the same level as customers, celebrities were accessible. Murray's advertised itself as a playground where performers stopped in to sup and "incidentally gave just regular folks a close up glimpse of some favorite leading lady or man." The glimpse was not all, for all shared an equality with famous theatrical personages. Even "people who dance professionally for fabulous salaries," claimed the advertisement, "mingle democratically with other guests on the revolving floor for relaxation." Churchill's presented itself as the place to witness and socialize with the famous, "the men and women most talked of in society," such as "the famous theatrical folk—the well known business and professional men of New York, with their wives."[6] In seeking proximity with these personalities, the cabaret public was both grasping for tangible clues on how to lead the life of leisure and expressiveness and also investing their performers with these fabled features. The closeness and informality of the setting reveals a symbiotic pursuit of fun, a feature that made these performers more than just entertainers. In *The Presentation of Self in Everyday Life*, Erving Goffman distinguishes the backstage private area of a performance where the entertainers prepare for the event and where they are allowed to keep a different self free from the audience. In the public, stage area, however, the performers present a different face entirely, one calculated to please or engage the audience.[7] This separation of private and public served as the basis for the theatre. Actors and actresses played the roles on the stage and then retired backstage where they removed their makeup. Although the cabarets had their backstage areas, the line between the public performing area and the private backstage was blurred. Entertainers sat in the audience for a drink, greeted customers, and danced on the floor. They created the role of host or hostess, merging the private and public selves of the entertainer. They were always on display.

The elevation of the performer's personality as an object of emulation was made possible by the rise in respectability and status of the café entertainer. In an effort to raise the performers' standing, cabarets abandoned many of the practices associated with saloon backrooms. In the saloons, for instance, audiences rewarded underpaid entertainers by throwing an unspecified sum of coins onto the stage. If the performance was appreciated, the number of coins rose, but if the audience disliked an artist, the latter might have to endure the humiliation of receiving little or nothing. In the cabaret, however, artists received regular salaries. Cabarets also required patrons to remain seated during a singing performance rather than dancing to the music. *Variety* wondered why: "Since it is the dancing floor that draws the crowd, why not let 'em dance all the while."[8] Managers probably preferred that audiences not ignore the singer, and they also realized that a seated audience was likely to order more drinks. In either case, the singer got more attention. Entertainers themselves often sought respectability commensurate with their new place in the social hierarchy, and they utilized European imagery and bookings to get it. Initially the public considered rathskeller acts backroom entertainers, but in the lobster palaces, the term changed to *café singers*. By 1913, it had become *cabaret artist*. Pauline Loomis, considered the queen of the cabaret, went so far as to bill herself as a "delineator of high-class songs." Performers also earned status by going abroad. According to columnist Karl K. Kitchen, "It is the ambition of every cabaret artist to get an engagement across the rolling [seas]. It means 'class.' " Achieving European renown increased the artists' leverage with American audiences. This had been the case with dancers, "the aristocracy of restaurant life," who owed much of their domestic success to their having entertained the crowned heads of Europe.[9] In the twenties a bevy of black entertainers traveled overseas before receiving domestic acceptance, but it was Sophie Tucker who experienced all of the aspects of cabaret life. She called her act "Sophie Tucker and Her Five Kings of Syncopation" and always considered her varied European tours the high points of her long career.[10]

While the elevation of the entertainers' status made them suitable figures for audience identification, the cabaret structure itself enforced the necessity of a strong and recognizable personality. In the first place, the setting brought the entertainer and audience closer, and thus permitted personal qualities to operate. Second, according to *Variety*, a forceful personality was needed to overcome the very informality of the café. "In a theater, cold-sober, of course anything would do," the paper proclaimed, but in a nightclub "a place [to] while the hours away after the cares of the day are thrown off . . . it's difficult to arrest attention from a tired brain or a besotted individual."[11] The cheery smile and personal banter helped performers reach out and involve an audience concerned with their own personal lives.

The café room built a tension between the entertainer trying to perform and the indifference of the audience. Personality bridged the gap in the café as it would in modern management, the bureaucratic structures of corporate life, and the mass urban world. To succeed, performers had to learn to understand and ultimately to manipulate the desires and feelings of the audience and themselves. By relying on their private selves as the bridge, the entertainers thus played out the dilemma of their audiences. Personality would help one stand out from the crowd, the institution, the mass, but at the cost of making the self more vulnerable to the approval of the crowd, and hence more passive. Just as the entertainers showed their constituents a way out of the entrapment of institutional roles and identifications, therefore, they also represented the potential for fitting in and adjusting to this organized society and succeeding within it.

The nature of the cabaret highlighted personality in other ways. Performers remained as long as they drew crowds. This gave them the advantage of relative permanency and the opportunity to build a genuine following. The direct contact, remarked *Variety*, "makes it a personal proposition," while the stability of the cafés offered acts benefits over vaudeville bookings and the impermanency of the road. Playing the same place saved acts agents' fees. "When it is considered that the act may play in one place for any number of weeks with none, or at least only one commission to pay," remarked the trade paper, "it is not hard to understand why this sort of entertainment is popular with the turns."[12] Furthermore, the longer stays encouraged associating the various acts with particular cafés. It was not as if they were merely playing a turn, but rather it seemed that for a brief time the act resided in one place to which they invited their public. Originally scheduled for four weeks at Reisenweber's, for instance, Sophie Tucker enjoyed enough traffic to remain for eight months instead of the four weeks for which she originally signed. The relief from the road and the feeling of being settled in New York was something she had not felt for a long time.[13] Tucker was not alone in the length of her engagements. Isabella Patricola and her eight-piece orchestra stayed three months in Wallick's, while as of January 1913, Sheehan, Adams, and Schoaff held the record at thirty-eight consecutive weeks at Shanley's, with time on their contract left. Doraldina, the hula dancer, contracted for thirty weeks with Montmartre at the end of 1916, and by 1917 they had named a room after her.[14]

Music publishers quickly recognized the potential for song boosting arising from this special feature of the café. "Cabaret singers," noted *Billboard*, "usually play to audiences that know them personally and visit the same place frequently." Residing in the town where they performed, they "seem far more convincing to them than the vaudeville star seen upon a given night and holding the stage for a limited time only." In a "cheerful mood," the audience listened to "the melody more easily than in a theater," *Variety* observed, and "a girl will ask an escort to take down the title of a number being sung." And making the rounds to boost their product, songwriters increased the familiarity with the song through audience identification with the creator. "If songs are 'there' and writers sing them at a cabaret," said *Billboard*, "the natural interest audiences take in listening to a writer's rendition, accounts for many quickly developed hits."[15]

Performers who succeeded in building a personal following earned the highest rewards in the cabarets. In the 1910s, star entertainers received a percentage of the gross over and above a minimum guarantee. The greater their draw, the larger the gross, the greater their ultimate salary. Consequently Maurice and Florence Walton and Joan Sawyer in 1914 in the Winter Garden's cafés received 25 percent of the gross receipts. At the Forty-fourth Street Theater, the Castles had a comparable agreement. In addition to their $1,500 weekly salary, they received a share of all receipts above that amount. The most successful attractions had rooms named after them, perhaps the highest reward, so that a particular café became their personal showcase. In the 1910s, the dance stars most readily achieved this status, for they were the era's names. The Castles featured themselves at the Sans Souci in 1914 and later at Castles in the Air and Castles-by-the-Sea, successfully conveying the image that their cafés were personal rooms to which they invited their friends, the public. Others followed the same policy. There were Chez Maurice and Doraldina's Hawaiian Room, and the 400 Room at Reisenweber's became known as "the Sophie Tucker Room," which it remained during her initial engagements there. In the twenties the policy grew with the expansion of the cabarets, and many stars had clubs bearing their own names.[16]

To build and keep a personal following, performers played the roles of hosts and hostesses and thereby reinforced the sense of residing in a particular establishment and inviting the public to the intimate confines of their homes. The practice began with the aristocratic dance teams, who helped legitimize the café with their exclusive drawing-room air. Louis Bayo, "the Tango King of Paris," for example, advertised his stay at Bustanoby's Domino Room as if it were a formal invitation to a dinner party: "Mlle. Paulette Duval, Mr. Bayo's Dancing Partner, will receive with him." Similarly a local newspaper described Joan Sawyer as presiding over the Persian Gardens "with the grace and dignity of a society hostess on upper Fifth Avenue." She had an aristocratic image in order to refine the new dances, but as new aristocrats these deities of popular culture made themselves available to the public. Joan Sawyer was a queen, but a queen in a public house where all could see and meet her. By bringing herself into personal relations with her public, this near "high-priestess of a mystic cult" gave her public the intimate knowledge of the new-style popular elegance and consumption.[17]

While the dance stars refined the image of the cafés, they also helped make them part of show business, reaching out to an even wider public. A performer like Sophie Tucker, gregarious, cosmopolitan, and sociable, could entertain a more diverse clientele to

bigger profits on Broadway. During her long engagements at Reisenweber's, Tucker perfected the style of the friendly entertainer. Her life
exemplified the show business maxim that success lay in "your ability
to make and keep friends." According to Tucker, the performers who
endured were the ones who were not stiffed shirts. To hold your audience, "you've got to give something of yourself across the footlights."
Starting out in more plebian burlesque and vaudeville, she could treat
everyone as an equal, even those she met in the higher confines of the
café. For her, success lay in the "big hello" and the "glad hand."
Early in her career she started an address book, recording the names
of everyone she met who was connected with show business or who
showed an interest in her. Periodically she sent cards to those in her
book, letting them know in advance to be sure to come and hear her.
One advance letter reminded her correspondent that she was returning to New York with new gowns and songs for a big family gathering
at Reisenweber's.[18]

Having built a successful vaudeville career, her expansive personality fit well into the cabaret. Mingling with the audience to shake
hands and say hello, Sophie demonstrated that the café was the place
to become friendly with entertainers, much like Jolson or other ethnic
performers made the Winter Garden, the Follies, and other forums
their personal showcases. In Jolson's words, "I used [the runway] to
get confidential with the audience by running up and down on this
platform, stopping for a chat with people, and by kidding the audience
and the performers in general. And the effect of this method of entertaining or of selling my goods was, and is to-day, truly remarkable."
Jolson's and Tucker's personal style suggests also that friendship and
personality were marketable items for entertainers. Sophie enjoyed
meeting and greeting customers. It was something she always did in
the cafés because she believed a performer owed it to the patron. "*I
know it's good business.*" Patrons enjoyed the friendly feeling which
performers conveyed in the cafés. Someone visiting town on business,
she wrote, liked to be able to return home to tell his friends at the local
fraternal organization that he had met her. This resulted in return
business. The next time she played his town, or he came to the big city,
she continued, he showed up again, "because he feels he's a friend of
mine."[19]

As the host or hostess of a cabaret, an entertainer's role included
the introduction of numerous personalities who had dropped in to sup,

drink, relax, and visit others in the business. Consequently giving the feeling of being on friendly terms with other entertainers was an important step on the road to success. In the cafés the owners made things happen, Tucker recalled. Whenever professional entertainers were there, he would ask them to get out on the floor and entertain the crowd. "It was free and impromptu," she noted, "and it created a feeling of real camaraderie." This informal approach to entertainers appears to be part of the original cabaret idea. Julius Keller of Maxim's claimed he started it to relieve Sunday evening slowness by inviting singers, songwriters, song pluggers, and well-known actors and actresses as bait for customers. Scattering them about the room for effect and the illusion of spontaneity, he would wine and dine them and then call on them to perform their specialties. Sophie's introduction to the cabaret floor occurred in this manner. She and husband, Frank Westphal, went cabareting in 1915, and Henry Fink, the owner of the Tokio, asked them to entertain as a personal favor. Finding the audience appreciative of the unrehearsed performance, Tucker institutionalized the practice in Reisenweber's with her advertised Sunday evening "Bohemian Nights," which showcased a number of aspiring professionals.[20] In one form or another, most cabarets used the idea, for the unscheduled nature of the entertainment increased audience participation, making it seem as if the drop-ins had spontaneously entertained that evening because of the particular chemistry generated between the performer and his or her friends in the audience. Audiences thus shared the illusion that their presence sparked the performance, as if they shared something truly intimate with the entertainer on that evening, as if they had been allowed to participate in the private hijinks of the celebrities' world.

The cabaret also expanded the lobster palaces' role as celebrity gathering spots and made stars even more accessible to the public in an atmosphere dominated by the theatrical world. Cabarets functioned as in-group gathering places for successful entertainers. Desiring to get something to eat after work, see others perform, and keep up with business news, professional performers in New York City found the cabarets social and business centers of their world. As the theatrical center of the nation, New York City also attracted performers in all fields—burlesque, vaudeville, theatre, and films—and everyone who traveled the road came to the city periodically, adding to the already high number of resident professionals. By the 1910s, more-over, entertainment in all fields was highly structured. Performers were controlled by agents and managers, and further bookings de-pended on meeting them, exuding the aura of success, and keeping one's name before the public. As a central institution in show busi-ness, the cabaret was one place to make such an impression. Under-neath the friendly atmosphere, cafés were very much part of the business aspirations of professionals. Cabarets also were places to celebrate in flush times, to show off their high position in show busi-ness. Conspicuous consumption was part of the definition of a star's success, for in entertainment, success remained highly variable. The cabaret also provided publicity for particular entertainment ventures. *Variety* observed that managers of several Broadway shows an-nounced special nights in cafés for the casts of their ventures to famil-iarize the public with the faces and names of their play. Both the restaurants and the shows benefited from the publicity. By the mid-1920s, when columnists and press agents became a highly organized industry, the cafés already served as the setting of the columns for they had become known as the places where entertainers played. The entire image of the cabaret as the place to mingle democratically with the stars served an underlying business purpose.[21]

This practice ultimately led to abuses. *Variety* reported that the Green Mill in Chicago scheduled performers from local theatres as a regular part of their bill. The Chicago café had started by using friends as drop-ins, but by the 1920s it held special theatrical nights where a star received special billing and a portion of the cover charges. Be-cause of the regular use of drop-ins, the Green Mill set aside tables for performers to keep audiences away, so that the entertainers would not be bothered by requests for autographs and other invasions of privacy, and the audiences would not have their illusions of friendly camara-derie shattered. As *Variety* put it, "It is next to impossible for a pro-fessional of any reputation to visit any of the cabarets in the Times Square section without drawing a request for a number or hit from the 'host' or 'hostess.' "[22]

Doubling was another practice that featured performers in cabarets outside their stage roles. Depending on the changing policies of the-atrical and vaudeville managers, many Broadway and cabaret stars had several engagements at a time. The large block of time between the dinner show (7 P.M.), the after-theatre supper show (11 P.M.), and, in the 1920s, the 1 A.M. show permitted actors and actresses to appear in a Broadway play and then hurry over to a café to perform a singing or dancing stint. This increased their salaries and exposure. Immediately after the war, Sophie Tucker doubled at the Winter Garden on Sunday nights while also doing Reisenweber's, and then played in *Hello Alexander* during the week. This could be profitable, but hectic: Cashing in on her appearances at Reisenweber's she had to hustle to meet her other commitments. For the dinner show she would go on at the restaurant, then jump into a taxi and race over to the Winter Garden where she changed her clothes and closed the bill of the Sunday evening concerts. Then back she came to Reisenweber's for the late supper show and another costume change. The dance stars pioneered this practice. The Castles appeared in *Sunshine Maid* and in Louis Martin's Café in 1913, and in 1915, they starred in *Watch Your Step* while hosting later in the evening in their own cabaret. By playing cafés after the show, entertainers gave audiences the opportunity to enjoy their stage favorites at close range and in a more intimate, less structured environment.[23]

In a variety of ways the cabaret served as an informal stage for the appreciation of entertainers as sociable friends enjoying a free and easy leisure life and not as purveyors of a stage role. The mixing with celebrities was one of the appeals of the cabarets, and with barriers down, audiences and stars shared a symbiotic search for personal vitality and a new definition of success. In *Vogue*, Clayton Hamilton discussed the function of celebrities in modern life. Entertainers, he emphasized, were more "alive than others," and this marked their greatness. They communicated vitality as an electric transfusion, for it "tingles in them, is a central and creative source of energy that radiates an influence electrical through all of the environing ether." Although Hamilton did not have the cabaret in mind, his imagery is fitting. Those who were physically close to celebrities in cafés shared their brightness, for "nothing can be dark that sits unshadowed in the sun; and no human being can be dull when he comes into contact with a super-man." For the ordinary person, the celebrity represented superior vitality, communicating "unconsciously a sense of life to many other people who seemed dead before he walked among them.''²⁴ In the cabaret, the personable entertainer communicated the possibilities of a new life to aspiring audiences, a new life associated with leisure and consumption.

SOPHIE STEPS OUT

A number of different entertainers from widely varied backgrounds acted out the role of friendly entertainer. Most of the major stars of the 1910s and 1920s were from recent immigrant origins, and they brought to the job a vitality unrestrained by, and thus appealing to, Victorians. Maurice Mouvet, the dancer, was vaguely European; Texas Guinan, the master of ceremonies of the 1920s, was Irish Catholic, as was singer Morton Downey; Gilda Gray was Polish; and one of the great entertainers of the 1920s, Jimmy Durante, rose from the Lower East Side in New York, the son of an Italian barber. Sophie Tucker, the embodiment of personality, was Jewish, and she joined a long line of Jewish performers onto the American stage in this period: Harry Richman, singer; Al Jolson, singer; Eddie Cantor, comedian-singer; Ethel Levy, singer; Ted Lewis, clarinetist and band leader; Ben Bernie, band leader; Nora Bayes, singer; George Jessel, actor, singer, and comedian; Belle Baker, singer; Lou Clayton, dancer. For all of them, Sophie Tucker perceived a common story. "We all sprang from the same source, the same origin," she told fellow performers at her golden jubilee dinner. "We were all swept to the shores of this country on the same tidal wave of immigration, the same flight from prejudice and persecution. Our life stories are pretty much the same"²⁵ Although black artists and audiences were still excluded from the informality of Broadway cabarets, those same cabarets provided an openness for ethnic entertainers, who were white and still vital. While Broadway represented the loosening hold of Victorian gentility over the well-to-do it also presented an alternative to the traditional immigrant world from which Tucker and so many others sprang. For Sophie, playing out the rootless subjectivism of urban life as a positive experience was a road out of the restrictions of a traditional culture for immigrants, and in her case for Jewish women. Because the Jews played such an important role in New York, we will look more closely at them, but the fact remains that together both immigrants of many backgrounds and the host society were helping to create a mass culture removed in essential aspects from past traditions, offering visions of freedom of self and escape from limits in urban culture.

Tucker was born into the Abusa household in 1887, on the road from Russia to the United States. Her father had earlier escaped military duty, and by 1893 the family settled in Hartford, Connecticut, where they ran the Abusa Home Restaurant, a popular spot for traveling show people. Family life centered on the business. Sophie, sister Anna, and brothers Moe and Phil, together with their mother, contributed to the family enterprise. A poor, Yiddish-speaking orthodox religious family, the Abusas observed kosher regulations and bound their lives by Jewish tradition and a daily round of hard and difficult work. Sophie had to accept the restaurant as part of being poor, but she resented the long hours and drudgery that kept her inside and away from playmates her own age.

The tightly knit home life was bound by the traditions of Jewish life. As head of the household, orthodox "papa" dominated the family and the business. Mama was subservient to his wishes and desires. In the Old World, the man studied the Torah and the woman kept the home, often overseeing at the same time business affairs in this world and taking care of most practical matters. New World experience created tension between reality and tradition.[26] In America, men were to work and provide for the family, yet papa never held onto the little money he made. In good times, he expanded his operations, only to lose when things went bad. Several times the family moved to New York, only to return to Hartford and the Abusa Home Restaurant. His gambling kept the family in debt, much to the chagrin of Sophie's mother and Sophie herself. Mama belabored him for being a *paskudnick* (worthless person) and advised her young daughter to marry a good husband who would be a good provider unlike the man she married.[27] The cycle continued. Mama scolded, papa lost, and the family seemed destined to remain poor. Clearly the man of authority was a good provider; without that, women would remain subordinate to domestic entrapment.

Show business seemed to be a life of greater independence. Unhappy in her own drudgery, desiring the approval of her playmates and the chance to play, Sophie rebelled against following in her mother's footsteps. She realized that earning a living was preferable to endlessly working in the family kitchen and waiting on other people as had her mother. "I knew I would do anything to get away from that." Sophie also had to circumvent her family's traditional view that the only proper role for women was marriage, babies, and helping one's husband. Her mother's life convinced her that the words rang hollow, but Sophie could not convince her that she did not want a career, but rather "a life that didn't mean spending most of it at the cooking-stove and the kitchen sink."[28]

In America in this period, women potentially had greater options. Tucker could marry whom she chose, an act deemed revolutionary in Jewish life. She might also seek her own career. At first Sophie sought escape from the home and approval by her peers through singing at a number of amateur programs at fairs and parks, where she was able to earn enough to contribute to the family. She was also drawn to the idea of fun with men, not the subservience she witnessed in her own home. At the age of sixteen, fat and unhappy, she married without parental approval a young neighborhood boy, Louis Tuck, the first person to ask her out and promise her the married life of fun about which she had been dreaming. When her parents found out, they ordered an orthodox wedding, but Sophie banked on the freedom from the family circle. While her mother scolded, Sophie recalled singing underneath her breath, "*I'd leave my happy home for you-oo-oo-oo.*"[29] Instead of being fun, however, her marriage replicated that of her parents. The first of many men in her life, Louis became another papa, weak and irresponsible, incapable of supporting a family, expecting to be served. Pregnant and in despair, Sophie moved back to the family restaurant, stuck in the kitchen supporting a man once again. After the baby's birth, with the sense of entrapment growing, Sophie made her break to New York and show business. It was not easy. Challenging the Jewish woman's traditional role of wife and mother, she left her baby with her parents and braved the neighborhood's malicious gossip (that she was no better than a whore) on the theatrical roads. Her justification was a traditional one: her independence would help support her parents and child, and she would return home only as a headliner, a success.

The theatrical life offered independence, acceptance, and the chance to realize success.[30] When Tucker began exploring the possibilities as a singer and comedienne, she was encouraged by performers from the Yiddish theatre and the American vaudeville stage. Yet she rejected an offer by Jacob Adler and Boris Thomashefsky to go onto the Yiddish stage. In her mind, the ethnic theatre remained too close to home and was too much associated with failure and drudgery. Her father had sold tickets for Yiddish shows and provided meals and sleeping quarters for actors, but usually was left with unsold tickets, canceled performances, or other mishaps. But she did notice this sort of thing was unusual with regular American productions.[31] If the Jewish stage meant failure, the American theatre signified money and success, security, and advancement. Sophie looked outward. Alone in New York in 1906, she found work in rathskellers, eventually leaving to join a burlesque wheel where she appeared in blackface and experienced the rigors of the road. Earning good notices, she soon advanced to vaudeville. Although her career proved ultimately successful, the beginnings were lonely and difficult. She earned her apprenticeship through craft and hard work, acting out her stifled maternal longings by caring for others and worrying about whether the independent road would always be so lonely.

Following a path similar to that of many other ethnic entertainers, although more successful than the usual run, Sophie represents that great influx of Jewish performers into American show business that occurred from the 1890s through the 1920s. In Sophie's background lay the Yiddish theatre and a Yiddish folk revival, already under way in the *shtetl* and towns of eastern Europe. The renaissance of the Yiddish language sparked a wider cultural ferment in poetry, the arts, the theatre, the press, and literature. By creating a wall of language and habit around a common ethnic identity, Yiddish culture at first was designed to protect Jewish tradition from assimilation. Yet once the children learned English in the schools, their cultural bent made them susceptible to the wider American life. They could enter the larger society through the avenues of culture.[32]

Jews had a long history of surviving as a lower-class group with middle-class economic values. Living in the ghettos of eastern Europe, forbidden to own land, they had served as middlemen for both peasants and the upper classes, trading and selling; they already knew how to function among hostile cultures and in an ethnically diverse society. The experience of survival had attuned them to the habits and desires of their oppressors, and, as with the American slaves or the Irish, often they knew the host society as well as they knew their own. When Papa Abusa arrived, he quickly set his sights on economic advancement and economic expansion. He was also aware of the economic potential for the family should Sophie enter show business. Consequently the economic drive established the desire to look outward and upward, while the release of the common folk by the Yiddish renaissance also released their longings for personal advancement and experience of the larger world.

Jews were also somewhat removed from Victorian sexuality. Marriage and procreation were positive goods, not necessary evils to prevent sin. Although eastern European Jews did not view premarital sex as permissible, they were far removed from the idea that the human body was inherently suspect. Between husband and wife, sex was to be fully enjoyed. Although orthodox Jews limited the times of the month when sex was acceptable, when they permitted it women had the right to sexual fulfillment as a positive good. The greater positive evaluation of the body found parallel expression in the communal tradition. One found religious expression through the community in folk festivals, mutual prayer, and religious celebrations where emotional vitality was prized. Games of chance and liquor, in moderate form, were part of the communal ritual. In this community, the role of women was ambiguous. While men devoted themselves to the Torah, women were left to run businesses and handle money. They developed a tradition of strength and practicality, but the religion demanded their subservience to the male head of the household. And until the end of the nineteenth century and even into the twentieth, marriages were arranged by parents and marriage brokers. Love, if it came, arrived after rather than before the ceremony. By the time they came to the United States, however, young men and women, much like Tucker, sought mates based on mutual love and affection. The nonascetic heritage permitted Jewish entertainers in America to engage in moral experimentation without the deepest burdens of the past, while the freeing of romantic love propelled them toward the fantasies of popular culture which they had a strong hand in fashioning.[33]

The Jewish presence in mass entertainment also had more prosaic roots. They congregated in large numbers in and about New York

City, the central entertainment center, and as Irving Howe notes, by 1900, Jewish businessmen played important roles as owners of theatres, managers, movie exhibitors, vaudeville owners, agents and bookers, and Tin Pan Alley song company owners. The businessmen had the middleman's role of providing consumption to those who wanted it, and with less respect for traditional proprieties, they would better give people what they wanted. Consequently for a performer like Sophie Tucker, it was within her realm of experience to consider the theatrical business open to her talents. Entertainment, after all, was not a central industrial enterprise, and it was in the service industries that immigrant entrepreneurial ambitions found their home. Jewish vaudevillians encouraged Sophie; they gave her the names of Jewish songwriting firms in Tin Pan Alley in New York, and she worked with Jewish agents who booked her. Although entertainment was open to people of many backgrounds, a good portion of the business was controlled, or came to be controlled, by the Jews, and this further opened the doors to Jewish performers. In this milieu, most bookers and agents sought talent that would sell; they were less interested in a performer's religious or ethnic ancestry. Consequently while many of the central areas of the business world still excluded Jews, show business allowed them to express their talents. As Howe describes it, show business glorified a roughneck sort of egalitarianism, "with little concern for those who might go under, but at best it gave people a chance to show off their gifts." As one observer boasted, with some exaggeration, "The greatest star in the legitimate is Warfield; the greatest star in musical comedy is Jolson, the greatest star in vaudeville is Sophie Tucker."[34]

The release of energy of the folk propelled Sophie Tucker and others like her into the mainstream, bent on breaking out, roaming the streets to explore the new culture as the old was already in transformation. She and other Jewish entertainers became consummate all-around performers because they themselves were rootless in a society loosening its traditional boundaries. The restlessness, the desire to make their way unaided in directions yet uncharted, gave these performers energy and also the desire for acceptance across the boundaries with large American audiences. Gilbert Seldes of the *New Republic* noted these qualities about Jolson and Brice, and they apply equally to Tucker. According to Seldes, these ethnic entertainers had an intensity lacking in the host society. He considered Jolson's vitality "a force so boundless, an exaltation so high, that anyone could still storm Heaven with laughter and cheers." Raised on the streets, they could "go farther, go with more contempt for artificial notions of propriety, than anyone else." Tucker found strength in the masses and support for her drive to succeed. People turned against an entertainer, she related, only when she turned her back on them. And cutting oneself off from the people killed the spark in ones' work.[35] This hearty earthiness made Tucker a superb entertainer in general and a consummate cabaret performer in particular.

Her singing, in rathskellers, burlesque, vaudeville, and cabarets, expressed the aggressiveness of a woman and an outsider breaking through the boundaries of her culture, and reaching toward American life. She expressed changes in American culture as well. She sang coon songs and ragtime at a time when the slow-paced, weepy, nineteenth-century ballads, filled with virtuous maidens, orphaned children, and platonic love, gave way to a new vitality in song. Big and brassy, unafraid to sing loud enough to rock the halls of a theatre or a cabaret, Sophie was one of a number of formidable female singers from the 1890s through World War I. Theatre critic Ashton Stevens described her power: "She has a voice—well, if Julian Eltinge's [a female impersonator] singing voice was as virile as Miss Tucker's, he would be executing a long overdue male impersonation." She was aggressive in her pursuit of success, and she used her voice in similar manner, with inflections borrowed from both her Jewish past and Negro music. As she observed once to Eddie Cantor, "These are no vocal chords, kid, these are bands of steel."[36] Made doubly formidable by her bulk, Tucker expressed desires for physical love and joy with a voice loud enough to make it impossible for the public to deny these formerly hidden emotions. She was strong and physical, some would say vulgar, as she snapped her fingers and moved her body in time to the music, or acted out the emotions of her songs in minidramas. Like other ethnic entertainers after the turn of the century, she expressed her lower-class origins as she stormed the halls of respectability and swept away much of the old gentility of middleclass music. She had three basic styles of song: the sexually aggressive woman seeking physical love, the singer of dixie melodies, and the forlorn woman, a wise loser in the game of love. These genres corresponded to her life and to the culture of her period.[37]

In deemphasizing the ballad, Sophie Tucker and other prewar

singers in vaudeville and cabarets turned to the American streets and the Negro for the source of a new-style music. The coon song of the 1890s and then the ragtime ditty relied less on European forms than had the ballad, and this well fitted immigrants who saw their future in America and who expressed the rise from the city streets with its slang and vulgarity. The new American was a yankee doodle boy, just as Americans were more confident after the Spanish-American War of the strength of their native culture and society. Sophie Tucker also expressed another of the new aspects of modern music: the emphasis on men and women as physical beings, with women released from the old role of homemaker and chaste embodiment of perfect morality. Seeking her own emancipation, Sophie expressed hitherto forbidden desires in her songs. A quick glance at some of her early recordings in the teens shows women expressing desires for physical love, and for loving men: "That Lovin' Rag" (1910), "That Lovin' Two-Step Man" (1910), "That Lovin' Soul Kiss" (June 1911). In a bill of eighteen songs at Reisenweber's in 1919, she included "Everybody Shimmies Now," "I Must Have a Little Liquor When I'm Dry," "That's the Kind of June That Will Make a Rabbit Hug a Hound," "Please Don't Take My Harem Away," "If We Had 'Em Here Like They Had 'Em There," "He Goes to Work in the Night-time and She Goes to Work Every Day," "I'm a Jazz Baby," "You Can't Shake That Shimmy Here," and "I'm Glad My Daddy's in Uniform."[38]

Tucker's music expressed a range of emotions and derived from Tin Pan Alley. From the beginning of her career, she frequented publishing houses for songs, and as her fame grew, song pluggers sought her to introduce their tunes. This music was built on formulas and advanced quickly to meet changing tastes. Modern Tin Pan Alley was built on mass distribution of sheet music, and while the music mirrored the personal concerns of a heterogenous urban society, it had the danger of becoming machine-made fantasies and standardized dreams. Tucker's contributions lay in finding the songs that fit her image; thus her personality triumphed over the machine product. By 1919 she had secured the services of Jack Yellen, a prolific tunesmith who turned out numbers specifically geared to her image and personality and who helped synthesize her themes into her enduring image: The Last of the Red Hot Mamas. As much as Sophie remained an individual, however, she too had to change her songs quickly to keep up with national tastes, which changed with the increased pace of the machine. The modern Tin Pan Alley product was a mélange of sources—black, Jewish, Irish, urban rattle—without expressing any of them beyond their commercial possibilities. Hence the urban folk was a machine folk, and although the songs were capable of bringing release, they also brought standardized dreams and mass feelings.[39]

Black music continued to form a consistent base of American music, a common form associated with no particular European immigrant group and hence an American product. The black base also served the desire for greater expression of physicality and the plebeianization of music. When Sophie first broke into burlesque about 1908, she sang in blackface, largely because she was considered too ugly to perform naturally. The black face served as a mask, allowing performers to express themselves fully to the host society in the guise of blacks, the group considered most uninhibited. The mask also permitted a sentimental attachment to an organic past forgotten but replaced by the mythical ordered world of the plantations, or small town glorified in the mammy and dixie songs, which were a staple of popular music in the 1910s and 1920s. Moving out of their own culture, singers like Tucker or Jolson sentimentalized their "Mammy" or their "Yiddishe Mama" (1925) and the past world dimly desired but long ago forgone in the push for American life and success. Jewish entertainers also put on blackface for another reason. According to Ronald Sanders, both groups felt a deep woe, had suffered at the hands of oppressors, and lived close to their pain. Many of the new songs hailed the brighter day and the aggressiveness necessary to live in the new land, but the singers invested blackface with a plaintive note, which kept them in touch with their past though with the pain once-removed, hidden behind a black face. In a culturally ambivalent position themselves—Jewish-Americans after all—Jewish performers were capable of playing ethnic pastiche, which they dominated after 1910. They sang America's rootlessness because they were the most uprooted of the new immigrants.[40]

In 1912 Tucker abandoned the protection of the blackface mask, but she preserved a mixture of Jewish and black elements in her singing. By 1914 she also had given up the external objectification of emotions through the coon song, and she had taken to singing ragtime tunes. Still, she portrayed the role of "*Hard Hearted Hanna*," earthy aggressor, interested in sex, a vamp, capable of expressing her emotions, and capable of taking care of herself. She continued to sing songs by Tin Pan Alleyites, both Jews and blacks, and her theme song, *"Some of These Days"* (1910), was written by black songwriter Shelton Brooks. Her music also mixed Negro and Jewish inflections, with her Jewish speech overlying black diction and pronunciation. On several occasions, listeners mistook her for a southern black girl. Once Dutch fans who had heard her only on record were surprised to learn that she was not black. It is obvious that much of her black sound together with a robust singing style and expressive body movement combined to convey an image of sensuality. While the authors of coon songs often equated blacks with lovemaking and freedom from civilized restraint, Sophie Tucker became a redhot mama, and could get away with it in the 1910s because she was white. Both Sophie and her audience could explore the intense emotions associated with sensuality by holding them at arm's length.

In her vaudeville and cabaret performances, Sophie's finely honed act ran to a pattern. Starting with a lively rag, she went into a ballad, moved on to a comedy song, then a novelty number. She always finished with what she called her hot number, earning the title, "Last of the Red Hot Mammas," leaving her audiences laughing. It was during the 1910s that she became a master of double entendre, turning to verbal sophistication as she gave up coon shouting and drew more sophisticated audiences. The cabaret atmosphere proved congenial to the risqué songs that vaudeville, and later radio, censored for family audiences. Eddie Cantor declared that "Sophie's entirely a night-club singer. Her style and material are hardly what you'd want at a Holy Name breakfast. But in the night-clubs she's queen, she has no inhibitions and needs none, she sings the words we used to write on the sidewalks of New York. And you *hear* her." In an interview she remarked that she did not like radio: "You can't do this, you can't do that. I couldn't even say 'hell' or 'damn,' and nothing, honey, is more expressive than the way I say 'hell' or 'damn.'" Her risqué songs worked in the cafés because they appealed to the "wise mob" without offending innocent patrons who heard only the literal words.[41]

The double entendres and Tucker's overall style permitted the audience to laugh at the conventional institution of marriage and the traditional roles of men and women. She could present sex and marriage as something to be laughed at and hence questioned, and she displayed an ambivalence about these sacred subjects that mirrored her audience's. She had come to the double-entendre song in 1910 when songwriter Fred Fisher convinced her that her size and lack of sexual allure made her perfect to sing about sex without offending or enticing anyone. A pretty, well-proportioned girl singing something like that, he told her, would offend an audience immediately. "It's smutty without being funny." Singing these songs, Tucker discovered that jokes about sex got the biggest laughs. They were jokes about real life, a part of life that people would not talk about openly. Audiences loved the many risqué songs that laughed at sex, instead of shying away from it ashamedly. "They get a feeling of relief right away." For people with Victorian roots, Tucker found the best way to treat sex was to get them to laugh about it and release their tension. And in her estimation the songs were moral. "They have to do with sex but not with vice." That distinction, she believed, was the secret of their sure appeal to American audiences.[42]

Under the guise of humor, Tucker not only brought out the secret and private desires of men and women into the public light; she also sang about her own distress with the fun home and the ideals of a romantic marriage. From her theme song "Some of These Days" to "I Ain't Got Nobody" and "What Do You Mean Loving Somebody Else When Your Love Belongs to Me," she described her love travails. Although she sang of universal feelings, she spoke about herself. This enriched her performance more than if she sang about some vague other person. Especially she sang about her own failures in marriage (three divorces by the 1920s), and her own loneliness. Audiences found her distress funny and laughed at the situations in the song, implicitly recognizing that that could happen to them too. One woman wrote Tucker about her singing of "I Used to Love You But It's All Over," in 1921, and declared, "You might have read all my heartaches and dedicated the songs you sang to me. . . . If you had not witnessed some experience in your life you would not and could not have sung it with the feeling and expression which you did." While she talked of sex in marriage, of men and women running around, she did so in a comic vein. She could get away with it partly through a cover of respectability and because she was a comedienne. When she made fun of old-style marriage and created her song pictures of sexual women, she did so from a moral position; she was instructing her audience. As in "You Can't Sew a Button on a Heart," she pointed out to women that to keep their men, they would have to become physical. The sexual role required more than being a good homemaker.[43] She advised men that they treat women "right," or women, taking advantage of the lessening of the double standard, would be vengeful. For both marriage was to be sexually and personally gratifying.

Sophie's aggressive image often undermined the deeply emotional and sexual life she wanted from men, and this came out in her act and the songs she sang. In "Some of These Days," a model for many of her other songs, Sophie sang to a lover who had spurned her: "You're gonna miss me honey." She was unhappy with her men, though successful in her career. Always she sang of men leaving her ("I Ain't Got Nobody") and herself as the victim, but she also contributed by marrying men who were younger than she, less independent than she, and making less money than she. When she found them either playing around or wasting her money, it was too late; all she could do was realize that her success had contributed to their lack of self-esteem. Second husband Frank Westphal, a younger man, worked for her as an accompanist. As her career skyrocketed, he became increasingly morose. She bought him a garage to give him an independent career and called it the Sophie Tucker Garage. The marriage did not long survive the business venture.

While her songs sang of the need and desire for men, they also sang of an aggressiveness and independence which made life with her man troublesome. Her strength expressed in song turned into problems. In "I've Got a Man," she argued that all life was bearable with a man. Regardless of what they might say, Sophie recalled, every woman felt as she did no matter what. All her life she wanted a "masterful man." Yet, she knew her successful life as a female entertainer kept her from her dream. She had started out wanting a life unlike her mother's, embarking on a career to become independent. She ended up releasing the energy of Jewish women, formerly directed toward the family, into an independent life. "Something happens to a woman when she does that." She is not likely to be a clinging vine kind of woman even when "the right man" appears.[44]

Tucker's career embodied a paradox. Her freedom from the cultural constraints of Jewish womanhood and her rise above the mass came through a continual drive for success: "I was never satisfied to sing a song," she remarked." "I wanted to know how to get more, how to bring that salary up, how to be a star."⁴⁵ Only by becoming self-supporting could she live the life of freedom about which she dreamt. However, she also dreamed about a romantic, sexual relationship with a man that her songs described, the relationship she was always left wanting. In her stage act, Tucker portrayed the aggressive woman, bent on independence, equal if not dominant to any man, a mother figure risen from the nineteenth century, capable in her bulk of succeeding and aggressively ordering men about. Her strong, successful life gave her freedom, an envious freedom, but it made her emotional life unhappy. As a model for women, she was either a threat to men or a pal, never a lover. Her aggression made her unfit for the love she wanted. Given the choice, most other women probably would have accepted the need for success but not chosen the emotionally disastrous model of Sophie Tucker. Men too might agree that the success of the star, the success that supposedly embodied an active, vibrant, sexual, and emotional life, was necessary, but men had to achieve it. Sophie's aggressiveness led her to unhappiness, and audiences got the message. In "Some of These Days," she sang of loss and longing but without subservience, for she tells the man, "You'll miss your fat mama." To achieve the new-style marital happiness and physical love, women must not step too far outside the home role; to do so, they would become too aggressive for men and scare them off, or else become a pal, a "good schnuck," humorous and able to survive in a male world, as Sophie clearly could, but not as the new model sexual creature.⁴⁶ For women, success outside marriage undermined the new model home.

HEY BIG SPENDER

While Sophie Tucker displayed the tensions between success for women and the new ideal of home, she and other friendly entertainers glorified success in the cabaret, making it clear that personal pleasure did not come to the unsuccessful. The friendly entertainer was malleable, capable of adjustment through a sociable personality, able to get along with everyone, to be a good sport. Freed from past ascetic character, entertainers represented the ability to adjust for success. However, they communicated a new definition of success: success lay in consumption. When Sophie Tucker, Will Rogers, or any other famous cabaret entertainer spied other well-known entertainers in the crowd, they pointed them out to the delight of the audience. In addition, Tucker, Rogers, and later, Texas Guinan publicized the successful. Fighters, beauty-parlor operators, songwriters, and others were introduced to the crowd and called on to receive applause.[47] A well-to-do patron could thus be like the star, removed from social constraint because of success in business. The high life, enjoyment of life, was not a threat to bourgeois values but an extension of them.

The cabaret thus paralleled the changing meaning of work in the early twentieth century. Success meant money to be spent rather than the overriding value placed on work itself. Success in the modern corporate society no longer meant ascetic glorification of the individual of character who produced wealth; rather success glorified the person of personality who could enjoy it. The tremendously abundant economy of the early twentieth century was less a battleground of character and more a system for the tangible fruits of enjoyment.

In this scheme of values, the individual had to have the money in order to consume; this definition of the good life was still individual and private rather than communal. The willingness to spend made the cabaret's life of consumption go. The "Pittsburgh Millionaire," "spender," "big shot," and "butter and egg man" were all terms associated with the café because the latter welcomed all who could spend money or impulses regardless of inherent moral worth. Money dominated the cabaret atmosphere, because money made its possessor stand out and generated acceptance wherever he went. The decor of the Broadway cabarets and restaurants was lavish, and high prices were paid for cover charges and drinks. Establishments that charged no admission enforced the appearance of "class as a prerequisite for admission." As Julian Street noted, "Practically any well-dressed person who is reasonably sober and will purchase supper and champagne for two, may enter." Captain Churchill, one of the more conservative proprietors, allegedly greeted prostitutes as politely as society women so long as they acted like ladies and spent well.[48] By 1917 increased prices in cabaret food, covers, and drinks brought on by higher entertainment costs and wartime inflation reinforced the emphasis on competitive spending and conspicuous consumption as the signs of success in the cabaret. *Variety* found that higher costs were attracting a particular crowd bent on spending and making an impression in the cafés. Tourists and strangers of all kinds in New York wanted to have a good time regardless of cost, and they frequented the cabarets. During and after the war, soldiers on their way to and from Europe made the Broadway spots their stomping grounds. Often another sort of patron frequented the cabarets. A fellow out with a girl he was trying to impress would take her to a cabaret. He wanted to show her a good time and show off his ability as a spender. She did not know him well enough to argue the extravagance. In these instances, and for New Yorkers in general, the cabaret acted as a place to celebrate special occasions—birthdays, raises, anniversaries. One went there to celebrate flush times, and one did so by spending big. The emphasis on spending also resulted from another source of patronage. New York was the business center of the country, especially in the fields of clothing and textiles, and buyers out with customers felt impelled to spend big in order to make a big sale. This was expense account living in its early stages.

In the atmosphere of the cabaret, the average patron showed off his luxury and status, signs of his having earned the right to play. The big spender and the average patron shared the view that success lay in conspicuous consumption. Attributes of work seeped into play, and elements of play—personality, friendliness, amusement—into work. Entertainers and celebrities combined both. They had succeeded in a world requiring friendliness, personality, and getting along, and now they could lead a life of expressiveness and play, whether on the cabaret's floor or at the tables.[49]

Unlike earlier comedians who stayed close to ethnic humor but like Jolson and others of her generation, Tucker represented the possibility of ethnic success and acceptance if one abandoned much of the ethnic content of one's culture and adapted to the larger world and market of American entertainment and social patterns. Tucker's name was anglicized (from Kalish to Abusa to Tuck to Tucker), her clothes luxurious, and by the 1920s her voice classy as she dramatically interpreted songs rather than belted them out. While she still used Yiddish expressions and sang "My Yiddishe Mama" in her native tongue, she had already begun to reach larger audiences by singing ragtime. While she stayed close to her family and Jewish life,

still she showed that malleability on the part of the friendly entertainer would produce success for other ethnics and for Jewish-Americans in the New World.[50]

NOTES

1. "Some of These Days," Shelton Brooks (1910).
2. *Variety*, December 22, 1916, pp. 15, 125, 127; also Sophie Tucker, *Some of These Days* (Garden City, N.Y.: Doubleday, 1945), pp. 155–56, notes that William Morris booked her and her Five Kings of Syncopation into Reisenweber's; she felt that this engagement was beneath a vaudeville head-liner, but Morris convinced her she would not lose prestige. She took an initial cut of $250 per week, from $1,000 in vaudeville to $750 in Reisenweber's, but she was soon earning closer to $1,500 because she drew business.
3. Leo Lowenthal, "Biographies in Popular Magazines," in William Peterson, ed., *American Social Patterns* (Garden City, N.Y.: Doubleday, 1956), pp. 63–117, discusses the concept of idols of consumption. I differ from Lowenthal's view only in seeing the pattern already in live entertain-ment before it becomes a part of these very popular and mass magazines.
4. *Variety*, April 9, 1915, p. 14.
5. Tucker, *Some of These Days*, p. 216, discusses her meeting and dancing with her third husband, in the audience of Reisenweber's.
6. *New York American*, September 28, 1919, p. 7; *New York Times*, April 26, 1914, III, p. 8.
7. Erving Goffman, *The Presentation of Self in Everyday Life* (Garden City, N.Y.: Doubleday, 1959), pp. 112–34, discusses the idea of backstage regions for human behavior.
8. *Variety*, March 28, 1913, p. 6.
9. Karl K. Kitchen, "The Cabaret Is No Longer a Fad—It's a Business," *New York World*, April 13, 1913, metropolitan section, p. 2.
10. Tucker, *Some of These Days*, pp. 177–221, discusses the fun and prestige she found in Europe. Black performers from James Reese Europe through modern jazz and blues musicians have found the same thing.
11. *Variety*, March 10, 1926, p. 18.
12. Ibid., March 14, 1913, p. 18.
13. Tucker, *Some of These Days*, pp. 152, 161.
14. *Variety*, January 9, 1915, p. 8, March 26, 1915, p. 5, March 30, 1917, p. 8, January 17, 1913, p. 17, discuss the terms of engagement for various entertainers.
15. *Billboard*, January 25, 1913, p. 9; *Variety*, April 4, 1913, p. 18, and September 26, 1913, p. 6, have material on personal song boosting.

16. For unique salary arrangements, see *Variety*, March 10, 1926, p. 18, October 17, 1914, p. 13, April 24, 1914, p. 18, January 23, 1915, p. 13. For stars with their own rooms, see *New York Telegram*, December 12, 1913, May 1, 1914, n.p., clippings in Castle Scrapbooks, Robinson Locke Collection, New York Public Library, Lincoln Center; *Variety*, January 16, 1915, p. 13; Tucker, *Some of These Days*, p. 152. For star-named clubs in the 1920s, see *Variety*, March 10, 1926, p. 18.

17. *New York Times*, January 3, 1915, IX, p. 7 [italics added]; *New York Review*, March 7, 1914, n.p., clipping in Robinson Locke Collection.

18. Tucker, *Some of These Days*, pp. 27, 15, 45; Sophie Tucker Scrapbooks, New York Public Library, Lincoln Center, has collections of cards and letters to and from numerous friends, as well as Tucker letter, March 1, 1921.

19. On Jolson, see Robert Toll, *On with the Show—The First Century of Show Business in America* (New York: Oxford, 1976), p. 309; Tucker, *Some of These Days*, p. 157.

20. Julius Keller, *Inns and Outs* (New York: G. P. Putnam's Sons, 1939), pp. 130–31; Tucker, *Some of These Days*, p. 136 (italics added); *Variety*, January 6, 1922, pp. 9, 45; *New York American*, November 18, 1917, p. 4.

21. For star system, see Albert F. McLean, Jr., *American Vaudeville as Ritual* (Lexington: University of Kentucky Press, 1965), p. 53, and Churchill, *The Great White Way* (New York: E. P. Dutton & Co., 1962), pp. 71–75.

22. *Variety*, August 26, 1921, pp. 1, 2, December 16, 1921, pp. 1, 2, January 6, 1922, pp. 9, 45, for regularization of drop-ins.

23. Tucker, *Some of These Days*, p. 160.

24. Clayton Hamilton, "Great Actors, as Other Great Men Are More Alive Than the Herd," *Vogue*, December 1, 1917, p. 17.

25. Tucker, speech, quoted in John E. Dimeglio, *Vaudeville U.S.A.* (Bowling Green: Bowling Green University Popular Press, 1973), p. 60.

26. Alice Kessler Harris, introduction to Anzia Yezierska, *Bread Givers* (1925; reprint, New York: Persea Books, 1975), pp. v.–xviii, discusses challenges to the old model of father in the New World. For more information on Jewish women, see Charlotte Brown, Paula Hyman, and Sonya Michel, *The Jewish Woman in America* (New York: New American Library, 1975).

27. Tucker, *Some of These Days*, p. 7.

28. Ibid., p. 12.

29. Ibid., pp. 15–16.

30. Ibid., p. 124, notes the lack of approval she found among her family and in Jewish culture in general even after she had become a headliner.

31. Ibid., p. 11.

32. For material on Yiddish language, theatre, art, literature, see Moses

Rischin, *The Promised City* (New York: Corinth Books, 1964), pp. 115–43, and Irving Howe, *World of Our Fathers* (New York: Simon & Schuster, 1976), pp. 417–551.

33. Howe, *World of Our Fathers*, pp. 12–13.

34. Ibid., p. 557; Jack Lait, "The Stage—and the Jew," *Cleveland Jewish Bee*, July 8, 1921, n.p., clipping, Tucker Scrapbooks.

35. Gilbert Seldes, "The Daemonic in the American Theatre," in *The Seven Lively Arts* (1924: reprint, New York: Sagamore Press, 1957), pp. 175–83; Tucker, *Some of These Days*, p. 133.

36. Tucker, *Some of These Days*, p. 91; "Trotting Forward," *Nation*, April 10, 1913, pp. 352–53, comments on cabaret singers in general as primitives. Eddie Cantor with Jane Ardmore, *Take My Life* (Garden City, N.Y.: Doubleday, 1957), p. 34. For general changes in music, see Russel B. Nye, "From Ballads to Blues," in *The Unembarrassed Muse* (New York: Dial Press, 1970), pp. 306–25; H. F. Mooney, "Popular Music Since the 1920s: The Significance of Shifting Taste," in R. Serge Denisoff and Richard A. Peterson, *The Sounds of Social Change* (Chicago: Rand McNally, 1972), pp. 181–97; H. F. Mooney, "Songs, Singers and Society, 1890–1954," *American Quarterly* 6 (Fall 1954): 221–32; and Isaac Goldberg, *Tin Pan Alley* (1930; reprint, New York: Flungar Publishing Co., 1961), pp. 84–177, 234–58.

37. *Variety*, January 10, 1919, p. 23, lists the nineteen tunes she did at Reisenweber's, and January 31, 1919, prints additions to the repertoire.

38. Brian Rust, *Complete Entertainment Discography from Mid 1890's to 1942* (New Rochelle: Arlington House, 1973), p. 641.

39. Goldberg, *Tin Pan Alley*, pp. 226–32, discusses the standardized song formula.

40. Ronald Sanders, "The American Popular Song," in Douglas Villiers, ed., *Next Year in Jerusalem: Jews in the Twentieth Century* (London: Harrap, 1976), pp. 197–219, notes the affinity of Jews for blackface entertainment after 1910.

41. Cantor, *Take My Life*, p. 34; Tucker, *Some of These Days*, pp. 94–95; *New York Times*, February 10, 1966, pp. 1, 31, has her remarks on radio.

42. Tucker, *Some of These Days*, pp. 94–6.

43. Tucker, *Some of These Days*, p. 96; Letter to Sophie Tucker, March 1, 1921, Sophie Tucker Scrapbooks.

44. Tucker, *Some of These Days*, p. 126.

45. *New York Times*, February 10, 1966, pp. 1, 31.

46. Tucker, *Some of These Days*, p. 126.

47. Ibid., p. 153. In the 1920s, Texas Guinan did the same thing. Also see Richard Ketchum, *Will Rogers* (New York: American Heritage Publishing Company, 1973), p. 147.

48. *Variety*, December 25, 1914, p. 8; Street, *Welcome to Our City*, pp. 10–11; Jimmy Durante and Jack Kofoed, *Nightclubs* (New York: Alfred A. Knopf, 1931), p. 195.

49. *Variety*, December 28, 1917, p. 16.

50. Tucker's father (Kalish) was running away from the Russian army and took the name Abusa from a comrade in similar circumstances. She married Tuck and added "er" to the name. Tucker also had a large Jewish following in vaudeville and in Reisenweber's, but except for Yiddish expressions, she did American entertainment based on a group with no European connotations, the blacks.

7 BROADWAY BABIES: GLORIFYING THE AMERICAN GIRL, 1915–1922

> Woman at her best nerver outgrows adolescence as man does, but lingers in, magnifies and glorifies the culminating stage of life with its all-sided interests, its convertability of emotions, its enthusiasm, and zest for all that is good, beautiful, true and heroic.[1]
>
> G. Stanley Hall

Psychologist G. Stanley Hall thus articulated the sentiments of an era and inadvertently explained the appeal of the cabaret's chorus girl revues which made their appearance on a regular basis in 1915. Girly revues became an important staple of cafés and nightclubs. Revues presented scantily clad young women who stepped out of the chorus line to appear more informally on the restaurant floor in close proximity to patrons in the audience. In simple ways the revue expressed tensions that women and men found with the new informal personality, the lowering of barriers, and the subsequent inability to discern confidently which women were "true" and which were not. Both men and women had changed their expectations of themselves and others; yet, for both the spectre of a life role for women like Sophie Tucker, independent, aggressive and lonely, proved unsettling and unattractive. As chorus girls, forever young, vibrant, and malleable, women would be able to catch men and avoid the problems of independence. As chorus girls, they would be fun as partners for men who recognized that their success could provide them with the good life.

The form of the revue is not difficult to discern, but its origin remains somewhat sketchy.[2] Featuring a number of song and dance acts loosely strung together under a common theme, the revue burlesqued and highlighted the "follies" of the day by giving individual performers a few action-packed moments in the spotlight. Apparently the revue originated in the music halls and early cafés of France, where entertainers mocked politicians and current foibles. Robert Baral has traced it to the Folies-Bergère's Place aux Jeunes, which opened in Paris on November 30, 1886.[3] Encouraged by his wife, Anna Held, a former Follies entertainer, Florenz Ziegfeld presented the first revue in America with his Follies of 1907. Apropos of its cosmopolitan origin, the master showman staged his sketches of the days' events atop the New York Theatre Roof, which for the occasion he renamed the Jardin de Paris.[4] During the next twenty-five years Ziegfeld and his competitors strove to outproduce each other with beautifully mounted productions, each featuring gorgeous scenery, snappy comedians, and, most important, beautiful women, beautifully presented.

With a spectacular string of successes behind him, Ziegfeld in January 1915 inaugurated the first modern cabaret revue in the Midnight Frolic atop the New Amsterdam Theater. A sumptuous cabaret, serving superb food, dancing, and elaborate chorus girl productions to the best of the carriage trade, the Frolic set a model of revue entertainment. From its inception until 1922 when prohibition forced its closing, the Frolic mounted sixteen revues, two a year. As in other cafés, audience participation figured importantly. Patrons applauded with little wooden hammers, snapped balloons, blew noisemakers, raced with pogo sticks, and talked from table to table by telephone. Chorus girls were the major attraction. Ziegfeld launched the café with "Nothing But Girls," starring singer Norah Bayes and twenty-four chorus girls, paid $30,000 per week in operating and salary costs, and met expenses by charging an unheard-of two-dollar cover at the nine o'clock show and three dollars at midnight.[5] Entering the café business with dash and flourish, Ziegfeld further solidified a wealthy clientele for Broadway entertainment and placed his own stamp on the nature of cabaret amusements. Where he led, other cabarets soon followed.

By March 1915 at least eleven other cafés were planning or had already presented revues. *Variety* wondered if the average café could afford the lavishness of the Frolic; Maxim's proved they could. Under the direction of Percy Elkeles and Lea Herrick, Maxim's put on "Keep Moving" with eight chorus girls and three principals for $750 in salaries and production costs without instituting admission charges. "Keep Moving" did business from the start, and other cafés were encouraged to follow suit. Soon two Bustanoby cabarets, Chez Maurice, the Tokio, Healy's, Reisenweber's, Wallick's, Pekin, and the New York Roof mounted chorus girl revues. Broadway restaurants were no longer afraid to invest in production numbers, better salaries, entertainment staffs, and more extensive advertising.

The cabaret's proven popularity made possible the featuring of vaudeville headliners, Ziegfeld's entry into the café business, and the inauguration of chorus girl revues. In 1912 and 1913 managers had toyed with the idea of more elaborate stage shows, but the theatrical licensing laws deterred them. Under the law, the use of stages and costumes required theatrical licenses costing $500, and this seemed risky for an unproven institution of entertainment. After adverse court decisions, owners opted for variety acts on the dance floor.[6] By spring 1915, however, the issue reemerged, for promoters needed substitutes for the ballroom dancers. Assured now of the money-making propensities, managers were willing to risk the extra expenses of theatrical licenses and costs. Through World War I, however, the issue of licenses remained uncertain. Theatres complained about competing cabaret revues, and magistrates issued contradictory decrees. One judge declared that costumes made a license mandatory, while another decreed that the absence of a stage rendered the license unnecessary. Because of their confidence in the cabaret's ability to make money, owners weathered the period of uncertainty and continued to offer large-scale revues. To meet the added expenses, some places raised menu prices a bit, and the Century Roof and the Midnight Frolic raised admission charges. Overall cabaret managers realized they could expend more on elaborate entertainment and continue to tu.n a profit.[7]

KEEP MOVING: SPEED AND TIME

The revue focused impulses toward vitality, presenting them in an organized manner with a common theme. The theme of the revue might be something as innocuous and informal as "the follies of the day" or "a day at the seashore," anything that served as an organizing framework for a number of disparate song and dance numbers. In his memoirs, Julius Keller recalled that he consciously deviated from the early cabaret formula of presenting unrelated variety acts when he introduced the cabaret revue as a Broadway musical in capsule form.[8] Instead of a series of disconnected performances, the cabarets now featured singing and dancing turns connected to each other. Most important, the revue filled its space with pretty women in dazzling and, for the period, daring clothing. Although individual acts continued to shine, their time in the limelight was brief, the overall production was emphasized, and the speed and time—the pacing—dominated, as did the choreographers and dance directors who now produced and ran the shows.

The revue worked well in the cabaret. As a fast-paced form of entertainment, it left the impression that the cabaret was a place to enjoy life in a stimulating manner. Gone were the nineteenth-century's elaborations of plot. Here was excitement, freedom, and release from routine. Here was the sense that the city was home to all sorts of pleasures and excitements, as the revue tossed at the audience a quick array of stimuli, much like the modern city: pretty girls, dances, songs, costumes, which conveyed their message on an emotional, subliminal level, with "something razzling and dazzling, of legs and tom-foolery, of nondescript entertainments which aim at making cheerful noise, of productions which introduce plenty of light and color and pretty dresses."[9] Seated against the cabaret's backdrop of high life, audiences could not fail to come away from a performance with a sense of participating in a fast life made possible by the city. Where else could one "See Broadway," enjoy life to the hilt, and have time "pass quickly"?[10] The modern world had moved from the sense of rationalized restraint to a quest for experience which could be found only in an exciting urban world. The sense of liberation emerged from and in conflict with organization and efficient production, for it was through direction, efficiency, and pacing that the individual performer stood out for a few moments in the spotlight. Rather than being destroyed by efficiency, the performer in the café was liberated by it, or so it appeared to the audience. If the revue often had the appearance of an assembly line with interchangeable parts, created as such because it was cheap, it also reflected the great faith that efficiency would produce freedom, not restraint.

Often the themes of the revue presented the city as the home of a free, new fast life. In the Midnight Frolic's "Just Girls," the city appeared as a place of freedom rather than entrapment. In the opening number, "The Girl from My Home Town," girls from twenty-four cities and one small town came to New York for adventure, men, and a new life, freed from the constraints of the small town. As the principal singer waits for his small-town true love, he and she see New York, where, the following numbers quickly tell us, "Dreams Come True," young women and men pursue success and love, and find them in the arms of the opposite sex. Audiences watched the male singer meet the girl from his home town, viewed couples dance in "Tango Girl," and saw the wish for love in "If Dreams Come True" and "I Want Someone to Make a Fuss over Me." They also explored the excitement of city life in a song about a Mrs. Kelly's table d'hôte restaurant, and they were able to feel like insiders to the fast life of riches when they watched a performer caricature Diamond Jim Brady dancing. The city, then, produced personal freedom.[11]

The structure of the revue and its underlying elements contributed to this vision of the city as a land of pleasure and the fast life. Pacing emphasized it. The essence of the performance was speed. Ideally running anywhere from twenty to forty minutes with the maximum of one intermission, the revue was much shorter than the conventional Broadway musical. In that short time span, choreographers presented, and audiences expected, nonstop activity. Both choreographers and *Variety* considered anything that slowed the production as inimical to the purpose and style of the revue. In 1916 *Variety* proclaimed that the cabaret show at the Garden was an ideal model, for despite a length of twenty minutes, the show seemed to have taken only five, "so active is the continuous entertainment that never lags for an instant."[12] The short time period, packed with acts, gave the audience the impression of continuous excitement and release.

Commenting on various shows, *Variety* never failed to suggest ways to accelerate the pace. One problem was intermissions, which interrupted the flow of the performance. A Castles in the Air presentation, the "Bull Ring," illustrates this point; it had three long breaks for dancing. *Variety* recommended that the producers reduce the number of intermissions to two in order to hold the attention of the crowds better. The worst sin consisted of performers staying longer on the floor than required, or for the revue to drag on past a point of satiation.[13] Programming was another problem, for the wrong kind of entertainer or number destroyed the pace. *Variety* advised Reisenweber's to curtail the tenor in "Full of Speed" or else cut the two ballads that he sang in succession. By nature slow, too many ballads could clog the proceedings.[14] The first revue at Michaud's in 1913 ran into trouble because it had not yet found the right rhythm. Edward Paulton, the author of the book and music, "was necessarily as much at sea as any one else as to what the restaurant clientele would demand." Making the mistake of including some bright and timely dialogue, he found it failed to get across without actions to accompany the words. The timelier skits employing dialogue flopped, prompting *Variety* to pronounce that "low comedy, songs and action seem to be the thing for cabaret production. The less dialog the better."[15] Julian Alfred, Percy Elkeles, and Lea Herrick, on the other hand, found the ideal in an appropriately named production, "Keep Moving," which put "nothing but speed into the revue, keeping the girls continually on the move in the small space Maxim's allows for its dance floor."[16]

Cabarets utilized many devices to increase the fast pace. Principals walked in on each other's exits, starting their own acts without waiting for the previous performer to finish. Commending the Garden in 1917 for its production, "Seeing Broadway," *Variety* proclaimed it a model of speed despite its forty minutes running time: "It's bing bang all the time, with succeeding artists or numbers walking on as others finish, cutting out even the opportunity for applause and necessarily encores." The lightning speed with which principals and chorus girls made their numerous costume changes enhanced the feverish pace. In one Garden revue, the six girls made four costume changes without leaving the stage. Sometimes performers would merely step behind an on-stage screen and reappear instantaneously in new costumes. No matter how they did it, the entertainers changed hurriedly and came and went quickly.[17]

While the speed and pacing produced a world of constant pleasure and excitement, the names of the revues created an image of vitality, good cheer, and sparkling urban enjoyment. "Follies of the Moment," "Spice of Life," "Cut Ups," "Dance and Grow Thin," "Seeing Broadway," and "Too Much Mustard" conveyed the idea that life was open and enjoyable, capable of being lived "Full of Speed," with "The Spice of Life," consisting of innumerable "Merry Moments." The innumerable follies and frolics were perfect entertainments for tired businessmen and their wives, for their constant activity, their

sense of liberation and fun filled with urban high life and sexual hijinks could easily make them forget the drudgery of the office and the
isolation of the home. They reveled in a world of "Keep Smiling,"
where the serious constraints of time, place, and class were absent.

The revue's approach to pacing also reveals American attitudes toward pleasure. While seemingly an alternative to the business world
and an escape from the routine institutional roles of men and women,
the revue in actuality was part of the logical and rational time
sequence of a hierarchical and technological society. The excitement
and speed worked to undercut rationality, to reorient one's logic away
from the utility of the daytime, but instead of moving to a sense of time
in which many acts and impulses would bombard the viewer at once or
to a sense of life, experienced slowly, the revue stuck to a time scheme
more compatible with industrial society. Within a fast-paced sequence, one ate, danced, watched an exciting show, and perhaps
found some measure of release. Committed to individual progress and
achievement, patrons sought to add excitement to their normal lives
by accelerating the already established patterns of regularity. The
world of pleasure and the irrational would be only a specialized seg-
ment added to normal life rather than a potentially reorganizing force.
Experiential living, informality, and individualism were removed for
leisure and the weekend, extended perhaps later into the night, but not
into the everyday world where business, success, and order dominated. In such a time scheme, leisure itself had the potential to become
fast paced, quickly offered, quickly enjoyed, and quickly over. Leisure and work followed the clock, and experience was packaged for
quick consumption. Personal liberation between men and women
would be worked out within those constraints.[18]

BALLOON GIRLS: THE CHORUS GIRL GLORIFIED

In this period of changing sexual and social mores, the chorus girl
formed the backbone of the revue. As the principals, showgirls, and
chorus girls, women supplied the "spice" in the "Spice of Life," and
the "mustard" in "Too Much Mustard." With the popularity of
revues in the theatres and in the cafés, chorus girls could be seen dancing and singing up and down Broadway, on and off the stage. As
theatre critic Alan Dale put it, the chorus girl had found national emi-

nence. She was "the frosting on life's cake."[19] Yet before her heyday in the 1910s and 1920s, the chorus girl had a long history in American popular culture. During the season of 1847–1848, women began posing in tights as "living statuary," portraying classical subjects and famous sculpture, such as "The Greek Slave" and "Venus Rising from the Sea," in all-male saloons and variety theatres. It was only after the Civil War, however, that women in tights became part of the mainstream of show business.

A combination of melodrama and ballet, *The Black Crook* opened in 1866 in New York City as the nation's first musical comedy. The marriage of a threadbare melodrama and a stranded British ballet company, *The Black Crook* offered one hundred singing and dancing young women for the delight of the audience and the outrage of moralists. "The first thing that strikes the eye is the immodest dress of the girls with short skirts and undergarments of thin, gauze-like material, allowing the form of the figure to be discernible," fumed minister Charles B. Smythe. "The attitudes are exceedingly indelicate, *ladies* exposing the figures from the waist to the toe except for such coverings as we have described."[20] The resulting furor drove audiences into the theatre, and *The Black Crook* became an enormous hit, encouraging many other musical comedy imitators. Musical comedy continued with chorus girls, but only as one of many attractions, including spectacle, extravagance, and melodramatic plots that enshrined ascetic virtue against aristocratic luxury and vice, thereby undercutting the appreciation of the sexual content of the female form. The combination was an almost perfect Victorian compromise between sensationalism and reputability.

A purer form of the girlie show eventually developed into burlesque, where the female form and figure dominated the other attractions. When Lydia Thompson and her British Blondes opened in New York City in the classical *Ixion* in 1868, they played male roles in revealing, tight-fitting tunics, a common guise for exposing women's physical charms during the Victorian era. Burlesquing the classics while paying them lip-service, Thompson's troupe by 1873 had formed into the standard chorus line, using high kicking and saucy songs; their classical allusions soon became Americanized. In 1870 M. B. Leavitt created the first American girlie show with Mme. Rentz's Female Minstrels, sparking imitation within the year by

eleven other such troupes. Specializing in scanty skirts, male impersonation, and living statuary, which they added to routine minstrel
fare, these aggregations, according to one performer, put the body
first: "The main thing, you see, is shape. All they have to do is put on
their costumes and let the jays look at them. . . . All they need is a pair
of tights." Eventually the troupes dropped the minstrel pretense, declared themselves burlesque outfits, and openly presented female
bodies for male viewing in all-male theatres and variety houses.[21]

Forming the lowest, all-male level of entertainment until the early
twentieth century, the girlie show was transformed during the first
decade of the new century by Florenz Ziegfeld into something acceptable for mixed audiences at the highest levels of society and entertainment. Borrowing the idea of the revue from Paris, he added musical
comedy production numbers, snappy comedians, and girls of all
kinds. Ziegfeld glorified chorus girls as glamorous creatures whose reputability and wholesomeness could appeal to both sexes. Borrowing
from the Follies, cabarets also presented chorus girls to mixed-sex
audiences and brought the female body out of its associations with
low, all-male burlesque and beer halls. The cabaret revue presented
the body as glamorous without the attendant spectacles and guises of
musical comedy; female physical charms entered the public realm
where both women and men could view them and learn from them. As
one ex-chorus girl and nautch dancer who had entertained middle-
aged businessmen put it, the ethics of cafés had to be high, for men
took "their wives, their sweethearts and, very often, their daughters."[22] The fact that the revealingly clad chorus girl appeared amid
reputable men and women contributed to a changing nature and
meaning for the chorus girl revue.

As the chorus girl entered the public realm, her image changed.
Prior to Ziegfeld, chorus women in burlesque were picked for their
bulk rather than their skill. In the 1880s, May Howard, the first burlesque queen, employed no one under 150 pounds. The Billy Watson
Beef Trust serves as the best example of the large chorine. An organization of "husky, capable-looking ladies of forbidding bulk," the trust
represented the "pre-flapper school of Broadway chorus." Less
active, agile, or graceful than the post-Ziegfeld chorus girl, the Beef
Trust's main function was pictorial and decorative. Under Ziegfeld,
the chorus developed from a static and inactive picture to a dynamic
and well-precisioned ensemble. Little attention was paid to glorifying

early chorus girls. According to one chronicler, their wardrobe "consisted of a couple of pairs of tights with sateen trunks, and perhaps an abbreviated frock or so."[23] Add to this their obvious maturity and lack of beauty and one has a picture of hardened chorines, fixed in a fallen life, inviting to men on one level but defining the women to be avoided in real life.

From the late 1890s through the 1910s, women of the chorus made a transition from this static, forbidding image of sinful womanhood, to the more acceptable image of the modern girl. Much like Irene Castle, the chorus girl of the Ziegfeld stage and the cabaret revues combined some of the sensuality of the evil woman of the past with the respectable aura of the girl. The modern chorus woman's character was not fixed, she was not hardened; in fact, the aura of the girl helped legitimize the expressiveness of the female body and make it more tangible for respectable men and women in the audience. The image of the chorus of young girls represented possibility and freedom rather than entrapment. The ideal body type resembled that of the girl next door, not the formidable bulk of a Sophie Tucker acting the bad girl or the dangerousness of a vampish Theda Bara. Fresh youth, arrayed in an optimistic light, was the ideal. When the chorus girls got older or fatter, they were dropped from the ensemble. In 1925 Chorus Equity, an organization for "ladies of the ensemble," established an elocution school because on the average chorus careers lasted no longer than the peak five years between ages seventeen and twenty-two. The chorus girl was just that: a girl. As *Variety* observed about one show, "The girls in them all look healthy, fresh and wholesome, eight of the trimmest girls around."[24]

While the image of women in the revue changed as both women and men made up the audience, only women displayed their bodies expressively on the floor. "Restaurant audiences do not want men," remarked *Variety*. "They want women, the more the better and the less they wear also." During variety acts, diners often kept on eating, but "at the finale when some of the girls appeared in short skirts the diners approved immediately." As the journal concluded, "A restaurant crowd wants women."[25] On another occasion, *Variety* commented that the idea of the revue was "youth with looks. One principal seems enough with these short shows. It's a matter of girls with them, not men. One fast bright and light singing juvenile to help the girls along is plenty." As the boy, the male juvenile played the love interest, an often necessary ingredient for bringing sexual attraction into play and resolving it in favor of true love. However, few men appeared. The September 1915 edition of the Midnight Frolic "Just Girls" was in fact just that, as thirty young women singers and dancers cavorted before the audience. Lacking Ziegfeld's funds, most restaurant revues used only an occasional principal and from six to twelve chorus girls. Dressed in short skirts and tights, though increasingly with legs and backs bare and flesh showing around the upper chest, chorus girls were so much the dominant part of these shows that Will Rogers once commented humorously on the superfluous quality of men in revues. As the only male star of the Midnight Frolic, he informed his audience that he was forced "to dress with two of the chorus girls' chauffeurs and Melville Ellis' [a costume designer] valet."[26]

Unlike burlesque, where enjoyment of the female form was permitted only at a distance and in a voyeuristic fantasy, the cabaret floor show brought the chorus girl into intimate proximity with the audience and made the young women tangible models of youth. Working close to the customers, they enticed men with face, figure, and personality. At the tables the women had to appear interested, using smiles, light chatter, and some forms of personal charm to make public contact with the customers. As friendly and personable, they were blank slates upon which members of the audience might write their hopes and fantasies. Their ever-present smiles invited customers to project their desires onto their faces. One observer described the sense of personal attraction the women conveyed: "They glance mischievously down at you. One, with the beauty of Circe, swings her foot over the railing above you, smokes a cigarette and smiles. That smile is no impersonal dental display. It strikes a responsive chord. For the first time in your life you turn dizzy looking up. Is it champagne or girl?" There was only one answer: "You glance up again and know it is a girl."[27]

In nearly every café revue, producers created a gimmick number that permitted men in the audience to express their attraction to these vivacious creatures. In "Venus on Broadway," for example, at the Palais Royale, the chorus tossed balloons to the audience and sang:

> If you catch the ball
> And throw it back to me,

Then I'll know, you see,
That you're my affinity.

In the hit of the March 1915 Midnight Frolics, the girls showed their power to make men become little boys and come out to play. "Balloon Girls" presented chorus girls wearing balloons on their costumes and headresses. Taking obvious pleasure from the interaction, male customers burst the balloons with lit cigars or cigarettes, producing squeals of delight and exclamations of surprise all around the room. Other revues were quick to include variations on this device. At the Hotel Martinique in February 1916, chorus girls engaged in a snowball dance, so they could get the men out on the floor and dancing. Maxim's "Wild West Revue" used a different approach. Toward the end of the show—all of these served as the climax of the revue—the management supplied lariats for roping the girls, and the girls kissed those who were successful. Maxim's also innovated another widely copied routine. They dressed their chorines with special pockets and invited the men to throw cotton balls into them, receiving either smiles or kisses as their reward. At Reisenweber's, Ruby Norton and her chorines performed "Won't You Take a Little Kiss from Me," arrayed in candy-striped dresses. At the climax of the song the girls threw small boxes of candy kisses to men in the audience, acting out a ritual of physical attraction between men and women.[28]

Moral critics witnessed the intimate aspects of the chorus but failed to discern its deeper meaning. The Committee of Fourteen considered that the chorus girl was "open prey for the disreputable patrons, who, demoralized by drink, force their attentions upon her." One committee undercover agent, J.A.S., viewed with alarm the lariat number in which girls lassoed men and a routine in which they placed glasses on the table so that they might take a drink. "There is a dirty appeal all through it, and a fine set of professional prostitutes to make the appeal."[29] The reformers had a point. Sometimes the girls were available, and sometimes business representatives hired them to sit with good customers. However, the actual chorus girl routine as a theatrical attraction went beyond prostitution. In so many of the gimmicks, women presented themselves as young, attractive, insinuating creatures, but the responsibility was for men to win them. The women might act coquettish, but still the active role, and hence the sense of mastery in this drama of attraction, was left to men. In order to win the women, men had to perform well at some task, an extension of their traditional role. Then they could earn the right to play. From a male point of view, the chorus girls were presented as playmates; they were fun, not demanding. Unlike Victorian women, they imposed no moral judgments, they were youthful, and men found it easy to play with them since they need not fear moral disapprobation or deep involvement. The ever-present smiles of approval and the youth of the performers worked to ease their interest in sexuality, as male mastery and control seemed intact.

Whereas during the Victorian era men and women separated sexuality from refinement, in the twentieth century they expected women to be both sexual and refined. In essence, men continued to project sexuality onto women; only the values changed. Women were to show their bodies and be expressive, while men remained aloof. Still committed to success, men made women stand for the vitality they wanted in their own lives without having to create emotional vibrancy out of the depths of their own beings. In the new style relationship, women were responsible for keeping the relationship vital and alive, for luring men out of their preoccupation with work and achievement.

WOULD YOU LIKE TO SEE A LITTLE MORE OF ME?

Although the glorified girl hit a responsive chord in American men, she would not have been such a successful staple of revues unless she could appeal to both sexes. Modern women were not ashamed to be present when their men were sexually excited; they could benefit emotionally and sexually when they got home. Moreover, the revue probably was not that threatening to them. Although chorus girls danced among the tables, they ultimately retreated to the anonymous chorus line for the ensemble numbers. "Some may be principals, who can tell," *Variety* asked of the Palais Royale revue. "What's the difference? They are all in the bunch, on the floor as well as on the program."[30] In the long run, the chorus girl embodied the values necessary for appealing to men. Featuring young women in luxurious clothes and skimpy outfits, the revue presented chorus girls as active, modern women capable of enjoying big-city freedom equally with their men. These were not old-fashioned small-town girls filled with moral constraints but women with the ability to attract their men and keep them interested, all the while enjoying life alongside them as companions and playmates.

In one of his many discussions on beauty, Ziegfeld noted that attractiveness of face and figure was the major asset he sought in hiring. Beauty caught men's eyes, and so too did his second priority, personality, a mystical quality defined as making men's heads turn. Talent brought up the rear.[31] The distinguishing appeal of the chorus girl was that mysterious quality that caught a man's eye, that required constant attention, yet could be cultivated through industrious care. Modern women could work at holding their men, and the chorus girl represented a democractic model of beauty: cultivation, makeup, and dress all contributed to every woman's beauty. In order to appeal to a man, the chorus girl was active and forward, but not so active that she represented a threat to fragile male egos or posed a challenge to his mastery. In the gimmick numbers, for instance, the women put themselves in the way of the men, but then it was up to the men to do something to catch the women. The women might use their wiles, their perfumes, their charms, and their bodies, but it was the men who actually had to win them. This ambivalent style of sexuality also carried over into clothing and beauty. In Ziegfeld's words, the overtly sensual beauty of the vamp was left out, for "the vampire is not a popular household pet."[32] For Ziegfeld, this meant excluding Jewish women, who matured early, from his beauty choruses, in favor of those who more nearly approximated the ideal of the youthful girl.

The ideal chorus girl thus combined a sensuality with niceness, and this showed up in the clothing she wore. She had to look good in luxurious clothing, in the skimpy outfits that showed her body. The approach to dressing was a peek-a-boo style, with neither customers nor performers having to admit the full sexual, and hence dangerous, potential of the women. The "Cut-Ups" at the Hotel Martinique, for example, featured "Would You Like to See a Little More of Me?" The chorus girls entered in full-length gowns, showing that they were ladies, and then proceeded to remove their dresses and dance about in tight-fitting underdresses. The women appeared coy, not openly inviting. During both winter and summer months, revues also used bathing beach costumes. In "All the Girls Are Lovely by the Sea,"

Maxim's girls wore bathing suits. This oft-repeated device drew on the body as healthy, and the water rendered sex clean. The peek-a-boo style perhaps reached its apogee in "My Pajama Beauty," in which the choristers remained in pajamas during the first part of the show. Throughout the 1910s and early 1920s, it was as if choreographers and audiences continued to think of the body as naughty and accordingly went about showing glimpses of it in a "naughty but nice manner." Perhaps it is for this reason that *Variety* declared that "one of the faults with the revue choristers is that the producers dress them up, rather than undress them. They may be frightened at taking a chance with the girls in clothes working on the floors so close to the tables, but it's worth trying."[33]

The luxuriously dressed girl formed the other side of the naughty chorus girl's image. Not only did women attract men with their bodies, they also demonstrated that they were ladies. Rector's emphasized this side of the revue by decorating its walls with life-sized sketches of elegant women taken from the covers of fashion magazines. Commending Maxim's, *Variety* noted that "no more costly nor more tasty dressing has been seen in the restaurants." Just about every revue had at least one gorgeously gowned number, for which the management paid a great deal of money. The finale of "The Spice of Life" at the Palais Royale, for example, costumed the chorines in luxurious clothes costing $150 apiece or more. According to the journal, the Palais and its owner had discovered the essence of the cabaret: "And in the 'flash' of clothes and women, Paul Salvain has at last struck the actual germ of the real cabaret performance in a high grade restaurant." For the patrons, undeniably, "it's women and clothes. Why try to make it anything else?" Percy Elkeles, responsible for the first revues at Maxim's, distinguished his shows with odd and costly costumes, garbing his chorus girls, even for bathing suit numbers, artistically, "not too daringly and yet real cabaraish." In all of his productions, according to *Variety*, the dazzling use of makeup and clothes made the chorus look handsome. In fact, the trade paper considered it a sin to have anything but expensive clothing. Speaking disparagingly of Reisenweber's revue of 1916, *Variety* declared it "very ordinarily dressed. The clothes looked as though they had seen long service."[34]

The costly clothing signified to men and women in the audience that

these girls were exciting playmates and also ladies, capable of reflecting a man's success and status. Whether ladies or not, their
clothes and upkeep cost money. Figures of high consumption, chorus
girls were women of leisure upon whom a man could lavish a good
deal of money in return for her pleasing him. Sometimes the choristers
changed costumes from eight to eleven times on stage, each time to
another and more or less costlier set of clothes. The goal was to
change, to represent novelty, to play the dual image required by men.
The high-priced clothes took money. For both women and men, high-
class glamour was the reward and meaning of success. The women in
the chorus appealed always to the "Johns," as *Variety* called them,
the big spenders seated at ringside. If women wanted to succeed, they
still had to find a man with money. Both men and women thus engaged in the process of encouraging success for men because success
brought them status. In playing to the front row tables, the chorus girls
demonstrated that the modern cosmopolitan woman sought not her
own identity but rather a successful man. To catch and hold and enjoy
such a man, the modern woman was to please him, attract him, change
her own identity as she changed her clothes, to fit his whims and
moods. In order to win the modern woman, the modern man still
needed to achieve success to pay for the consumption of wine, women,
and song. Because he, not she, was responsible for economic success,
women would have to adapt to male needs, would have to undergo the
greatest reorientation of character. The chorus girl, like the modern
woman, banked on novelty and external cosmetic changes in fashion,
face, and dress in order to catch her man and keep her relationship
vital.

The chorus girl was exciting, but she was not taken seriously as a
person. Men wanted a new-style woman and women wanted a new-
style man. But men also needed to retain control in order to achieve
the success that would hold the woman and provide the appropriate
rewards of life, hence their desire for a chorus *girl* as a playmate, who
could be enjoyed and sent back to the line. Perhaps it was for this
reason that popular mythology characterized the chorus girl as both
stupid and a gold digger. The gold digger was seemingly mastered by
stronger, richer men, but she actually manipulated them into fur coats
and expensive meals. As men saw in the expressive woman someone
to be used, they also had to worry about themselves being controlled

by sexuality, rendered masterless. Indeed since women had the only supply of sex and beauty, they held power and could easily manipulate men. This was the fear. In response, men and women also considered the sexually charged woman as too stupid to pose a real threat. By picturing the chorine as brainless, men found a woman who attracted, yet one whom in fantasy they could hold in check. This belief had a long tradition and lasted at least into the 1930s. Gossip columns and publicity material even promoted one woman, Dumb Dora, for her astounding stupidity. A chorus girl in the twenties felt compelled to try and dispel the myth. "One of the most ridiculous things believed about chorus girls is that they are uneducated. Some rich man's son is forever marrying 'an uneducated, stupid chorus girl.' "[35] Whether true or not, the tradition lasted because men and women wanted to believe that women, potentially anarchic in sexual attractiveness, could still be controlled. The woman as playmate and companion, but inferior intellectually, became the ideal. The demand for sexual attraction as well as lady-like behavior placed modern woman and man on a tightrope. Should she be too alluring she would become a gold digger, able to master men. If too much the lady, she would be unable to attract them. The new style of womanhood thus created new choices for women but also weighted those choices with tremendous anxiety. How far a good girl could go without becoming a bad girl became a primary question that both men and women asked. Were men interested in them for their bodies or for themselves? Movies and fiction of the 1920s explored the dilemma: how much sex was too much and how much made a woman unfit for a respectable male and marriage? It is no wonder that as the issue of sexuality opened up, the marriage age dropped to allay some of these anxieties.

BEHIND THE LINES

In the Midnight Frolics of 1915, "The Girl from My Home Town" opened the show with beautiful women from every state arriving in New York hoping for theatrical and/or emotional success. Many revues offered variants on this number, presenting New York as a magic city where fame, fortune, and excitement beckoned young women. Since the Floradora Girls in 1900 married prominent men about town and saw their names featured in lights, the chorus represented a potential stepping-stone to personal happiness and self-advancement. In fact, Theodore Dreiser's *Sister Carrie* moved from a small-town Wisconsin home to the big city, where after involvement with several men, she made her way through a Broadway chorus to eventual stardom. Evelyn Nesbit Thaw, the notorious woman in the Thaw-White murder case, hailed from a poor Pittsburgh background but worked her way up through the Floradora chorus. If one failed to get work as a singer, dancer, or actress on the stage, the Broadway cafés also beckoned as a place of work and a place to be noticed. Joan Crawford, Ruby Keeler, and Barbara Stanwyck, to name only a few, were chorus girls in nightclubs who went on to bigger things.

The salaries permitted them to lead lives of greater freedom. Some of the girls lived with families or sent their salaries home, but some managed to live single, independent lives, with money for personal exploration outside the homes of their fathers and husbands. Much like modern shopgirls, clerks, and secretaries who swelled the ranks of women workers from 1900 to 1920 and who read of chorus exploits in the newspapers, chorus girls were symbols of the single working urban woman. In an article on clubs for chorines, Charles Belmont Davis noted that most came from poor families and probably helped support their parents.[36] The chorus girl, like the modern working girl, was often on her own, responsible for advancing herself as well as her family.

The chorus nurtured the myth of Cinderella. The young aspirant would dance or sing her way to the top because the road was open to anyone with beauty or talent, and although there were limits on the latter, the former was a democratic entity, open to girlish caucasians. Blacks were not welcomed, and neither were overly mature Jews, but if one fit the standardized concept of the girl, one might have a chance. Perhaps Ziegfeld expressed the dream best in 1920 in *Sally*, starring his protégé Marilyn Miller, the epitome of the Ziegfeld girl. *Sally* opened with Miller as a lower-class orphan and then followed her rise through the chorus to theatrical fame, wealthy admirers, and riches. According to Robert Toll, Sally was the dream come true, the fantasy of glamour, fame, and wealth; the show portrayed that young women from limited circumstances could achieve social mobility through the theatre, catch husbands, and become desirable ladies.[37]

The chorus offered young women the experience of independent big-city living. One chorus girl noted that "American girls don't care much about 'Art for Art's sake.' They want *action*. They look upon the stage as a means to an end—an experience, or an opportunity." Not all sought success. "They want to see life, to know what's what, to experience and discover for themselves," as single young women. "You know women always used to take their look at life through a telescope—held stoutly in the hands of some male member of the family. Now they are permitted to get a close-up." They also learned much more about the opposite sex. "There's no denying that the chorus gives a girl all sorts of chances to meet men—all sorts of men, but not so much of the wealthy sort as is generally supposed." This freedom led not to anarchy but to greater personal responsibility. They became women of the world capable of handling themselves.[38]

For the most part, chorus girls did not fulfill their dreams. After a few years of youthful glory, they either moved up, changed jobs, or settled down. While it lasted, chorus work was hard and demanding; the women had to put up with unpaid rehearsals, long hours, and male producers, choreographers, and bosses who ran the theatres, the cabarets, and their lives. While more glamorous than the secretary and capable of earning more money, the chorus girl's situation was not all that different. The opportunities for succeeding as an individual were too few. Women were limited largely to the drudgery, the mass work; they made up the crowd of the modern city. In their cabaret work as well as in their private lives, the reasonable path to the Cinderella dream of upward mobility lay in marriage. This period witnessed the expansion of work experience for women, but it was not enough to sustain them for a lifetime. Instead they would take the newfound freedom of the wider world into the expanded private realm of marriage; they would also learn how to catch a man and how to please him. Their options were limited, their autonomy short-lived, and their beauty an asset that would be nurtured by an expanding cosmetics industry.

HAWAII CALLING

By the fall of 1916 a new craze was sweeping Broadway. In theatres, cabarets, and summer resorts, Hawaiian orchestras and hula-hula became the rage, and the exotic Doraldina, a woman in her early twenties who, depending on the source, was either born in Spain of an Indian mother and a Spanish father, or in Chicago, became a star in the Broadway cabarets. In 1916 she opened at Reisenweber's, had a room named and decorated after her, and then later in the year moved to the Montmartre. After European tours, she returned in 1919, doing a Turkish harem dance that *Variety* declared would "draw business to a cemetery."[39]

It is no accident that this craze coincided with the glorification of the modern chorus girl. Both the Hawaiian dancers and the chorus girls made their livings by transforming themselves into alluring creatures who could attract men to the cabaret and to themselves. Both acts represented the high value placed on women pleasing men as a respectable part of the modern relationship between the sexes, and soon after the Hawaiian craze, chorus girls themselves donned grass skirts as a staple of their costuming and performed hulas as a regular part of their act. That Hawaiian dancers were so successful is ironic, for their muscle dancing, while more refined, owed much to the disreputable cooch dance, which was done by Little Egypt at the Columbian Exposition in Chicago in 1893, and thereafter was the province of burlesque theatres and all-male audiences. Through her artistic and graceful approach, however, Doraldina helped make this exotic and primitive dance acceptable on Broadway. And similar to other cabaret trends, such as rag dancing and coon shouting, Hawaiian dances and ukulele orchestras made their way to New York from elsewhere in the nation, in this case, the West Coast. They were refined there and made acceptable for national consumption.[40]

In the hula, with arms undulating, young women wriggled their abdomens and rotated their hips in time to the languorous music. The skimpy grass skirts and bare legs were another attraction. Hawaiian dancers were exotic. Doraldina was noted for her "extraordinary [olive] skin and complexion." But stardom required refinement as well. The *New York Sun* found Doraldina perfect for the role, doing the hula in such a way that its "sensuous gracefulness and its exotic originality will be preserved at the same time so that the sensitiveness of Western audiences will not be outraged by the native hula in all its primitiveness." As they put it, "Only an artist could have modified the original dance in a manner as to have not destroyed its essential beauty. Doraldina has done this, and just to the degree that she neither offends by the least vulgarity nor disallusions *[sic]* by spoiling its originality by too great an application of western refinement."[41]

By 1917 the Hawaiian steps were commonplace. Single and double acts performed them all over Broadway, and Doraldina turned to Indian dances to keep ahead of the trend. While she maintained that balance between art and primitiveness that seems characteristic of cabaret entertainment prior to the war, the respectability she brought to the art also paved the way for the more violent muscle dancing of the shimmy, performed by Gilda Gray and Bea Palmer in 1919. From then on, shimmys, Egyptian dances, South Sea Island dances, and other exotic forms of body expression were popular in the cabarets. Each of these was performed mainly by women, who in their swaying, wriggling, and gyrating of legs, arms, and torsos, beckoned to men, attracted, and, as one observer noted of Doraldina, "represent[s] the exotic charm of the maidens of the South Seas, to whom are known the final ports of many missing men."[42] Getting away from it all would become part of the modern style.

CONCLUSION

In chorus girl revues and Hawaiian hulas, women made themselves attractive to men, and acted out the positive and negative possibilities of an informal identity for women. In playing to the front-row tables, the women demonstrated that the modern woman sought a successful man, not her own identity. Yet given the continuing orientation of men to the public world of success and women to the private realm of the home, the revue suggested ways in which men and women could solve the separation of sexual roles. Revues showed chorus girls acting in a world of leisure and fun. They were healthy, coy playmates fit for the realm of leisure. They rode horses, they engaged in sports, they portrayed nighttime activities. At Maxim's, Percy Elkeles dressed his charges in the uniforms of all the athletic departments in which a young modern woman might indulge.[43] They did not portray roles in the male world of business or politics, and when they did, it was only as humorous counterpoints. They mirrored, in a sense, the society, for in the larger dimension of life, upper-middle and upper-class women did not follow the model of the reformers and enter public life in the economy. They might work before marriage, but thereafter they channeled sexuality and new experiences toward the home. In the twentieth century, what made home appealing was its extension into the larger realm of leisure. There, in the cabaret, or in free-time activities, men and women would find excitement together. Thus men and women did not change their positions in the society; they did not have to alter their roles radically. They filled in with leisure activities around the edges of their established identities. And if the cabaret goers took cues from the chorus girl or from Irene Castle, for that matter, and through leisure and high consumption put romance into marriage, they soon found that leisure and romance cost large sums of money. For that, men dedicated themselves to the economy. The expectations of what life together could mean had been raised, but the tensions involved in producing that life remained.

NOTES

1. G. Stanley Hall, *Adolescence* (New York: D. Appleton, 1904), 2: 624, quoted in Dorothy Ross, *G. Stanley Hall* (Chicago: University of Chicago Press, 1972), p. 339.

2. For general works on the revue, see Robert Baral, *Revue: A Nostalgic Reprise of the Great Broadway Period* (New York: Fleet Publishing Co., 1962); Raymond Mander and Joe Mitcherson, *Revue: A Story in Pictures* (New York: Taplinger, 1971); and Cecil Smith, *Musical Comedy in America* (New York: Theatre Arts Books, 1950), pp. 119–20. These generally detail theatrical productions. I have relied on *Variety* for descriptions of cabaret revues.

3. Baral, *Revue*, pp. 243–45.

4. For Ziegfeld, see Charles Higham, *Ziegfeld* (Chicago: Regnery, 1972); Billie Burke with Cameron Shipp, *With a Feather on My Nose* (New York: Appleton-Century-Crofts, 1959); H. E. Cooper, "Glorifying the American Leg," *Dance* 7 (March 1927): 26–27. Gus Edwards, "The Kid's Clever," *Collier's*, January 5, 1929, p. 20, maintains that he invented the revue and Ziegfeld copied it on a much grander scale.

5. Baral, *Revue*, pp. 53–56, and *Variety*, March 26, 1915, p. 5.

6. *Variety*, October 17, 1913, p. 7, April 16, 1915, p. 7; Robert Toll, *On with the Show* (New York: Oxford University Press, 1976), pp. 295–326, for details on Midnight Frolic and revues.

7. *New York Times*, May 29, 1915, p. 20; *Variety*, June 18, 1915, p. 3; *New York Times*, May 30, 1915, II, p. 16, June 4, 1915, p. 20, June 5, 1915, p. 6, June 13, II, p. 2, and *Variety*, July 28, 1916, have information on caba-

ret revues and court problems. *Variety*, July 2, 1915, p. 8, discusses how cabarets met the added expenses of the revue.

8. Julius Keller, *Inns and Outs* (New York: G. P. Putnam's Sons, 1939), p. 134; *Variety*, December 29, 1922, pp. 15, 20.

9. "Revue: The Most Hopeful Sign on the Dramatic Horizon," *Current Opinion* (November 1918): 303.

10. *New York Times*, January 3, 1915, IX, p. 7.

11. For a description of "Nothing But Girls," see *New York Herald*, June 6, 1915; *New York World*, June 3, 1915; *New York Evening Journal*, January 18, 1915; *New York Telegraph*, January 7, 1915, n.p., clippings in Ned Wayburn Scrapbooks, New York Public Library, Lincoln Center.

12. *Variety*, February 4, 1916, p. 8. Though brief, *Variety*'s comments influenced producers of revues. After the paper pronounced, the choreographers set about working on the problems. The relationship may be only coincidental.

13. Ibid., September 29, 1916, p. 8, October 22, 1915, p. 7.

14. Ibid., October 29, 1915, p. 8.

15. Ibid., October 17, 1913, p. 7. The restaurant setting encouraged the abandonment of extensive dialogue until the invention of the microphone because it was difficult to be heard over the diners. Lyrical melodies were also a problem. Consequently exciting rag melodies were often used. See ibid., December 18, 1916, p. 113. To capture the audience, the performers needed an exciting style, one that appealed to the emotions. See ibid., February 28, 1919, p. 17. Also the acts had always relied on speed and nonstop action. Shanley's, for example, employed twenty acts that did twenty-eight turns, with no wait over thirty seconds. See Plain Mary, *Variety*, November 28, 1913, p. 21.

16. Ibid., February 27, 1915, p. 15.

17. Ibid., January 19, 1917, p. 8, January 26, 1917, p. 13, noted that an André Sherri show at Rector's had the twelve chorines change costumes eleven times.

18. Edward T. Hall, *The Hidden Dimension* (New York: Doubleday Anchor, 1969), p. 173, established the distinction between monochronic time, which is logical, orderly, and sequential, and polychronic time, which has many things occurring at the same time.

19. Alan Dale, "Among Other Things," *Variety*, October 6, 1916, p. 2.

20. Robert Toll, "The Girlie Show," in *On with the Show*, pp. 207–38; Smythe quoted, pp. 214–15. See also pp. 173–76 on "The Black Crook"; for comments on leg shows by an actress, see Olive Logan, *Apropos of Women and Theatres* (New York: Carleton Publishers, 1869).

21. See Toll, *On with the Show*, pp. 215–22.

22. A dancer [probably Bee Jackson], "Hey! Hey! Charleston," *Collier's National Weekly*, December 10, 1927, pp. 12, 34.

23. See Toll, *On with the Show*, pp. 215–22, for early chorus girls, and *Variety*, July 7, 1922, p. 15; Richard Watts, Jr., "Musical Comedy and Revue Dancing—How Did It Develop?" *Dance Magazine* 9 (January 1929): 16, 63; H. E. Cooper, "Glorifying the American Leg," *Dance* 17 (March 1927): 26, 27.

24. *Variety*, November 18, 1925, p. 19.

25. Ibid., April 20, 1917, p. 8; John Murray Anderson, *Out Without My Rubbers* (New York: Library Publishers, 1954), p. 58, producer at Palais Royale, noted that "the show girls and dancers were the real draw, for they were the creme de la creme of all beauties, culled from many hundreds of applicants."

26. *Variety*, March 26, 1915, p. 13, September 3, 1915, p. 7.

27. For pictures of balloon girls, see Wallace Morgan's sketches in "Every Night at Midnight," *McClure's* 45 (June 1915): 26–27. Quote is from Ada Patterson, "Ziegfeld's Midnight Frolic," *Harper's Bazaar* 50 (April 1915): 49.

28. Descriptions of revues are in *Variety*, January 12, 1917, p. 7, September 27, 1918, p. 19, February 28, 1919, p. 17, February 18, 1916, p. 113, April 9, 1915, p. 8. Affinity number at Palais Royale in ibid., November 9, 1917, p. 17.

29. Committee of Fourteen, *Annual Report for 1918*, p. 20; J.A.S., *Investigative Report*, May 3, 1919, Committee of Fourteen Papers, Mss. Room, New York Public Library.

30. *Variety*, October 4, 1918, p. 19. Margaret McIvor-Tyndall, "The Truth About the Chorus Girl as Told by One Who Played the Game," *Dance Lover's Magazine* 1 (April 1924): 14, notes the tendency of the public to stereotype chorus girls: "It always strikes me as funny—the way people talk about chorus girls. Why, you'd think they were a distinct species by themselves—a kind of bug, one so much like the other you couldn't tell which was which."

31. Florenz Ziegfeld, "Picking Out Pretty Girls for the Stage," in Roderick Nash, ed., *Call of the Wild: 1900–1916* (New York: Braziller, 1971), p. 258.

32. Ibid., p. 260, notes that Jewish girls are too mature for chorus girls; men prefer small girls; p. 262 has vampire quote. Add to this the idea that she must be "both pretty *and* nice."

33. *Variety*, October 22, 1915, p. 7, for cut-ups; ibid., March 26, 1915, p. 13, has material on beach routines and style of dress.

34. Ibid., September 27, 1918, p. 19, October 4, 1918, p. 19. On Elkeles,

see ibid., February 28, 1919, p. 19, and September 27, 1918, p. 19. On Reisenweber's, see ibid., October 13, 1916, n.p., clipping in Robinson Locke Collection, New York Public Library, Lincoln Center. On fashion decor, see ibid., September 22, 1916, p. 14.

35. Nils T. Granlund, with Sed Feder and Ralph Hancock, *Blondes, Brunettes, and Bullets* (New York: David McKay, 1957), pp. 230–31; and Thrya Samter Winslow, "Chorus Girls Aren't Like That!" *Dance* 8 (July 1927): 16.

36. James R. McGovern, "The American Woman's Pre-World War I Freedom in Manners and Morals," *Journal of American History* 55 (September 1968): 320, notes that the increase in women working occurred in the years 1900–1920. Charles Belmont Davis, "A Chorus Girl's Club," *Collier's National Weekly* 47 (May 20, 1911): 18, 29–30.

37. Toll, *On with the Show*, p. 321, and "A Dancer, Hey! Hey! Charleston" [probably Bee Jackson], *Collier's National Weekly*, December 10, 1927, p. 34, note clubs are a golden road for ambitious girls.

38. McIvor-Tyndall, "The Truth about the Chorus Girl," p. 14.

39. *Variety*, May 30, 1919, n.p., clipping in Doraldina File, Robinson Locke Collection.

40. "New York's Newest Dance-Craze," *Green Book Magazine*, September 1, 1916, pp. 481–83, has material on Doraldina's career, clipping in Doraldina File, Robinson Locke Collection.

41. *New York Sun*, July 2, 1916; *New York Times*, July 9, 1916, clippings in Doraldina File, Robinson Locke Collection.

42. Picture and caption of Doraldina in Robinson Locke Collection.

43. *Variety*, March 3, 1916, p. 13.

Part Four **THE FRAGMENTATION AND FLOWERING OF AMERICAN CULTURE**

8 INTO THE JAZZ AGE

> It is to this music that America in general gives itself over in its leisure hours, when it is not engaged in the struggles imposed upon it by the exigencies of present-day American life. At these times, the Negro drags his captors captive. On occasions, I have been amazed and amused watching white people dancing to a Negro band in a Harlem cabaret; attempting to throw off the crusts and layers of inhibitions laid on by sophisticated civilization; striving to yield to the feel and experience of abandon; seeking to recapture a state of primitive joy in life and living; trying to work their way back into that jungle which was the original Garden of Eden; in a word, doing their best to pass for colored.
>
> James Weldon Johnson[1]

The evening of January 15, 1920, had a bittersweet air. Crowds surged up and down Broadway searching for their last legal drink. Midnight brought prohibition, and no one knew what else. The celebration thrown by the Salvin organization to mark the beginning of prohibition and the end of an era differed from other parties that evening only in its explicit symbolism. The party for five hundred guests in the back room of Rector's got off to a rousing start as shimmy dancer Gilda Gray, portraying the handmaiden of Bacchus, led an effigy of the honored guest through the thirsty crowd. Patrons rushed upon them, tore the dethroned god from his handmaiden's grasp, and struck him down dead. After being laid to rest, he was carried about the room in a coffin provided for the occasion by the management. Then for the last time in thirteen years, wines and spirits flowed legally in a public cabaret. While few could predict the future, most people, friend and foe of night life alike, assumed that night life as they had known it was dead.[2]

The question remains how much prohibition and the world war, its immediate cause, affected the patterns of nightlife in the 1920s. For most historians, the reaction to the war and prohibition led to a moral letdown, a debauch, as the generation of the 1920s reacted to the deflation of moral idealism and high purpose by rebelling against authority and the standards of civilization. For these historians, the 1920s was a beginning. But the purpose of this study is to show that the 1920s were a culmination, building on the trends under way in social and sexual life since the 1890s.[3] Clearly the war did raise moral idealism. Men and women of this generation found in the war an outlet for the tensions in their sense of manhood and womanhood. Entertainers and movie stars joined the war effort and proved their dedication to civilization. Sophie Tucker, Al Jolson, the Original Dixieland Jazz Band, James Reese Europe, Vernon and Irene Castle, Douglas Fairbanks and Mary Pickford aided the preparedness and war cause. During the war, cabarets inserted tents and other military apparatus into their revues. As Vernon Castle went to war to serve his country, he also vindicated his manhood; Irene, in *Patria*, the preparedness serial, defended the nation and her own womanhood against sensuous Mexicans and Japanese spies. This generation found in the kaiser the greatest white slaver of them all, bent on destroying home, womanhood, democracy, freedom. In fighting for the home, men were fighting to preserve the traditional image of woman from the threat of both aristocratic and lower-class brutal sexuality. The war, for the moment, called men and women back to moral civilization, to duty.[4]

In New York nightlife, mayors and moral reformers found the opportunity to enforce the traditional values they had seen slipping during the 1910s. Reform groups such as the Committee of Fourteen supervised army camps and amusement zones in New York, policed cabarets selling liquor to service men, and stepped up their attacks on "pleasure hounds," "lounge lizards," and other sexual aberrations bent on weakening men and women amid the ravages of war. In New Orleans, reformers closed the red-light district, and many of them supported the War Time Emergency Prohibition Act. In New York, Mayor John Purroy Mitchel placed tighter clamps on the cafés. A fusion candidate of the Republicans and Progressives, Mitchel had achieved a reputation as the dancing mayor because of his penchant for fox-trotting. He had also worked out a more liveable curfew of two o'clock that somewhat mollified reformers and late-night cabarets. The war, however, put him in a different mood. He proposed a one o'clock curfew to protect the scarce energy of young men from depletion by pleasure. "I have decided," announced the mayor two weeks after the declaration of war, "to cancel for the period of the War all existing all-night licenses for the sale of intoxicating drinks." For good taste and proper sense, he wanted cabarets to end their drinking and dancing at an early hour. "The conservation of our resources, national and personal, human and material, should begin now." Unlike previous curfew campaigns, Mitchel's decision met with the patriotic approval of the Hotel and Restaurant Men's Association and went into effect on May 1, 1917. Reformers and critics, male and female patrons saw in the war a necessary defense of traditional, frugal values.[5] Noteworthy, of course, was that Mitchel continued the progressive approach to amusements; instead of outlawing cabarets entirely, he limited excesses through licensing and brought them under government control.

While urban areas had worked out compromises in entertainment and in reform with the new sexual styles, others saw in the urban culture a threat to Protestant, small-town moral existence. In this sense, as Henry May has pointed out, the war, and for that matter Prohibition, contributed to the destruction of old values. Defended as the savior of moral democratic civilization, the war destroyed the importance of civilization for ordering experience; the grim war undercut the idea of restraint of the passions for social duty by the excesses to which the idea had been put. The fact that authority and propaganda committees justified violence and aggression in ascetic, refined terms tended only to undercut authority as propaganda; why follow cultural leaders who stood for civilization? Moreover the war ushered in prohibition. Urban reformers during the 1910s had cleaned up the excesses of the new amusements in order to bring morality to play. They utilized licensing, surveillance, and curfew laws, but they were often split on prohibition because its enforcement in cabarets seemed impossible. During the war, they worked to enforce prohibition in army camps. Moreover, the fight for prohibition became the province of small-town Protestants bent on establishing the primacy of their values on the encroaching, more glamorous culture of the ethnically and sexually heterogenous urban areas.

Prohibition to urbanites was an excess of civilized zeal. Reformers and conservatives increasingly assumed a puritanical image bent on outlawing all pleasure that threatened them. They were not human, merely overly zealous ideologues. In one famous cartoon, *Vanity Fair* in 1925 pitted a sober commissioner of prohibition, Mabel Willebrandt, against Texas Guinan, the loud and raucous nightclub master of ceremonies as the two poles of civilization in the twenties. Guinan, like the best people who visited her clubs, made a career out of evading the prohibition law and its officers. She clearly came off best by comparison. As the *New Yorker* hit the stands as the epitome of sophisticated urban life and "not edited for the old lady in Dubuque," the split between city sophistication and small-town morality widened.[6]

By establishing the forces of morality against already won urban pleasures, prohibition encouraged further individual rebellion from society. The cabaret already represented freedom from institutional roles that were compromised by a new view of public success and status. Men and women had adopted the new sexual and social trends by relegating them to the world of home and leisure, while safeguarding the public male world of sobriety, diligence, and success in the economy. Instead of using these new values to create a new-style public life and economy, most urbanites were content to compartmentalize these new trends in leisure. They saw the high life as the reward of the economy. Prohibition exacerbated this trend. Discontent with the Eighteenth Amendment led to increased emphasis on drinking and sexual styles as private rights that were not the business of the state or the society. People wanted to be left alone to enjoy themselves, and thus they failed to link their new social and personal values to social transformation.

While concentrating on the twenties, most historians have missed these earlier developments. By examining the changes in nightlife since the 1890s, we are now prepared to treat the twenties as a culmination of a long process rather than the beginning. The defense of drinking as a private right in the 1920s was possible because during the 1910s new sexual changes had been oriented toward the private realm and made compatible with public success for men and a continued private role for women. We saw this in the structure of the café. While the cabaret provided a life that was cosmopolitan and more open than the cloistered home and social life of the nineteenth century, it also offered a safe environment for acting out new values, which in turn could be taken back to the private social worlds from which people came. Neither the critics' nor the patrons' worst fears were realized. Publicly expressed intimacy and informality did not undercut class status. While groups merged in behavior and values, their private social worlds remained protected.

For men and women, new sexual styles were limited largely to leisure, an extension of the home. After 1910 both men and women included elements of passion, expressiveness, and a wider conception of self into their formerly formal culture and broke down the barriers between men and women, upper- and lower-class culture, blacks and whites. However, these trends were the province of leisure, an expanded realm where the nonauthoritarian and individualistic aspects of the culture would find an outlet. As society accepted sexual women, it confined them to safe areas of life. Leisure could absorb sexuality and consumption, could indeed even become the reason that men worked, but it would not challenge the public world of the economy where both men and women counted on men making their way, earning their incomes and their status. The leisure area, made safe, became the realm for consumption values. Once the new synthesis was developed, this bourgeois order saved, women and men could more deeply investigate the sexual dimensions of their lives. By the time of the war, this intensification of private pleasures, divorced from the public world, was already under way. Men and women of the prosperous classes could go further in their exploration of a new inner life in the twenties because they did not have to worry about destroying civilization. The war had already discredited the notion of submission of personal desires to external authority, and one's personal allegiance to the public world was now fractured. Instead of working as an agent of moral progress, to extend one's private morality and character into the economy, men worked to get the money for more leisure, enjoyment, and consumption. Prosperous women no longer felt duty-bound; they helped promote pioneering conceptions of the home and marriage as self-fulfilling and self-gratifying. This emphasis on a separation between the values of work and leisure arose when urbanites, progressives, and feminists could find few ways to link new private styles to public order and because of the contradictions inherent in Victorianism from which urbanites were moving away. The increased emphasis on personal consumption, enjoyment, and leisure in the twenties used the individual's concern for a fuller private life and the sense that the individual's social style had little public import. The revitalization of American culture meant a revitalized self.

RESPECTABLE CRIMES

Prohibition threatened to disrupt the operation of nightlife. Drink fueled the cabaret by blotting out the routine world and loosening constraints. When drink was threatened, so were the profits of the old-style restaurants. Many old-style lobster palaces had to choose between breaking the law or going broke. Thomas Shanley of Shanley's explained that "eating places pay, of course," but they were "not what I call a restaurant, where a man or a woman can get the best of food and the best of wines, a cocktail and a liqueur." In sum, he observed, "We can't go on at a profit on soft drinks. We obey the law and lose money, and we can't afford that." Some places tried to make a profit on soft drinks and other soda fountain delights, and others became cheap dance halls to fill empty coffers in the troublesome years of 1920 through 1922.[7] It was clear that alcohol was necessary for profits and the style of the cabarets. Those who continued selling liquor were brought low by the padlock, a costly matter because the fine and loss of income added to the amount of fixed rent that had to be paid.

Prohibition thus destroyed a number of the old respectable cabaret owners and opened the door to bootleggers who could supply the liquor. As *Variety* put it in 1925 in the midst of a nightlife revival, "A survey of the situation generally finds a bootlegger as the usual Ethiopian in the lumber-heap." Three groups, mirroring New York's major ethnic divisions, entered the café business. First were Irish gangsters, like Owney Madden, formerly of the Hell's Kitchen Gopher gang and one of the big liquor suppliers. He held interest in Broadway's Silver Slipper and Harlem's Cotton Club. Larry Fay owned the Club Napoleon, El Fey Club, and a piece of several Texas Guinan ventures. Second, Italians were prominent in speakeasies and clubs in Italian areas such as Greenwich Villiage. And third, Jews, such as Arnold Rothstein, owned pieces of Broadway and Harlem clubs and were rumored to have supplied money to other operators, small businessmen who opened other clubs. Like Al Capone, New York criminals made crime a business by providing a consumption service in the 1920s.[8] While the presence of criminals produced some violence in and about the nightclubs, especially in the late 1920s and early 1930s, for the most part they helped keep the peace in Harlem, making it safe for people in "ermine and pearls" to go uptown, and they also emphasized the entertainment-drinking end of the business rather than the overarching attention to decorum and civilization.[9] They emphasized, in other words, the trend after 1915 of drawing patronage by girlie revues and big-name entertainment.

The danger of raids made expensive decorations and elaborate surroundings unwise, and it also drove down the cost of opening nightclubs. With the exit of old cabaret operators, many with roots in restaurants rather than entertainment, many small businessmen entered the field, and nightlife became competitive. While the early 1920s was a period of relative slump because of the aid local New York City police gave federal Volstead agents, the period after 1924 witnessed a new blossoming, and New York voted to abandon local enforcement; only a small federal force was left to monitor Manhattan. Because of the fear of raids, however, these clubs often sought the relative anonymity of cellars, basements, and backrooms of brownstones in the sidestreets of the forties and fifties. There, with membership cards to elude curfew and speakeasy mannerisms to elude officials, the nightclub emerged as a cheaper place, with a few drapes, some silk splashed on the walls, and a tentlike effect over the dance floor. Everything was portable after a raid. The reduced costs necessary to compete opened the door to marginal businessmen, who with a few partners concentrated on the relative profit-making aspects of nightclubs: entertainment for the draw and liquor for the bank.[10] In this highly competitive atmosphere, redolent of all small business, operators who could find the right atmosphere, could appeal to the customers' wants directly, and could supply the best entertainment and atmosphere, could perhaps out-survive their competitors for a season or two.

In concentrating on quicker profits in entertainment and for some in drink, nightclub operators cut down their emphasis on food, services, and other extras. They needed a headwaiter with a quality list of patrons to get started, and for the rest, they could rent out the concessions on a percentage. Specialization entered the business, and the quality of the food declined. Proprietors wanted food just good enough to keep patrons interested; the majority of profits came from increased cover charges, the surreptitious sale of liquor, and higher volume business. Partly the higher prices arose from the desire to make quick profits before the clubs were put out of business and partly because of the higher costs of entertainment. However, by catering to patron desires, the nightclubs sought to increase attendance, and to do this they emphasized even more the entertainment, the exciting qualities of the Broadway cabarets under way since 1915: the use of vaudeville stars, headliners, bigger monied acts, and, on Broadway, girls who were increasingly scantily clad.[11]

Prohibition also made running nightclubs even less reputable. Society women might open an exclusive establishment on the East Side like Lido-Venice, but many of the smaller clubs fell into ethnic hands, many of them Jews and Italians, whose dominance has lasted to this day. Like the ethnic entertainers, these proprietors had a feeling for the rough equality of Broadway life and a desire for success and celebrity that came with being close to the elite of the theatre and entertainment. The ethnics, arising out of the theatrical profession or other consumption businesses, such as bootlegging, rather than the elegant prewar restaurant or hotel business, perceived that the nightclub could appeal more directly to people's nighttime fantasies, their desires and hopes, and also to a more democratic merchandising of exclusivism and exotic pleasure. The mass roots of the nightclub lay in the prewar Broadway cabarets, but the war, prohibition, and the opening of the field to new people expanded the desire to attract and hold large audiences. As *Variety* observed in 1918, "Like Paris was framed for Americans, so is Broadway now staged for the country folks."[12] With less commitment to the civilized apparatus and gracious style of the lobster palaces, the ethnic small business owners succeeded at giving people what they presumably wanted.

At one end of the spectrum, the cafés reproduced a good deal of their low-life male origins in the 1920s. Given the speakeasy and the hidden nature of cafés, proprietors often sold liquor, introduced B-girls once again to lure male "suckers," and raised the prices. All through the 1920s, sucker places were part of the nightlife for men looking for women. However, when it came to places serving respectable men and women, the cabaret seemed to expand its audience. It certainly expanded its number. By one reporter's count, there were seventy decent places running by the late 1920s; these often went in and out of fashion, with new novelties constantly entering the fray. The life of a café, while relatively long in the prewar period (Shanley's, Churchill's, Reisenweber's, Murray's, Pekin, and others lasted the duration), now enjoyed a season or two at most. Prohibition could end the life, but so too could the new nature of the business. Set up to sell dreams of romance and escape, the nightclubs of the twenties had to be ever on the watch for new novelties. Moreover, a bust or an unpleasant incident like a fight could show the seamier side of cafés and easily dissuade patronage. Although the new conditions reduced the emphasis on civilized decor and imperial imagery, the wider audience for nightlife still required silk on the walls, an aura of class and status, the velvet rope, society people in the audience. While civilization as a hierarchical social value for controlling the passions, confining the will, and mastering anarchic society did not survive, the desire for class and exclusivity, even for large Broadway audiences, was necessary to legitimate sexual pleasures, to give them bourgeois respectability, and to make leisure the reward for self-control and success. It was all still expensive, even more expensive given the cover charges of two or three dollars for popular places and three to five dollars at more select spots, but the idea of civilization as an organizing framework for life was reduced on Broadway. More people could share in the rewards of success, and, as the 1920s progressed, they could appreciate more fully that money from an organized business society, instead of civilization, could offer them fantasy, escape, and a fuller private life removed from the rationalized control and order of public life.

PUTTIN' ON THE RITZ

After the initial years of the twenties, the nightclub business expanded to include some seventy clubs, not including speakeasies, East Side rooms, Greenwich Village dance places, and Harlem nightclubs. The number and variety increased as civilization's hand was reduced; novelty increased, and so too did the image of the nightclub as a fabulous urban experience, the epitome of New York, the height of romance and adventure. While within urban areas the cabaret had achieved a measure of legitimacy before the war, by the late 1910s and early 1920s, other agencies of popular opinion trumpeted its charms to the nation. In *Why Change Your Husband, Old Wives for New, Affairs of Anatole*, and other domestic dramas, Cecil B. De-Mille, the premier director of the late 1910s and early 1920s, explored changes in marriage for a mass audience, which the New York theatre had been doing since the turn of the century. In his features, respectable, prosperous, unexciting husbands and wives, tired of each other but with few ideas on how to change, divorce. One partner leaves for what he or she considers a more exciting glamorous urban existence, for a chorus girl or a musician. Once the divorce occurs, however, the duller partner begins a personal transformation. Women who wanted to be homebodies suddenly realize they must attract their husbands, must use makeup, put on exciting lingerie and fashions, must go out at night and dance, must learn to enjoy nightclubs and cafés if they want to avoid the mistakes of the past. Husbands learned to devote less time to the office, more to family and women. In the end, the original partners discover each other in new guises, remarry, avoid the debilitating nature of urban sin, but privatize the experience for themselves and thus revitalize and reorient their lives. Movies—and so many urban movies seem to have had a nightclub scene—used nightlife as an image of what marriage and life would be, even when criticizing nightlife.[13] In and around the cities in the twenties, early radio hooked up nightclubs and played dance music into people's homes. Urban tabloids carried Broadway columns after the mid-decade, detailing nightlife shenanigans in tones of envy and dismay, and so too did the front-page newspaper stories. Consumption heroes, living off the fruits of the system, were avid topics of interest.[14]

A large variety of people in increasing numbers went to nightclubs in the twenties. Young people made up a large proportion. During the 1910s, the well-to-do young, spurred on by the dance craze, visited the cafés, but in the 1920s, several clubs catered specifically to them, playing the favorite music of a college crowd. Young people from prosperous backgrounds had the time and money to indulge in nightclubs, at least now and again, and as Paula Fass has suggested, the young had a peer culture that found its heroes and heroines in popular culture. Caught partly between an affectionate family and a competitive society, the young found in nightclubs and movies values that brought the two together; one competed for the status, success, and leisure that provided the pleasure, affection, and enjoyment of life. Gilman Ostrander adds that a technological society placed great weight on youth as consumers because each wave of technological innovation placed youth in the forefront of society. In this, however, the nightclub was not age specific. The rise of youth culture was part of the tensions of the larger culture. Because both men and women desired a new style of consumption, a new personal existence within a tradition of male success and work as the distributor of private rewards, only the prosperous and the young, with occasional family trade, could enjoy this style of life. Because the old could only take part vicariously, the entire culture focused on the lost stage of youth, as seen in revues when people could pursue romance and mutuality, and gave over to that period of life the actual means and time for its pursuit. Youth culture derives in part from the failures of the larger society to resolve its own tensions.[15]

An older crowd might visit certain nightclubs or they could dance in the popular ballrooms of the Biltmore, Pennsylvania, Commodore, and New Yorker hotels. Featuring rippling waterfalls, starry-lit skies, and the sweet dance music of Guy Lombardo, George Olsen, or Vincent Lopez, the hotels provided a touch of romance for those out on a budget. Neither innovative nor raucous, these rooms filled the gap for an older, often suburban, crowd, out for a big night in the city. They too could get away from family and friends and find a measure of privacy in public.

Members of society broke down some of the barriers of privacy in the 1920s and entered nightlife on a more regular basis. Even before the war, society members visited certain places, like Sans Souci, Midnight Frolic, Moulin Rouge, and in the mid-1920s they were fond of East Side spots like the Lido, the Flamingo, the Matador, and later the Central Park Casino, where the prices were higher and the clientele more exclusive. In 1928 Rudy Vallee noted that the Heigh-Ho Club on the East Side did not permit Jews, a group considered too pushy for intimate mixture. On the East Side, the crowds were much more controlled, and the game of status in public was played out much more by society people who had few standards left, other than money, for delimiting status. One way was to create exclusive places, keep out the Broadway crowd and the tourists who seemed to flock there.

Society men and women also went to Broadway for a good time, however, and there in public broke the barriers between themselves and the theatrical crowd. Public nightlife also gave some of the wealthy young the chance to escape society. Young Ellin Mackay, daughter of Clarence Mackay, a communications tycoon, attempted in 1925 to answer "Why We Go to Cabarets" in the *New Yorker*. As she put it, society itself had become too formal and public, too over-run by people not of one's choosing, with whom one was supposed to mix, meet, and, presumably, romance. Nightclubs were removed from the parental eye, allowing the young to achieve intimacy with friends of their own choosing, now that society had turned into a cir-cus and was not quite so exclusive. Instead of having to dance with numerous young men, she and her friends could find greater privacy along Broadway. Public space allowed for private romance and per-sonal choice, removed from family and institutional social expecta-tions. For Mackay, this stance culminated in a highly unusual action: the marriage to Jewish songwriter Irving Berlin.[16]

By the 1920s nightclubs were no longer risqué, and many rich young people had become interested in themes of popular culture, especially as they touched personal choice among the sexes. While some retreated to the private life of townhouse and Long Island estate, a number of them found a public role, made possible by the leaching of social commitment. As the public became increasingly interested in society figures, stars, and their grand lives of play and romance lived publicly through tabloids, gossip columns, fan magazines, and popular stories, it became apparent that the by now widely dispersed social group known as New York society had to compete for public attention in the newspapers. A new means of status was the notice of the newspapers, the attention of entertainers, and spending of money on a spree. Publicity and celebrity—living a role the popular press desired—provided status in a competitive social order. For women, the public's notice gave them a chance to grace the theatre and fashion, as well as society, pages only now in terms of worldly sophis-tication. Without challenging male prerogatives, women especially could devote themselves to the business of play, to being smart, to knowing what was fashionable all over the city. They could remain leisured, and yet have purpose. Café society gave them a chance. With endless new money, social place could be won by turning to the future, to the new, to what was daring.

An important by-product of the use of nightlife by society was the elevation of entertainment stars to near parity with the wealthy as celebrities. The celebrity of the twenties was the apotheosis of the consumption idol that had been forming in the 1910s. The star entertainer, making fabulous sums, living in luxury, was a democratic figure, one who offered the tangibility of the new life to an ever wider audience, who took both the conspicuous consumption of the rich and the liveliness of the bottom and merchandised them within the parameters of success. Gossip columnists Cholly Knickerbocker in the society pages of the *New York American* and Walter Winchell on the entertainment pages of the *Evening Graphic* and later the *New York Mirror* wrote about stars and society figures whose activities came under their notice. Celebrities, and particularly stars, were coming to represent the hopes, wishes, and fantasies of the readers of the popular press. The star was removed from all concern with politics or social duty and instead was someone who had achieved personal harmony and freedom, youth and beauty, a life of consumption as the reward of success, above and beyond the restraints of background or class.[17]

A case in point is Harry Richman, singer of romantic ballads, man about town, theatrical and nightclub star of the 1920s. From a Cincinnati, Ohio, Jewish family who had high ambitions for him as a classical violinist, he soon gave up his ethnic heritage and pretensions to culture, but he kept his high aspirations for a life in show business. Knocking about the country, Richman worked his way from saloons and vaudeville to theatres and Broadway. By the end of the 1920s he starred in the *George White Scandals* with his trademark song, "Puttin' On the Ritz," written by another Jewish boy who had transcended his background through Broadway, Irving Berlin. In tuxedo and top hat, Harry was a star who lived lavishly, was linked in the columns to numerous Broadway and Hollywood women, among them Clara Bow, and who romanced numerous society women. In effect, with his Long Island parties, world airplane trips, and conquests of society and its women, Richman never quite got over proving himself to a non-Jewish world and his first-generation parents. His nightclub, Club Richman, was a popular spot that drew Broadway and Fifth Avenue clientele. As the featured performer, he appealed to the ladies in the audience as a romantic figure, vaguely swarthy, dreamy, and intense.

When he noticed someone he wanted, he would send her a note to come to the ladies' room. He had cut a doorway through to his office. A woman would come through the washroom to his office for fifteen minutes of pleasure and would then return to her escort. Through popular entertainment, Richman became an American celebrity, combining ethnic vitality with status and class derived from both Americanization and from hobnobbing with those high in the social order. Richman indeed put on the ritz.[18]

HELLO SUCKER!

The entertainer as a figure of impulse followed from the developments of the 1910s. In pursuing greater mutuality, both men and women learned to separate a more pleasurable personal world from the more rational, hierarchical realm of business. As the private realm became more sexual, men and women removed it from the purposeful world of the economy. This separation fragmented the old unity between character and the public world that had been an underlying motivation of Protestant culture. By the twenties, however, urbanites, having preserved order in the public world, were free to indulge themselves in the private world of consumption and fun.

During prohibition, clubs were much smaller than the early cabarets. These offered privacy and romance, away from the prying eyes of others. Indeed the use of corners, private tables, and smaller spaces increased the sense of privacy that the individual enjoyed, removed from the outside world. In that smaller space, moreover, they could enjoy an even more intimate relationship between themselves and with the entertainer. In the smaller space, more people had the sense of interaction with the entertainer.

The inclusion of the master of ceremonies in cabaret entertainment in the early 1920s was part of this trend. Although the Folies Bergère had introduced the master of ceremonies as a continental invention as early as 1911, it did not catch on in the restaurant cabarets. The large restaurants were too noisy to hear someone talking, and for that reason, both masters of ceremonies and verbal comedians were not strong presences in the early cafés. The advent of smaller clubs, however, meant that someone could talk and be heard, and during the 1920s some of the greatest stars were the masters of ceremonies.

Texas Guinan was one of the most famous hostesses of twenties nightclubs. Born Mary Louise Guinan in Texas of Irish Catholic parents, Texas received her nickname after appearing in several wild west shows as a sharpshooter. An expert rider and markswoman, she also made a career in Broadway musicals and movies in the 1910s. In her nightclubs, she often acted as if she were still in a rodeo. Loud and raucous, Texas attracted celebrities and big spenders to every one of her numerous nightclubs. The columns called her clubs human zoos, so filled and various were they. Living alone with her family, she radiated strong, single womanhood, but as was the case with Sophie Tucker, her position of strength, aggressive behavior, and humor left her as one of the boys, a pal. This neuter quality gave her greater leeway, however, and she was able to set the tone of her clubs with raucous good humor and hearty candor.

As master of ceremonies and hostess, she dominated her clubs. Announcing "give this little girl a big hand," she introduced her vaudeville acts and revues with a liveliness that overlay the mechanical nature of the form. And just when the revue threatened to eclipse audience participation, Texas activated the audience. She was a figure of intimacy, though not threatening, and when she called out "Hello sucker!" in her bawdy voice, she alerted the rich men that they had to pay for their cheap thrills, and of course they knew it. She was honest about the superficial nature of the entertainment, and through this honesty made herself a celebrity, whose liveliness and ability to get along with people became the mark of the successful master of ceremonies. She knew everyone, and in her friendly manner with politicians, society figures, and stars of the stage or screen, she could induce them to get outside themselves; she could get them to stand up and introduce themselves, she could get even respectable folk to play leapfrog at late hours. In her jam-packed spots, she got people not to take themselves so seriously.

The successful master of ceremonies smoothed over the rough spots in the shows, kept the entertainment moving along at a fast clip, enhanced audience participation, and, most of all, kept alive a sense of audience sociability and friendliness. Extending the model set by Sophie Tucker, Guinan was a more consummate friendly entertainer. She knew everybody and was extremely friendly to everyone she knew. And she was the apotheosis of the consumption idol. Texas's fame rested not on her talent as a singer, dancer, or actress; she made fame through that particularly modern talent of getting along with all kinds of people up and down the social hierarchy. As such, her continued celebrity was perpetuated by getting her name in the papers. She was a celebrity because she knew other celebrities. She was reminiscent of Jimmy Walker, "Beau James," the entertaining mayor of New York in the 1920s, who had friends among celebrity people in all walks of life as well, and much of whose fame rested on his ability to get along.[19]

Part of Texas's appeal lay in her resistance to law and order, personified by the Volstead agents who repeatedly shut her down only to have her open again; she encouraged her image by staging a "Padlock Revue" in 1927. She stood for the public's right to privacy in their personal and leisure life, and she was only one of the celebrities of the 1920s who played on the taste for rebellion by testing restrictions set on social behavior and sexual display. Two other popular acts of the twenties, Clayton, Jackson, and Durante and "The Mad Waiter," developed the critique of gentility. Clayton, Jackson, and Durante was composed of a singer, a dancer, and all-around piano-player-comedian (Jimmy Durante). Until 1923, Durante was known as Ragtime Jimmy and played authentic jazz and ragtime at Coney Island and at the Alamo Café, an early rathskeller underneath a burlesque theatre on 125th Street. In the early 1920s he teamed with his partners, and began a series of small clubs—Club Durant, Dover, Parody—which originally drew the "wise" mob and then began to attract a wider Broadway audience. To many nightclub commentators, Clayton, Jackson, and Durante were the hottest café act of their day, and even intellectuals of the *New Republic* found Durante an expression of the *Seven Lively Arts*.[20]

The trio seemed to have tailored their style to the requirements of the cabarets. They improvised as they went along, they worked back and forth with the audience, and they starred in their own clubs so repeat business would come to see them. One of the central features of their humor was that the audience, respectable people, while treated courteously, were also made objects of humor; nothing was sacred. When a well-dressed couple walked in, for example, Jimmy might seat them at different tables or start dancing with the woman. The implicit point was whether they were good sports. They employed Fifi, a rather bad French singer, and, during her song, the trio would yell at her, dance in front of her, make fun of her histrionics, and generally try to distract her. The fun came from the interaction and the improvisation. They also had the habit of introducing their washroom attendant as someone interested in getting ahead, thus poking fun at Horatio Alger and success. In their famous wood number, they grabbed every piece of wood in the club and piled them on stage while singing the virtues of wood as described in an advertisement written by the Lumber Association. They took the sacred principles of order, success, and propriety and turned them upside down. They turned the formalities topsy-turvy.

Frank Libuse, "the Mad Waiter," extended the informality of Guinan and Clayton, Jackson, and Durante. From Chicago, Libuse acted the role of the waiter, who, when guests arrived, took them to all corners of the room, leaving them stranded. In seating someone, he might pull the chair out from under, making them the object of the joke. This was audience participation indeed. Respectable-looking people apparently drew his attention, and they went along with the various jokes, waiting for the next "stuffed shirt" to come in, so that they could be on the inside of the humor next time. For all three acts, the stuffed shirt was an object of humor. While the distinctions between the classes remained in fact, these nightclub acts deflated the formal distances. In popular culture, the public sought to ape the style of the wealthy and to reduce the difference between "them and us," while wanting to be like "them."[21] In glorifying the good sport, all these acts thus tested whether members of the audience were stuffed shirts or had the personal qualities necessary to fit into a more sociable and more malleable style of life.

Just as Durante and the Mad Waiter stretched the bounds of the socially acceptable, Gilda Gray—and dancing in general—extended the acceptable limits of sexual display. A Polish immigrant from Milwaukee, Gilda was discovered in Chicago doing the shimmy—a black torso-shaking dance—and moved on to New York cabarets in 1919. Having changed her Polish name, Michealski, to May, Gilda underwent another transformation at the hands of Sophie Tucker into Gilda Gray, a name that combined luxury and glamour (gilda) with class and reserve. Gilda presented this theme in her dancing. She followed Doraldina in the cafés and presented a body-shaking dance to blues and jazz music. While performing these wicked torso movements, she kept an impassive innocent face, which assured patrons she was respectable. Moving to her own cabaret, the Rendezvous, in the early twenties and to Broadway shows and movies, Gilda remained a big star. She followed the path of many women stars, marrying her manager, nightclub entrepreneur Gil Boag, and moved to the suburbs to enjoy the good life in a colonial home.[22]

The shimmy, while performed in and about the cafés, remained largely an exhibition dance. Moralists tried to outlaw it and other jazz dances in the early 1920s, and although Gilda was arrested, she eventually moved on to the alluring South Sea Island dances. For most urbanites, the shimmy contained too much exhibitionism and body, and they remained content with variations on the one-step and fox-trot. About 1925, however, young people began to do more energetic and more athletic dances, which utilized the full torso, legs, and hips. The source of dances like the charleston and the black bottom lay in black culture, and they found wide introduction in New York after the popularity of *Shuffle Along*, a black musical of 1921–1922. The charleston assumed popularity when it was combined with the one-step so that couples could dance close, and then open out and display their bodies to each other. The couple remained at the center of the dance. Also whites removed hip and pelvic thrusts, making the dance athletic instead, showing more leg than in the 1910s but in a romping, fun spirit. While more body was displayed, it was done again along the lines of good fun. Despite their restraints, young men and women felt they had advanced years ahead of their parents. Doing these athletic dances, the young pictured the old culture as too restrained and civilized, the epitome of the stuffed shirt.[23]

The Broadway compromise between restraint and rebellion is perhaps best epitomized by the history of jazz. Although a number of bands have laid claim to being the original jazz band, the Original Dixieland Jass Band (ODJB) introduced New Orleans–style brass band music to New Yorkers when they played in Reisenweber's in late 1916 and early 1917. Sophie Tucker, at the same spot, also at one time billed herself as the Queen of Jazz and Her Five Kings of Syncopation. The Original Jazz Band, composed of five young men, many of them second-generation Italians, picked up their music from the brass bands—black and white—in the New Orleans area prior to World War I. Their music differed from ragtime in its greater syncopation and in its large component of improvisation. Untutored musically, the band members rarely wrote down their scores, unlike ragtime. They also broke open the semiformal quality of ragtime by making their instruments duplicate animal sounds, such as a horse whinnying or a tiger growling.[24] Being brassier in sound than early bands, the ODJB forced patrons to experience a wild, anarchic music, which seemed to be without structure.

After the ODJB demonstrated the power and the draw of the new music, a number of other black and white bands, composed largely of young men, began working northern dance halls and cafés. No one was sure what jazz was or even how to spell it, but the music meant that the dancing would become more energetic, with even more room for body movement and personal expression. Dancers did faster fox-trots, the less inhibited ones could shimmy, and the band played them on, the music being a perfect companion to the dances.

With its roots deep in black culture, jazz relied heavily on personal expressivism, outside of formalism, expressed through improvisation. It also offered white musicians and audiences an outlet from their own particular cultures. In his investigation of jazz in the twenties, Neil Leonard suggests that Benny Goodman, Mezz Mezzrow, Hoagy Carmichael, and Bix Beiderbecke were attracted to jazz because it offered a standard of music and life different from the gentility of midwestern values. As Hoagy Carmichael quoted one black musician, "You may not make much money, but you won't get hostile with yourself." The music itself gave vent to one's experience of life. The underlying appeal of the legendary Bix Beiderbecke, a cult figure in life and death, lay in his living the jazz life, searching the purity that came out of his cornet. According to contemporaries, Beiderbecke cared little for surroundings, food, or clothes, drank a good bit, and died young from the fast but happy life. For many musicians, the authentic jazz life was an experiential life outside the conventions of white America.[25]

It is perhaps no wonder that in the twenties these hot jazz players were for the most part outsiders. Most people in the early twenties did not listen to real jazz. Instead they might have heard "nut" jazz, played by Ted Lewis, the clarinetist-comedian who began making his way in the Broadway cabarets from 1919 on. Nut-jazz men picked up the anarchic animal sounds and unusual instrumentation but gloried in the comic effects rather than in the music.[26]

While the nut-jazz men discounted the potential of jazz and emphasized the happy-go-lucky nature of the music, commercial and refined jazz players defused the potential of jazz in other ways. Paul White-man, perhaps the best-known band leader of the 1920s, was the son of the conductor of the Denver Symphony Orchestra. Abandoning clas-sical music early, he went into the dance music field, becoming a major attraction in his own right. Perhaps it is no accident that white musicians of the twenties achieved star prominence, moving out from supporting roles to the dancers, a role played by the black bandsmen such as James R. Europe in the 1910s. Whiteman made his first ap-pearance in New York in 1921 at the Palais Royale on Broadway. He became a star by doing for jazz what the Castles had done for black dances. Black music could not be absorbed in unadulterated form; re-formers, church leaders, and parents in the early twenties were up in arms about the new music. Whiteman perceived that he could make jazz respectable by uplifting it and demonstrating its classical, har-monic qualities. Starting out as a commercial bandleader, playing smooth music that downplayed improvisation and raucousness, by 1924 he gave concerts at Aeolian Hall, in which George Gershwin performed his "Rhapsody in Blue." While using jazz shadings, Whiteman relied essentially on written scores and European har-monics. The result was harmonious rather than anarchic, and the public made him a star.[27] In a culture that had learned to see love as the justification for sex, popular white dance bands played romantic, smooth, or athletic music, with the passionate and wild side down-played.

THE APOTHEOSIS OF SLUMMING

The styles that whites worked out in the Broadway cafés along the lines of romantic love, the private fun home, and personal experiences were not the only important elements of the 1920s. In the early 1920s, the split between the public world and the private personal world per-mitted the exploration of greater impulse and passion. Prosperous youths and adults explored the more adventurous implications of the cabarets of the 1910s, turning to Greenwich Village for drinks. The Village, an authentic bohemian and Italian ethnic community in the 1910s, had increasingly become a tourist area and nightlife zone for uptown whites since 1917. The cafés offered secrecy to young and old of college and noncollege background. The area had other potent associations. As a bohemian section, the Village became a playground where uptowners could indulge in wilder forms of sensuality. The Village's overtones of free sexuality attracted uptowners and out-of-towners, for in the Village they could see people apparently uninterested in success, caring little about money, desiring only to live the good life without responsibilities. Beyond that, the Village, then as now, had the reputation for homosexuality, and conventional whites could see lesbians and homosexuals on the streets.

Uptowners were in a strange relationship to these trends, for in leisure they desired the same lack of responsibility, but in everyday life, they were committed to the world of respectability. Consequently Greenwich Village existed as an area of fantasy, where uptowners could easily buy an experience, where they could vicariously partake of a wilder imaginary world. The area specialized in atmospheric spots, first with tearooms where tourists went in the late 1910s to see poets, intellectuals, and perhaps actual bohemians, and then with clubs designed to attract the visitors. Bohemian areas often pave the way for more conventional nightlife. While having an image of being irresponsible, bohemians usually come from respectable families, draw a large number of young people, and thus make uptowners feel safe enough on the streets of what had been an ethnic ghetto. As the area attracted uptowners, the nightlife itself became geared to tourists.[28]

Some Village nightclubs capitalized on the area's bohemian reputation by creating environments designed to convey a total fantasy or experiential image. A few large institutions had pioneered this departure from rationality as early as 1915. Briefly in 1915, Castles in the Air had transformed its space into a Spanish atmosphere, replete with bullring. And Reisenweber's was in the habit of periodically transforming one of its rooms into different concepts to match an entertainer or revue, such as for Doraldina's Hawaiian Island in 1916. The Montmartre, moreover, in late 1916 developed the bohemian implications of the café, by using red table cloths, spiderwebs in the corners, and wine bottles on the tables to create a Parisian atmosphere for fashionable urbanites. With wooden benches and rough-cut tables, the Montmartre attempted to have the room itself become the experience and the audience become the stars.[29]

By the 1920s the variety and style of cabarets had increased. The classical, imperial style of the lobster palace cabarets had given way to the fantasy orientation of clubs which reproduced South Sea Islands, the boardwalk, gypsy camps, Russian lands, and others. The break with public accountability removed the individual personality from rationality and opened up a realm of private experience. Greenwich Village was known for atmospheric cabarets. Don Dickerman's Pirate's Den with an atmosphere of lawless pleasures is perhaps the best example. Painter N. C. Wyeth and a friend visited the Den in 1926 and described it in a letter to his father: "We entered by a small but heavily bolted oaken door—a pirate, 6'6" in great coat, cocked hat, heavily belted, bristling with flintlock pistols and a cutlass at his side, let us in." The fun only began there. "We crept along a narrow hallway dimly lighted by flickering candles in ships' lanterns. At the tunneling end of this passage came the sound of a brawl, yells and clashing steel. . . . Through the dim light we could make out the kaleidoscope movement of figures, the flash of metal and an occasional report of a pistol." After submerging themselves in this tunnel, "We entered through this bedlam, so it is that all patrons are received. As we groped our way up twisting stairways, along ships' balconys [sic], captains' walks, and suc-like paths, we reached a large room stacked with guns, racks of cutlasses and hundreds of pistols. Ropes, tackle of all description, boarding irons, culverines, brass cannon, cages of parrots and monkeys—all lighted with ships' lanterns!"[30]

It was not just Village cafés that exploited the potentials of fantasy. The Rendezvous on Broadway, where Gilda Gray performed the South Sea dances, alternated its atmosphere from a South Sea Island one season to a Russian outpost the next. Also in 1923, Lew Leslie's Plantation Club attempted to duplicate the success of the all-black Broadway production of *Shuffle Along* and opened an all-black revue on Broadway. On entering the Plantation, customers found themselves on a southern plantation, complete with log cabins, Negro mammies, picket fences around the dance floor, a twinkling summer sky, and a watermelon moon. Aunt Jemima herself stood in one of the cabins flipping flapjacks.[31]

The Plantation Club anticipated the rise of Harlem as a nightlife zone for whites. Just as whites had looked to the Village as a place to experience real life while keeping it at a distance, they did the same in

Harlem, but with more dedication, especially after the Village became too touristy and lost its exotic attraction. New York had long had black and tans, but police, citizenry, and reformers considered them dangerous. In the Tenderloin, blacks and whites often intermingled, but this produced violence in 1900 and again in 1910 as whites attacked blacks, especially black performers. By the late 1910s and 1920s, however, blacks were living in their own segregated zone, too far away to be dangerous yet close enough to be exciting. A number of Tenderloin places, tiring of police harassment, began moving to Harlem in the mid-1910s. By 1925 whites began making the trek north in large numbers, partly for the wider opportunities for alcohol and partly because of the aura of exotic release surrounding the area and blacks. *Shuffle Along* in 1921–1922 publicized black entertainment, the Plantation made it acceptable in the intimate space of a cabaret, and Carl Van Vechten's novel, *Nigger Heaven*, opened up Harlem itself to white eyes. While attempting to analyze the black community and its various social groups, Van Vechten was fascinated with the expressivism of the Negro, and the sexuality of the cabarets played a large part in the book's success. The true Negro conformed to a white vision: he represented joy in life unfettered by civilization.

To meet the influx of people, a number of nightclubs opened their doors on 133rd to 135th Streets between and on Lexington and Seventh avenues, and those already in existence began to accept white patronage. The Cotton Club, Connie's Inn, and Ed Smalls's Paradise were the most famous, but the area was also home to innumerable small clubs, some of which did not open until the late hours after the others had closed. Most of the big clubs were white owned, and they appealed to a white vision of Harlem life. Blacks made up the entertainment core, but the creative and business talent was usually white. While many of the big clubs presented revues that were merely extensions of broadway ideas, whites had the image that black men and women, unlike themselves, really enjoyed performing. More than this, they were not performers in the conventional sense; this was the real thing. Black entertainers were perceived as natural, uncivilized, uninhibited performers, naturally smiling, because they had what whites lacked: joy in life. Guidebooks advised visitors to go to Harlem late, after the unadventurous whites downtown had gone to bed. The lateness of the hour added to the sense that one was venturing to the heart of darkness, the city of night where all things forbidden during the day were available in those few hours stolen from conventional life. In hard-working New York, Harlem was the Montmartre of America, its dramatic counterpoint. The numerous descriptions of driving up to Harlem, through the park by cab, made it seem as if one journeyed out from civilization, to the heart of impulses. Whites could find anything they wanted in Harlem, a city that never slept. Out for an evening, thus, whites created an entire fantasy land out of Harlem. From the mid-1920s to the early 1930s, Harlem represented the apotheosis of slumming.

The "real life" of Harlem was the creation of white fantasies. It is commonplace to assert that black entertainment serves white needs; this is particularly true where Negroes are perceived as natural entertainers, comics, and buffoons for whites. In the 1920s, the image of the Negro entertainer underwent a subtle shift at the same time that white culture's perception of what was respectable for themselves also changed. In minstrelsy, whites had played blacks on stage. It was only in the 1880s and 1890s that blacks began playing out the stereotypes of the happy-go-lucky Sambo or Jim Dandy that whites had already established in the form. By then minstrelsy itself was too tied to an ascetic and rural mode—the plantation—to mirror new urban values fully. Moreover, black composers and performers at the turn of the century were moving the form of black musicals slightly out of the old formal definitions of what roles blacks could play. By extending the roles into forms of musical comedy and a love interest, they helped break out of the tight, formal style of minstrelsy itself. By the mid-1920s, black culture was still perceived in the older sensual terms, but now the emphasis was on the positive nature of that sensuality. In the Harlem clubs black men and women were portrayed as primitive dancing fools, whose sensuality civilized whites could not hope to match. The only soul left had to be black.

Harlem clubs catered to these white fantasies of a natural race. Duke Ellington's band played "Jungle Music," the waiters at Ed Smalls's charlestoned in the aisles as they served the food, and the women in the revues were "tall, tan and terrific." Dancers like Earl "Snakehips" Tucker and Bill "Bojangles" Robinson danced in a happy and sensual way with their feet doing all the work, uncontrolled by the mind. The women, too, appealed to white tastes, for the revues presented light-skinned women who could appeal to white concepts of beauty, but had a touch of darker exoticism and hence animality. In all the clubs, white visitors felt they were experiencing real life, hotter music, hotter dancing, life lived at its quickest.

The Cotton Club, Connie's Inn, and several others were also segregated. Blacks performed; the audiences were largely white. Ed Smalls was warned by local police that he would be ill advised to permit mixing of blacks and whites in his club. Moreover, white visitors tended to crowd out the blacks, making it uncomfortable for them. Consequently while Harlem clubs broke from the minstrel form by presenting sex as desirable, Negro women as beautiful, and blacks in general as capable of love, they also retained the underlying element of minstrelsy. Blacks wore masks and served whites. The setting in the big clubs rendered the experience safe because whites did not have to mix with blacks on equal footing; instead blacks played the role they always did, the servant of and performer for the more powerful race. The fact that blacks were denied admittance to Broadway clubs unless they worked there reinforces the inequality of the Harlem experience. While whites had the power in the situation to define the relationship, blacks had little control over the exchange. Whites, however, felt they could relax with the blacks precisely because the latter were their social inferiors. They were less civilized, yet they were also of a lesser racial stock, and need not be taken seriously as a model of how to live one's life in the daytime world of reality. Whites thus enjoyed a safe Montmartre in Harlem, one that gave them the chance to act black and feel primitive personally without having to change their downtown, public lives.

The divided nature of the Harlem experience matched the divided nature of the twenties. Whites wanted to go up to Harlem for fun, adventure, and the aura of nighttime sin. As Gilbert Osofsky suggests, they missed the other side of Harlem, the reality of daytime life, the poverty that was as much part of black life as was joy in life. But when the lights went off and the sun came up, whites had gone back to their own world. Here in Harlem they stepped outside many of their cultural definitions of the past, but they refused to step across the barrier of race. When they went to Harlem, whites of all ethnic backgrounds were white and hence American. In Harlem, though, they could find the group outside their compromises, outside the fun home, the group defined by race as passionate. In Harlem they could come home to the life outside their selves—to passion and impulse and experience. What permitted them to do this was the compromise they had made with themselves, with the idea of containing fun, passion, and impulse within the framework of success and status. They continued the tensions between leisure and work, between enjoyment and diligence, and in doing so, not only could they step out in leisure, they also needed to find the passion, life, and enjoyment they had established as desirable within their own personal lives. With blacks at the bottom, whites could step out and step back to success, home, and the sanctity of privatized dreams.

The nightclubs of the twenties continued to bring diverse groups together for an evening in the exploration of a new and vital popular culture that offered a way out of many of the limitations and controls of nineteenth-century society, culture, and institutional identity. Yet the nightclub embodied a dilemma. As Gilbert Seldes discovered, businessmen found the late nightclub "everything against which he is working; leisure and laziness and incontinence; carelessness of time and money; what seems to be an impertinent indifference to getting on." In this kind of fast-paced leisure, men and women sought relief and naturalness. But they failed to consider leisure and sexuality as the natural business of the week, as an approach to the economy. Men and women of the business classes thus remained trapped by their economic perspective. "Into two or three hours we concentrate the release from practical affairs," Seldes lamented, "which in another age might be spread over three weeks."[32]

Although confined to private aspects of individual lives, this pursuit of a release transformed American popular culture, opened up a vision of an expanded and deeper home life, and helped develop personalities more capable of self-development, self-gratification, and self-adjustment. The new model for an affectionate home was less dutiful, giving men and women the hope of more vibrant personal lives. That women would mostly find their identities in the home and men still in business was unfortunate, yet both sexes supported the new personal styles as a reward of success rather than a challenge to it. New personal styles allowed men and women to see social progress through self-fulfillment. Instead of re-creating the society or the economy, instead of seeing the family as the basis of duty to the state,

prosperous urbanites sought to throw off the weighty hand of civilization and their parents from their true, more vital selves. In their pursuit
of self liberation, they often turned to lesser, more primitive or less
restrained groups, such as blacks and immigrants and transformed
their culture into a popular one, more identified with America than
Europe. To achieve personal freedom, one had to step out from the
crowd and define one through all kinds of experiences. The cabaret
offered vicarious experiences at a price for the prosperous. New experiences, newer personal styles often became the province of an
expanding consumer economy, offering powerful visions of liberation
and adjustment for personalities still trapped in the normal routines of
everyday life.

NOTES

1. James Weldon Johnson, *Along This Way* (New York: Viking Press,
1968), p. 328.

2. Gil Boag, as told to Dorthie Bobbé," *When Night Clubs Were in
Flower–Gil Boag's Story"* (unpublished manuscript, 1956), pp. 109–10.

3. Frederick Lewis Allen, *Only Yesterday: An Informal History of the
Nineteen-Twenties* (New York: Harper & Bros., 1931), pp. 88–122, views
the war and prohibition responsible for the changes in manners and morals, as
does William E. Leuchtenburg, *The Perils of Prosperity: 1914–1932* (Chicago. University of Chicago, 1958), pp. 158–77. In reconsidering feminist
ideology, William O'Neill, "Feminism as a Radical Ideology," in *Our
American Sisters: Women in American Life and Thought*, ed. Jean E. Fried-
man and William G. Shade (Boston: Allyn & Bacon, 1973), pp. 301–23,
holds to a prewar-postwar dichotomy prevalent among writers on women's
suffrage. Before the war, women sought higher service and political roles,
goes this view, but after the war they turned toward personal pleasure. My
work suggests that this search for pleasure occurred before the war, and in
fact, many feminists drew strength by opposing this idle woman. Paula Fass,
The Damned and the Beautiful (New York: Oxford, 1977), holds to this
prewar-postwar dichotomy and sees birth control as the cause of the affectionate family, and youth culture as a phenomenon of the 1920s. The question is why did people use birth control devices before and during the early
1920s? Does this not call for a shift in values to explain the use of the technology? Gilman Ostrander, *American Civilization in the First Machine Age:
1890–1940* (New York and Evanston: Harper Bros., 1970), explains the

change as due to the dominance of technology. My point is that the technology merchandised a particular set of social values.

James R. McGovern, "The American Woman's Pre-World War I Freedom in Manners and Morals," *Journal of American History* 55 (September 1968): 315–33, undercuts the older view of the war as casual. The kitchen revolution as cause among upper-middle and upper-class women seems unconvincing. David M. Kennedy, *Birth Control in America, The Career of Margaret Sanger* (New Haven: Yale University Press, 1970), pp. 70–71, notes that the new woman no longer seemed so new by World War I. He sees the changes as a result of changes in intellectual thought and the diminishment of older roles. John C. Burnham, "The Progressive Era Revolution in American Attitudes Toward Sex," *Journal of American History* 59 (March 1973): 885–908, sees changes toward sexuality arising from attempts by conservative doctors and reformers to educate the public to the dangers of syphilis. I see this more as a symptom than a cause. These external causes all played their part, but so too did the gradual collapse of Victorian ideology from within.

4. *New York Times*, April 18, 1915, V, pp. 19–20; Cholly Knickerbocker, "Society Is Cultivating the Work Habit," *New York American*, March 23, 1919, editorial section, p. 5, notes how young society women took to war and relief work; Peter Filene, "Men and Manliness before World War I" (paper delivered at the Organization of American Historians, April 1972), suggests briefly that men found in war a temporary answer to the problems of manhood raised by associating with women. Henry May, *The End of American Innocence* (Chicago: University of Chicago Press, 1958), pp. 363–67, saw in the war an attempt to promote genteel values.

5. Announcement by Mayor John P. Mitchel, April 17, 1917, Mayor Mitchel Papers, New York City Municipal Archives. Allen F. Davis, "Welfare, Reform and World War I," *American Quarterly* 19 (Fall 1967): 516–33, discusses the achievements of social justice reformers during the war. See also the Annual Reports and Papers of the Committee of Fourteen, Manuscript Division, New York Public Library.

6. *Vanity Fair* and the *New Yorker* both identified themselves as big city magazines of sophistication, cosmopolitanism, and broad culture, albeit with a certain superiority over the culture they promoted.

7. Obituary, Thomas Shanley, *New York Times*, October 3, 1932, vertical file, New York Restaurants, Local Division, New York Public Library. See also *Variety*, March 17, 1932, p. 4, July 14, 1922, p. 30, and Jimmy Durante and Jack Kofoed, *Night Clubs* (New York: Alfred A. Knopf, 1931), p. 192, for cabarets' becoming dance halls in the early 1920s.

8. Stanley Walker, *The Night Club Era* (New York: Frederick A. Stokes Co., 1933), pp. 86–125, 246–49, and Robert Sylvester, *No Cover Charge, A*

Backward Look at Night Clubs (New York: Dial Press, 1956), pp. 3–25, discuss in breezy fashion the role of criminals in nightclubs of the 1920s. Ethiopian quote from *Variety*, December 30, 1925, p. 11.

9. Noble Sissle, interview, August 1971, and Ed Smalls, former owner of Smalls's Paradise Club, interview, October 1971. See also Sylvester, *No Cover Charge*, p. 45, for similar remarks.

10. *Variety*, December 30, 1925, pp. 11, 20.

11. Ibid.

12. Ibid., December 27, 1918, p. 157.

13. Lary May, *Screening Out the Past*, 1980 describes the themes of De-Mille movies such as *Why Change Your Wife* (1920), *Old Wives for New* (1918), *Don't Change Your Husband* (1919), and others.

14. Warren Sussman, "Piety, Profits and Play in the 1920s," in Howard H. Quint and Milton Cantor, eds., *Men, Women and Issues, American History*, vol. 2 (Homewood, Ill.: Dorsey, 1975), pp. 191–216. Often tabloids featured stories of some man or woman from New York or a small town who embezzled money from a firm and blew it on a long week-end spree in the clubs—a mass fantasy.

15. Fass, *Damned and the Beautiful*, and Ostrander, *American Civilization*, discuss the growth of youth culture (filiarchy) in the 1920s, which fed off the themes of the movies, theatres, and cabarets.

16. Ellin Mackay, "Why We Go to Cabarets, A Post-Debutante Explains," *New Yorker*, November 28, 1925, pp. 7–8.

17. Eve Brown, *Champagne Cholly: The Life and Times of Maury Paul* (New York: E. P. Dutton, 1947), details the life of Cholly Knickerbocker, chronicler and publicizer of New York society in the *New York American* and other newspapers. See especially pp. 277–82 for his recognition that café society existed, and men and women of fashion frequented certain cafés. Bob Thomas, *Walter Winchell* (New York: Berkley Publishing Corp., 1971), gives an overview of his career and his focus on personalities. In 1929 he moved to the *Mirror*. Walker, *Night Club Era*, pp. 128–48, shows how Winchell, from the Jewish Lower East Side, mirrored many of the celebrities he covered in his lack of respect for formal conventions.

18. See Harry Richman and Richard Gehman, *A Hell of a Life* (New York: Duell, Sloan & Pearce, 1966) for details on his life.

19. For material on Texas Guinan, see Texas Guinan Scrapbooks, New York Public Library of the Performing Arts, Lincoln Center; Edmund Wilson, "Night Clubs," *New Republic*, September 9, 1925, p. 71; John Stein and Hayward Grace, "Hello Sucker!" (unpublished manuscript, 1941), Theatre Collection, Lincoln Center; Texas Guinan, "How to Keep Your Husband Out of My Night Club," *Liberty*, April 30, 1932, pp. 50–51, which advises women to be like her and her chorus girls.

20. Durante and Kofoed, *Nightclubs*; Gene Fowler, *Schnozzola* (New York: Viking Press, 1951); Gilbert Seldes, "Jimmie Is Exhubilant," *New Republic*, January 16, 1929, pp. 247–48; Robert Benchley, "Where Are My Skates?" *Bookman* 66 (December 1927): 415–17.

21. Frank Libuse is described in Stephen Graham, *New York Nights* (New York: George H. Doran Co., 1927), pp. 147–50.

22. Gilda Gray is covered a bit in Gil Boag and Dorthie Bobbé, *When Night Clubs Were in Flower*, p. 93; "Enigmatic Folksongs of the Southern Underworld," *Current Opinion* 67 (September 1919): 165–66; *New York Herald Tribune*, December 23, 1959, and *Variety*, December 30, 1959, clippings in Gilda Gray File, New York Public Library, Lincoln Center.

23. For these dances, see file of *Dance Lover's Magazine*, 1924 (later, *Dance Magazine*), Dance Collection, Lincoln Center; Gilbert Seldes, "Shake Your Feet," *New Republic*, January 1, 1925, pp. 283–84, notes how the charleston adds motion of hips, buttocks, and thighs to the dance, along with patting one's own body.

24. H. O. Brunn, *The Original Dixieland Jazz Band* (Baton Rouge: Louisiana University Press, 1960), discusses early careers of this path-breaking group.

25. Neil Leonard, *Jazz and the White Americans* (Chicago: University of Chicago Press, 1962), pp. 47–72.

26. Ibid., pp. 12–13, discusses nut jazz.

27. Ibid., pp. 73–89; Paul Whiteman and Mary Margaret McBride, *Jazz* (New York: J. H. Sears, 1926), discuss symphonic and sweet jazz and Whiteman's career.

28. The Village clubs have received little study outside the popular periodicals and press. See Walker, *Night Club Era*, pp. 280–95; Graham, *New York Nights*, pp. 32–114. Caroline Ware, *Greenwich Village, 1920–1930,* 1935; reprint, (New York: Harper Colophon, 1965), pp. 52–62, 93–98, 239–57, distinguishes between tearooms and cabarets and demonstrates how the latter drew on the Village's reputation as an exotic locale. *Variety*, September 2, 1925, pp. 3, 5, surveys a number of Village spots.

29. Bohemian spots started with the Moulin Rouge at Forty-eighth and Broadway in late 1916; a number of Broadway cafés featured bohemian nights. See Boag and Bobbé, *When Night Clubs Were in Flower*, p. 87.

30. There are numerous descriptions of the Pirate's Den. This one is from Betsy Janes Wyeth, ed., *The Wyeths: The Letters of N. C. Wyeth, 1901–1945* (Boston: Gambit, 1971), pp. 717–23; see also the film, *Dancing Mothers*, which uses it as a setting. To this style of club should be added the Nut Club, the Village Barn, and others that banked on an unconventional image.

31. The Plantation can be found in Charles G. Shaw, "11:30 to 3:00 (A

Text Book for Students of Insomnia)," *Smart Set* 71 (June 1923): 87–89; *Variety*, June 9, 1926, p. 44.

32. Harlem clubs can be seen best in the reviews in *Variety*, articles in the *Amsterdam News*, and autobiographies of black performers. Also see Gilbert Osofsky, *Harlem: The Making of a Ghetto* (New York: Harper and Row, 1968), pp. 179–87; Nathan Irvin Huggins, *Harlem Renaissance* (New York: Oxford University Press, 1971), pp. 84–136; and more generally in Rudolph Fisher, "The Caucasian Storms Harlem," *American Mercury* 11 (August 1927): 393–98; and Archie Seale, "The Rise of Harlem as an Amusement Center," in Myrtle Evangeline Pollard, *Harlem as Is*, vol. 1, Appendix C (unpublished, CUNY, February, 1936), Schomburg Collection.

BIBLIOGRAPHICAL ESSAY

This essay highlights the available and significant primary and secondary sources that bear on the study of nightlife. Those seeking further sources should consult my "Urban Nightlife and the Decline of Victorianism: New York City's Restaurants and Cabarets, 1890–1918," Ph.D. dissertation, University of Michigan, 1974, and the notes to this book.

SECONDARY SOURCES

There are few serious works on nightlife, American cabarets, and the activities that occur in them. Among the most useful studies of cabarets and nightclubs are Jimmy Durante and Jack Kofoed, *Nightclubs*, New York: Alfred A. Knopf, 1931, which is the most detailed; Lloyd Morris, *Incredible New York*, New York: Random House, 1951; and Lloyd Morris, *Postscript to Yesterday*, New York: Random House, 1947, which has a sense of cultural sweep. Robert Sylvester, *No Cover Charge, A Backward Look at Night Clubs*, New York: Dial Press, 1956, gives a general description largely for the period after prohibition. Stanley Walker, *The Night Club Era*, New York: Frederick A. Stokes Co., 1933, has useful information on the 1920s. Having written for and edited *Variety*, Abel Green and Joe Laurie, Jr., have filled *Show Biz: From Vaude to Video*, New York: Henry Holt and Co., 1951, with information on all aspects of entertainment in the twentieth century. On chorus girls there is very little, and although biographies and photo essays of Florenz Ziegfeld and his Follies exist, none really brings his and their cultural importance to light. For an adequate biography, see Charles Higham, *Ziegfeld*, Chicago: Regnery, 1972. Broadway as cultural center, unique neighborhood, and symbol of modern life has received little critical attention. Arthur Meier Schlesinger, *The Rise of the City, 1878–1898*, 1933; reprint Chicago: Quadrangle Books, 1961, pp. 98–102, first noted that improved lighting opened up urban nightlife on a vaster scale.

Marshall Stearns and Jean Stearns, *Jazz Dance: The Story of American Vernacular Dance*, New York: Macmillan, 1968, is an insightful survey of changes in popular dancing, significant artists, and their roots in black culture, but it does not attempt to place its subject in cultural perspective, which two British-focused works at least venture. See A. H. Franks, *Social Dance—A Short History*, London: Routledge and Kegan Paul, 1963, and J. S. Richardson, *The Social Dances of the Nineteenth Century in England*, London: Herbert Jenkins, 1960.

While several good studies exist on ragtime and jazz, no one yet has forcefully analyzed the full sweep of American popular music in its cultural context. See William J. Schafer and Johannes Riedel, *The Art of Ragtime*, New York: Da Capo Press, 1977, a good introduction to its subject, and Neil Leonard, *Jazz and the White Americans: The Acceptance of a New Art Form*, Chicago: University of Chicago Press, 1962, an excellent monograph tracing the route to acceptance of jazz and in the process telling us much about American cultural and racial attitudes. Samuel B. Charters and Leonard Kunstadt, *Jazz: A History of the New York Scene*, Garden City, New York: Doubleday, 1962, complements Leonard nicely, is more detailed on the various bands and personalities, and offers some insight into James Reese Europe, who deserves his own biography. H. F. Mooney, "Popular Music Since the 1920s: The Significance of Shifting Taste," *American Quarterly* 20 (1968): 67–85, and Mooney, "Songs, Singers and Society, 1890–1954," *American Quarterly* 6 (Fall 1954): 221–32, provide an insightful overview of changes in American popular song. We still await an in-depth history of Tin Pan Alley in its economic, ethnic, class, sexual, and racial dimensions. Edward A. Berlin, *Ragtime: A Musical and Cultural History* (Berkeley: University of California Press, 1980), has just appeared.

On Greenwich Village clubs, see Caroline Ware, *Greenwich Village, 1920–1930: A Comment on American Civilization in the Post-War Years*, 1935, reprint, New York: Harper and Row, 1965, pp. 52–55, 235–63. On Harlem nightclubs, see Nathan Irvin Huggins, *Harlem Renaissance*, New York: Oxford University Press, 1971, especially chapters 3 and 6; the incomparable James Weldon Johnson, *Black Manhattan*, 1930, reprint, New York: Atheneum, 1969; Gilbert Osofsky, *Harlem: The Making of a Ghetto*, New York: Harper and Row, 1968. Be sure to see George Hoefer, *The Sound of Harlem*, photo-text booklet accompanying Jazz Odyssey,v. 3, The Sound of Harlem, C3L33, produced by Frank Driggs, filled with beautiful pictures of and data on Harlem entertainment. Breezily written but giving the basic information is Jim Haskins, *The Cotton Club*, New York: Random House, 1977.

On New York society members, who were vital patrons of the cabarets, I have profited from Frederick Cople Jaher, "Nineteenth Century Elites in Boston and New York," *Journal of Social History* 6 (Fall 1972): pp. 32–37, and his "Style and Status: High Society in Late Nineteenth-Century New

York," in *The Rich, The Well Born, and the Powerful: Elites and Upper Classes in History*, edited by Frederick Cople Jaher, Urbana: University of Illinois Press, pp. 259–84. See also Carrol Hunter Quenzel, "Society in New York and Chicago, 1888–1900," Ph.D. dissertation, University of Wisconsin, 1938; May King Van Rensselaer and Frederick Van De Water, *The Social Ladder*, New York: Henry Holt and Company, 1924; Ralph Pulitzer, *Society on Parade*, New York: Harper and Brothers, 1910; and of course, Thorstein Veblen, *The Theory of the Leisure Class*, 1899, reprint, New York: Mentor Books, 1953. There is, however, no full-length study of the wealthy in New York City that puts together culture, ritual, society, politics, and economics.

Youth culture carries much of the sexual revolution in the twentieth century, and young people were also important patrons of the cabarets. Paula Fass, *The Damned and the Beautiful*, New York: Oxford University Press, 1978, is mechanistic in its analysis but right nevertheless in seeing the birth of youth culture. Gilman Ostrander, *America in the First Machine Age, 1890–1940*, New York: Harper and Row, 1970, tries to connect youth culture to modern technology and consumption, as well as to the new modern affectionate family. I also agree that Anglo-Saxon culture had been transformed from within by the 1920s.

Suggestive general works on the broader field of amusements and leisure are Foster Rhea Dulles, *America Learns to Play*, New York: D. Appleton-Century Company, 1940; Russel B. Nye, *The Unembarrassed Muse*, New York: Dial Press, 1970; and Robert Toll, *On with the Show, The First Century of Show Business in America*, New York: Oxford University Press, 1976. There are several important monographs on other areas of amusement. For melodrama, see David Grimsted, *Melodrama Unveiled: American Theater and Culture 1800–1850*, Chicago: University of Chicago Press, 1968, an excellent study, which lacks a companion for the post-1850 period. On minstrelsy, see Robert Toll, *Blacking Up: The Minstrel Show in Nineteenth-Century America*, New York: Oxford University Press, 1974, and Alexander Saxton, "Blackface Minstrelsy and Jacksonian Ideology," *American Quarterly* 27 (March 1975): 3–28. Albert F. McLean, Jr., *American Vaudeville as Ritual*, Lexington: University of Kentucky Press, 1965, interprets vaudeville with a provocative anthropological perspective, but in so doing loses sight of changes in the nature of the entertainment, while John DiMeglio, *Vaudeville, USA*, Bowling Green: Bowling Green University Popular Press, 1973, focuses more on the vaudevillian's life and perspective. Robert Sklar, *Movie-Made America*, New York: Random House, 1975, is the best general account of the movies, while Lary May, *Screening Out the Past: The Birth of Mass Culture and the Motion Picture Industry, 1896–1929*, New York: Oxford University Press, 1980, is a brilliant study of the sexual, ethnic, and cultural changes brought on by the corporation, mass consumption, and modern urban life. Jon Kingsdale, "The 'Poor Man's Club': Social Functions of the Urban Working-Class Saloon," *American Quarterly* 25 (October 1973): 472–89, offers an interpretation of the saloon, and Sheri Cavan, *Liquor License: An Ethnography of Bar Behavior*, Chicago: Aldine Publishing Company, 1966, covers a number of different public drinking situations. As yet, there is no general history of American drinking (and eating) habits comparable to Brian Harrison, *Drink and the Victorians, The Temperance Question in England*, Pittsburgh: University of Pittsburgh Press, 1971. On restaurants there is very little, but see Lately Thomas [pseud.], *Delmonico's: A Century of Splendor*, Boston: Houghton Mifflin, 1967. J. Fred MacDonald, *Don't Touch That Dial, Radio Programming in American Life from 1920 to 1960*, Chicago: Nelson-Hall, 1979 is indispensable. On amusement parks, see the enjoyable and informative John F. Kasson, *Amusing the Million, Coney Island at the Turn of the Century*, New York: Hill & Wang, 1978, and Charles Funnel, "Virgin Strand, Atlantic City, New Jersey as a Mass Resort and Cultural Symbol," Ph.D. thesis, University of Pennsylvania, 1973.

There are many suggestive works by nonhistorians on leisure and amusement: Robert E. Park and Ernest W. Burgess, *The City*, Chicago: University of Chicago Press, 1967; Walter Reckless, *Vice in Chicago*, Chicago: University of Chicago Press, 1933; Daniel Russell, "The Road House: A Study of Commercialized Amusements in the Environs of Chicago," Master's thesis, University of Chicago, 1931; and Harvey Zorbaugh, *Gold Coast and Slum, A Sociological Study of Chicago's Near North Side*, Chicago: University of Chicago Press, 1929; all see the new urban amusements as part of urban pathology and breakdown rather than as the beginning of new choices and a new culture. Leo Lowenthal, "Biographies in Popular Magazines," in William Peterson, ed., *American Social Patterns*, Garden City, New York: Doubleday, 1958, pp. 63–118, suggests the concept of idols of consumption. Charles Keil, *Urban Blues*, Chicago: University of Chicago Press, 1966, offers ways to relate performers and performance to culture and everyday life, as does Richard Schechner, *Public Domain and Other Essays on the Theater*, New York: Avon Press, 1970. Edward Hall, *The Hidden Dimension*, Garden City: Doubleday & Co., 1969, sees space as a cultural product, and Marshall McLuhan, *Understanding Media: The Extensions of Man*, New York: McGraw-Hill, 1964, remains a vital starting point for considering the importance of any medium of communication. Ned Polsky, *Hustlers, Beats and Others*, Garden City, New York: Doubleday, 1967, does participant observation in pool halls. Erik Erikson, *Childhood and Society*, New York: Norton, 1950, shows that individuals carry and change culture and history. Finally Erving Goffman, *The Presentation of Self in Everyday*

Life, Garden City, New York: Doubleday, 1959, and *Interaction Ritual*, Garden City, N.Y.: Doubleday, 1967, shows the value of having a good eye and the importance of performance in human life and culture. Murray Melbin, "Night as Frontier," *American Sociological Review* 43 (February 1978): 3–22, articulates the notion of night having cultural properties usually associated with the American frontier.

PRIMARY MATERIALS

Archives

For scholars interested in further research into theatre and nightlife, the Theatre Collection of the Library for the Performing Arts, New York Public Library, Lincoln Center, has an enormous amount of primary source material. The clipping and photo file, organized by the name of individual performer and institution, is an important research tool but should be used carefully because, in the area of nightlife at least, most of its clippings are post-1933. These files can be supplemented by the extensive holdings in the Robinson Locke Collection, which has earlier material on important creative personalities, such as Gilda Gray, Maurice Mouvet, Doraldina, and others. The extensive Irene and Vernon Castle Scrapbooks, containing a large number of clippings on their career, sketches of their act, remarks of moralists, photos, and a good deal of information on the pre–World War I dance craze, is a must. The Theatre Collection also holds Sophie Tucker's massive collection of scrapbooks, which contain useful biographical, career, and general amusement information, as well as every greeting card she received. Scrapbooks, containing material on Ned Wayburn's tenure as revue director for the Midnight Frolic, offer material on cabaret revues and chorus girls. Among its holdings, the Theatre Collection also has the scrapbooks of Fay Marbe, Billy Rose (on microfilm), and Texas Guinan. The Dance and Music Collections of the library also have numerous clippings filed by name and subject on dance, dancers, music, and musicians. The Dance Collection contains a large number of dance instruction books and antidance tracts spanning the course of U.S. history. For descriptions of the dances and the Castles' approach, see Mr. and Mrs. Vernon Castle, *Modern Dancing*, New York: Harper Bros., 1914.

The Local and Genealogical Division of the New York Public Library houses a wide variety of nineteenth- and twentieth-century guidebooks to the city, as well as a number of books on all facets of New York City history. There is also a small Restaurant File with clippings on and by past hoteliers and restaurateurs. The only extant copy of *New York Plaisance*, 1908, devoted to a text-picture essay of Murray's Roman Gardens, is in the division.

The Schomburg Collection, New York Public Library, has a number of dissertations, clippings, and photos on famous black performers, as well as the *Amsterdam News* and the *New York Age*, which gave wide coverage to Harlem nightlife and the area's growing worldwide reputation, often reprinting news of Harlem that appeared elsewhere. A number of guidebooks to the city and to Greenwich Village (along with newspapers and periodicals of this area) can be found in the New-York Historical Society. It contains a huge collection of largely untapped material on New York City hotels in the nineteenth century. Gossip columnist Louis Sobol has given his large collection of clippings to New York University, and they are housed with the *New York Herald Tribune* morgue, which includes clippings and background material on New York personages, as does the *Daily News* morgue.

The Committee of Fourteen Annual Reports, 1905–1931, together with the committee's investigative papers, housed in the Manuscript Division, New York Public Library, offer invaluable insights into the activities and thought of urban reformers and their complaints against the cabaret and other urban amusements. The reevaluation of play can be followed in *Playground*, a central forum, much like *Survey*, but more specialized, for settlement workers, social workers, and reformers in the first two decades of this century. These should be supplemented by the works of Jane Addams and Louise De Koven Bowen, cited in the text, and by the papers and reports of the Juvenile Protective Association, University of Illinois, Chicago Circle Campus, and the Chicago Historical Society.

The connection between reformers and city administrations can be found in the papers of Mayor William J. Gaynor, Mayor John Purroy Mitchel, and Mayor James Walker at the New York Municipal Archives. These papers, supplemented by *Annual Reports, 1910–1925*, Police Department, New York City, provide information on official attitudes toward dancing and licensing and especially on Gaynor's campaign against the cabaret dance evil in April 1913. This material sheds some light on licensing and policing, but the most valuable resource would be the records on licensing violations. The New York City Police Department gave me no cooperation and insisted that the records had been burned.

The Oscar Tschirky Scrapbooks and the Menu Collection in the Hotel and Menu Collection, Library of the School of Hotel and Restaurant Management, Cornell University, contain much on the Waldorf and Waldorf-Astoria hotels, Sherry's, Oscar Tschirky, and turn-of-the-century hotel keeping in New York. They also contain much material on restaurants, the art of dining, and social behavior at the turn of the century.

Periodicals

No library or historical society could find the one specifically professional nightclub periodical, *Nightclub and Ballroom Management*, 1933–; its absence hinders an understanding of how nightclub managers consciously conceived of their business and designed their cafés. The business end can be gleaned, however, from local and theatrical newspapers, such as *Variety*, 1905–, which had a cabaret column as early as 1912 and which devoted coverage to entertainment in the cafés and the run-ins with the authorities over the years. *Variety's* yearly wrap-ups cover the main trends in nightlife, but since its main interest is the business side, one has to piece together the more general picture of entertainment. The *Dramatic Mirror* and *Billboard* provide some weekly coverage as well. Other important periodicals for nightlife are the *Theatre* and *Dance Lover's Magazine*, 1924–, which changed its name to *Dance* in 1925, and which published fiction, reviews, pictures, and instructions of current dances. See also the local magazines, *Broadway*, 1930–1931, *Broadway Zephyr*, 1918; *Shadowland*, 1920–1923; all are in the Theatre Collection, Library for the Performing Arts, Lincoln Center.

Because of the glamorous and/or scandalous nature of the subject, newspapers provided extensive coverage on cafés. I used the following: *New York Times, World, Sun, Tribune, American, Evening Graphic, Mirror, Daily News, Amsterdam News,* and *New York Age.*

Popular periodicals covered the cafés and entertainment for reasons mentioned above, and in the case of some, because they considered cafés a blot on the city. For the glamorous treatment, see: *Vanity Fair, Vogue, Theatre Monthly, New Republic, New Yorker,* and *Everybody's Magazine.* Some of the more genteel and reform-oriented periodicals are *Atlantic, Harper's Weekly, Harper's Magazine, McClure's, Forum, Cosmopolitan, Outlook, Literary Digest, Current Opinion,* and *Harper's Bazaar.* The solidly middle-class *Saturday Evening Post* and *Collier's* disapproved but found the cabaret glamorous nevertheless. *Hotel Monthly* covers a range of issues pertinent to the subject, and *Architecture Magazine, Architecture and Builder's Magazine, New York Architecture,* and *Architecture Review* devoted pictures and essays to the design of important restaurants and hotels.

Autobiographies

Participants in the cafés, whether as entertainers, owners, or audience, wrote a number of memoirs. For the most part, these must be used with extreme caution because celebrity autobiographies run to type; they often avoid the art and push the gossip. The fact that so many are ghost written adds another cautionary note. They are, however, indispensable for understanding a subject with a secret history (crime, prostitution, prohibition, gangsters, police). On lobster palaces and hotels, I found the following useful: Julius Keller, *Inns and Outs*, New York: G. P. Putnam's Sons, 1939; Belle Livingstone, *Belle Out of Order*, New York: Henry Holt and Company,

1959, which also details her life as a Park Avenue speakeasy operator; George Rector, *The Girl from Rector's*, Garden City, New York: Doubleday, Page and Company, 1927; Evelyn Nesbit, *Prodigal Days, the Untold Story*, New York: Julian Messner, 1934; Evander Berry Wall, *Neither Pest nor Puritan*, New York: Dial Press, 1940; and Albert Stevens Crockett, *Peacocks on Parade*, New York: Sears Publishing Company, 1931. For cabarets of the 1910s, see the autobiography of Jesse Lasky with Don Weldon, *I Blow My Own Horn*, Garden City, New York: Doubleday and Company, 1957; Irene Castle and Bob and Wanda Duncan, *Castles in the Air*, Garden City, New York: Doubleday and Company, 1958; Sophie Tucker, *Some of These Days: The Autobiography of Sophie Tucker*, Garden City, New York: Garden City Publishing Company, 1946 (English edition with Dorothy Giles, 1948); John Murray Anderson, as told to Hugh Abercrombie Anderson, *Out Without My Rubbers: The Memoirs of John Murray Anderson*, New York: Library Publishers, 1954; Gil Boag, as told to Dorothie Bobbe, "When Nightclubs Were in Flower, Gil Boag's Story," unpublished manuscript in Bobbé's possession 1956; Eddie Cantor, *As I Remember Them*, New York: Duell, Sloan and Pearce, 1963; Elsie De Wolfe, *After All*, New York: Harper and Brothers, 1935; Perry Bradford, *Born with the Blues*, New York: Oak Publications, 1965; Elizabeth Marbury, *My Crystal Ball*, London: Hurst and Blackett, 1924; Maurice Mouvet, *Art of Dancing: An Autobiographical Sketch with Complete Descriptions of Modern Dances and Full Illustrations Showing the Various Steps and Positions*, New York: G. Shirmer, 1915; Willie "the Lion" Smith, *Music on My Mind*, Garden City, New York: Doubleday and Company, 1964. For material on nightclubs of the 1920s (and much more), see Jimmy Durante and Jack Kofoed, *Nightclubs*, New York: Alfred A. Knopf, 1931; Harry Richman with Richard Gehman, *A Hell of a Life*, New York: Duell, Sloan and Pearce, 1966; Billy Rose, *Wine, Women and Words*, New York: Simon, Schuster, 1948; Rudy Vallee and Gil McKean, *My Time Is Your Time The Story of Rudy Vallee*, New York: Ivan Obolensky, 1962; Ethel Waters with Charles Samuels, *His Eye Is on the Sparrow: An Autobiography of Ethel Waters*, Garden City, New York: Doubleday and Company, 1950; Betsy Janes Wyeth, ed., *The Wyeths: The Letters of N.C. Wyeth, 1901–1945*, Boston: Gambit, 1971; Ben Gross, *I Looked and I Listened*, New Rochelle, New York: Arlington House, 1954; Nils Granlund with Sid Feder and Ralph Hancock, *Blondes, Brunettes, and Bullets,* New York: David McKay Company, 1957; Louis Sobol, *The Longest Street, A Memoir*, New York: Crown Publishers, 1968; James Weldon Johnson, *Along This Way, The Autobiography of James Weldon Johnson*, New York: Viking Press, 1968; Edward "Duke" Kennedy Ellington, *Music Is My Mistress*, New York: Da Capo Press, 1976.

Biographies

There is supplemental materal in a varied group of biographies: Jane Ardmore, *The Self-Enchanted, Mae Murray: Image of an Era*, New York: McGraw-Hill, 1959; Eve Brown, *Champagne Cholly: The Life and Times of Maury Paul*, New York: E. P. Dutton and Company, 1947; Gene Fowler, *Schnozzola: The Story of Jimmy Durante*, New York: Viking Press, 1951; Richard Ketchum, *Will Rogers, The Man and His Times*, New York: American Heritage Publishing Company, 1973; Irving Shulman, *Valentino*, New York: Simon and Schuster, 1968; John S. Stein and Hayward Grace, " 'Hello Sucker!' The Life of Texas Guinan," unpublished manuscript, n.d., Library for the Performing Arts, Theatre Collection, New York Public Library, Lincoln Center.

NAME INDEX

INDEX OF CABARETS, HOTELS, AND THEATRES

SUBJECT INDEX

About the Author

LEWIS A. ERENBERG is Assistant Professor of History at Loyola University in Chicago. A specialist in social and cultural history, he has published in *Feminist Studies*. STEPPIN' OUT won Honorable Mention in the Ralph Gabriel Prize Competition in American Studies.